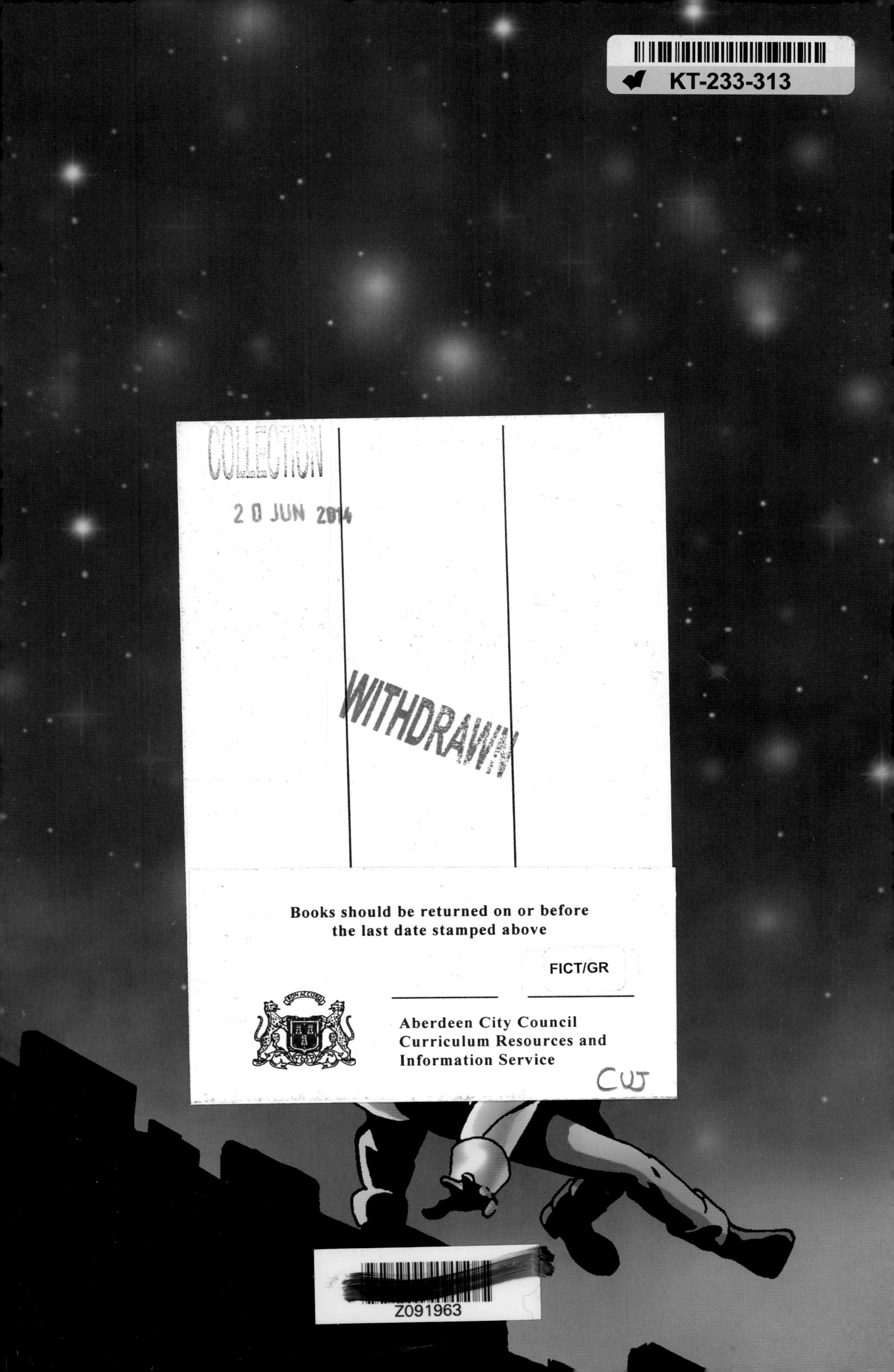

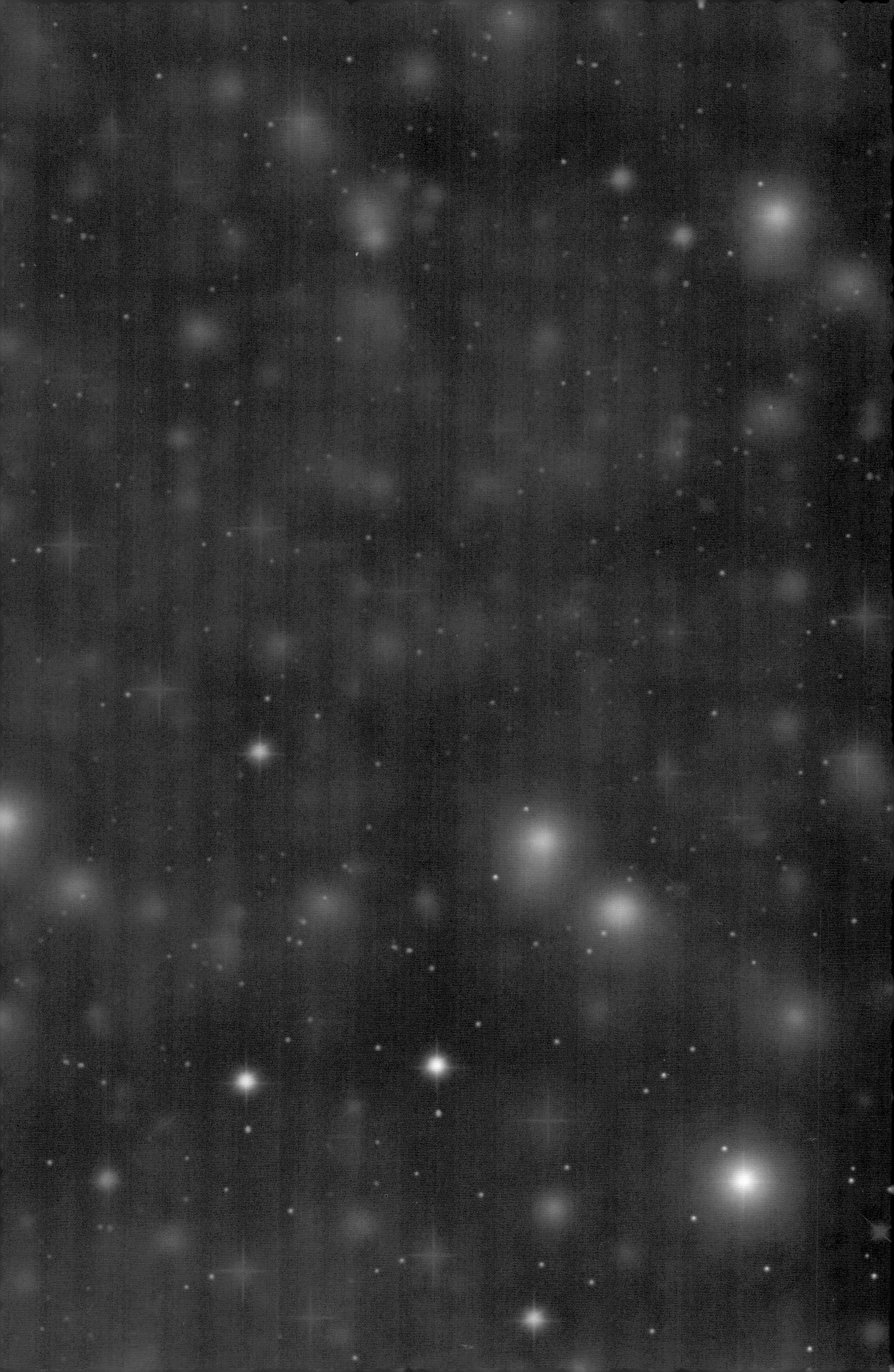

LEAVE IT TO CHANCE

ROBINSON • SMITH • FREEMAN • COX

image®

JAMES ROBINSON & PAUL SMITH

WITH

GEORGE FREEMAN
INKS

JEROMY COX
COLOR ART

AND

AMIE GRENIER
LETTERING

LEAVE IT TO CHANCE VOL. II: TRICK OR THREAT published by Image Comics, 1071 N. Batavia St. Ste. A, Orange, CA 92867. Copyright © 2002 by James Robinson and Paul Smith. All rights reserved. Originally published as LEAVE IT TO CHANCE Vol. I #5-8. LEAVE IT TO CHANCE, its logos, symbols, prominent characters featured in this volume and the distinctive likeness thereof, are trademarks of James Robinson and Paul Smith. Any similarities to persons living or dead is unintentional and purely coincidental. With the exception of artwork for review purposes, none of the contents of this pubication may be reprinted without the express permission of James Robinson and Paul Smith. PRINTED IN HONG KONG

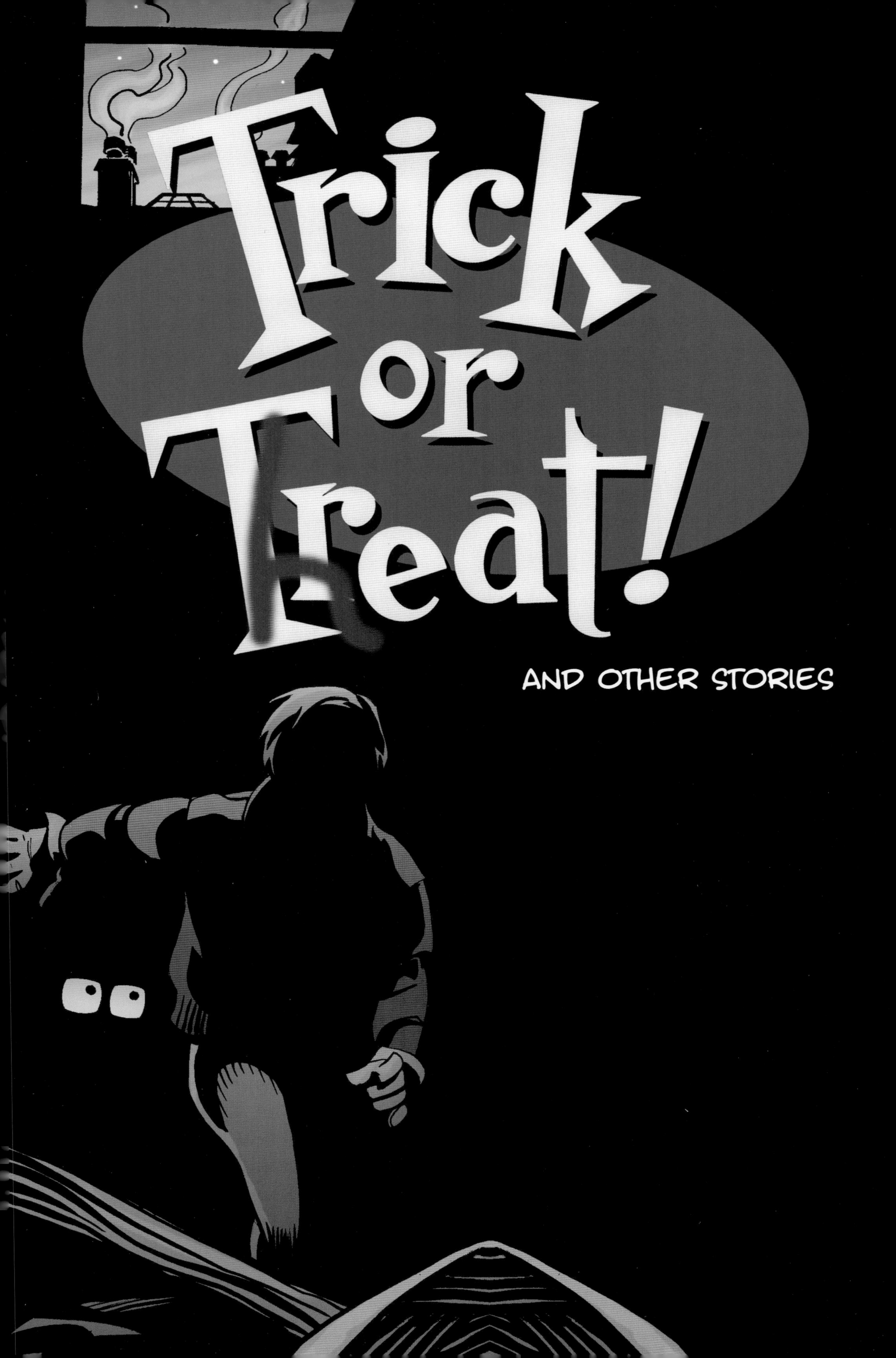
Trick or Treat!
AND OTHER STORIES

BIOGRAPHIES

JAMES ROBINSON

James Robinson came into America from the cold, gray climes of England. He stumbled into comic books like a drunken sailor and among his many works, most notable are The Golden Age, Firearm, WildC.A.T.s, Batman: Legends of the Dark Knight, 67 Seconds, London's Dark, Bluebeard and Illegal Alien. He recently finished his seven year opus Starman for DC Comics.

At the same time, James has entered the film world, adapting the League of Extraordinary Gentlemen for 20th Century Fox starring Sean Connery.

He resides in Hollywood.

PAUL SMITH

The victim of an abnormally happy childhood, the artist was born on 9/4/53 in Kansas City, Missouri, the youngest of three boys.

A former animator and storyboard artist (now in recovery), he has pretended to be a comics professional since the early 80's. Some of his various works include his rookie year on the *X-Men, Dr. Strange, Mike Mahogany, Nexus,* and *The Golden Age* (the latter in collaboration with James Robinson).

Highly opinionated and a royal pain to work with, the artist resides in southern California with his motorcycle, Lockheed. He has never met a deadline in his life.

GEORGE FREEMAN

George Freeman has been penciling, inking and colouring comics from his wintry Canadian home for the last twenty-four years.
Starting with *Captain Canuck*, he has since drawn *Black Widow, Elric, Batman, Green Lantern, Jack of Hearts, Mr. Monster, The Challengers of the Unknown* and various *Big Book* stories. In 1996, he and his wife, colourist Laurie E. Smith, were nominated for an Eisner Award for colouring the *X-Files* comic book. (Chris Ware won.)
He still enjoys *Acme Novelty Library,* British Mac magazines, Frank Giacoia inks and red-headed women.

JEROMY COX

Jeromy worked for four years as an animator for film, television, and video game projects. Jeromy started coloring comics for Wildstorm three years ago and hasn't stopped since.

Jeromy's self published comic book, *Zombie Love,* is on hiatus because he's working so much. Plans are to resume production later this year. Jeromy is currently coloring *Leave it to Chance, Mage The Hero Defined,* and is the Art Director on a super secret virtual reality project for Angel studios.

He likes bacon, coca cola, red vines, butterfingers, Star Wars and mayonnaise. Not necessarily in that order.

CONTENTS

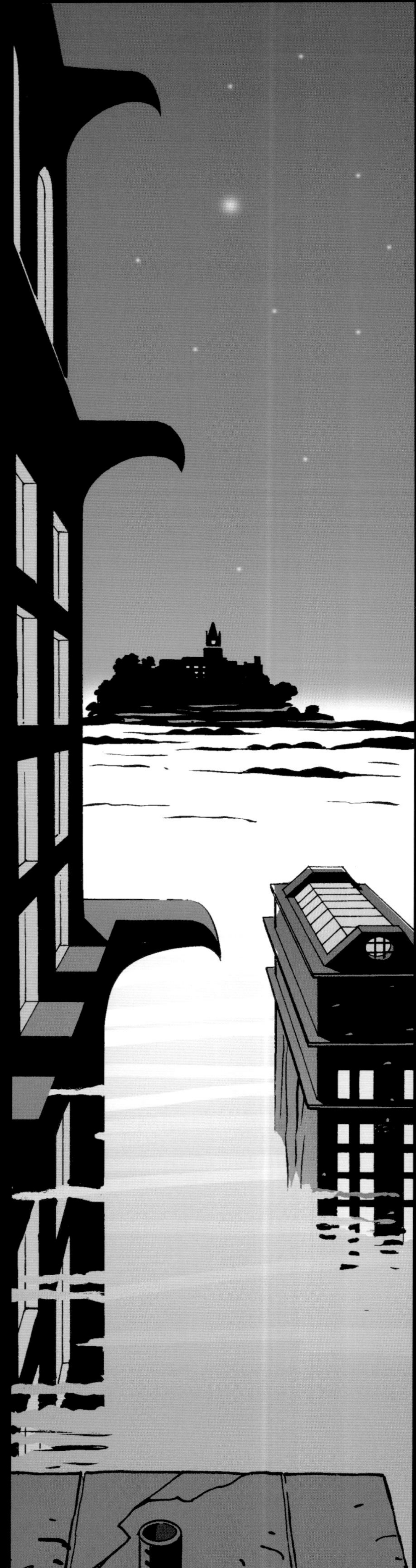

INTRODUCTIO

"Do what you believe in."
–Jack Kirby

Passages, circles, time. It's difficult to say exactly where some things start or stop. For m it was the day we laid Jack Kirby to rest. After Mike Lake (who brought James to America as I recall,) and I just stared at each other. This changes everything. The end of an era, of chil hood, of innocence. For the younger readers w are wondering, there aren't enough pages in t book to explain Jack's importance to comics. was the King.

We talked all afternoon. About everything. We played the "What's wrong with the industr game. The list was endless. The solution, in o infinite wisdom, was simple. We needed new readers, especially girls, and heroes you could look up to.

James calls the next day. Unable to attend service, he was curious how it went. I mention the conversation with Mike and how I'm workin on an idea. An entry level adventure book. N gratuitous sex, violence or foul language. Non age specific, non gender specific. With a stron female lead you could take home to meet you mother. (Not to mention a cool little dragon.) felt I was on the right track and that he might take a crack at it himself.

Maybe a week later, he calls back. What if we cross Nancy Drew with Kolchack, the Night Stalker? There's a city where magic works. A family who's been investigating the city's arcane

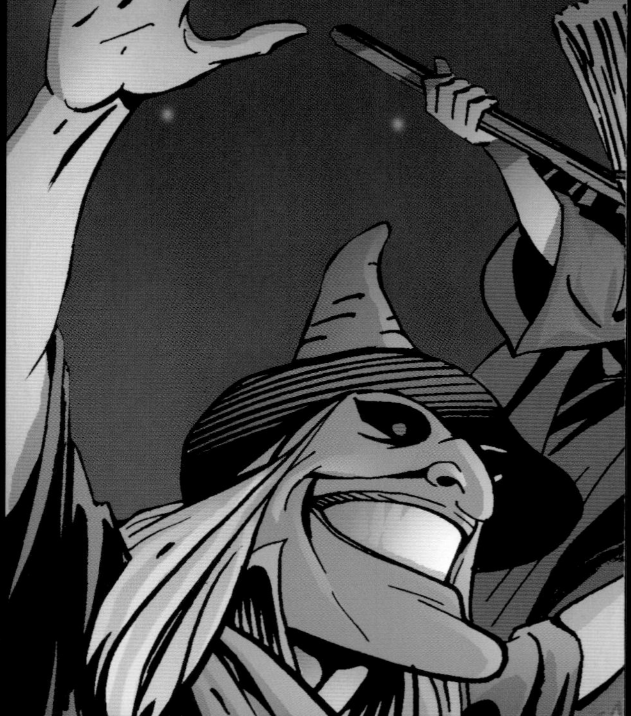

of years. Until now. The father's a widower. His only child a daughter. She's waited her entire life to begin her training. Dad says no, you're a girl, it's too dangerous. Grow up, get married. Your son shall carry on the family honor. Devastated, but not daunted, she'll prove she has what it takes.

Silence. I blink my brain. "James, this is a billion dollar idea." I tell him to secure all rights immediately. Hire whatever guns you need, but don't share this with anyone. He says no, he needs a partner. He needs someone willing to bleed.

I need to think about it. My own story is coming together. But, somehow, it turns left at Albuquerque. Taking on a life of her own, my heroine had become dark, convoluted. I'd lost sight of the goal.

I couldn't stop thinking about James' idea. Pure, simple, on target. My standing offer to writers has always been, write me a story I can't refuse... and I won't.

I'm in. Ideas are flying. Things are coming, going, changing (see the sketchbook section in the back for a few examples.) She's older. Her name is Sadie? The city is a futuristic metropolis with a Victorian bent. Somewhere, the dragon jumps ship. Slowly, things solidify. James strikes again, "Let's call it Leave it to Chance."

We flood the market with our proposal. What didn't happen next still amazes me. Nothing. The response was universal. Show us the book

James likes to razz me about the time it took to get Chance from this point to publication. Good or bad, I can't do a hundred books a month like James can. There were other projects I'd promised, and a couple I took for the money. I was going to need a war chest.

My strength was that of ten because my heart was pure. I would create a universe from scratch. Reinvent myself as an artist. Do it for love. Do it for free, with enough money left over to publish it myself. Chance's fight had become my own. We would make them believe.

I'd like to say it was effortless. Ha! I'm an inept hack without a clue. I throw out more than I keep. James threatens to beat me with a Virgo stick. He tells me I'm the only one who knows it's wrong. So? It's still wrong.

Mistakes are wonderful things. It's how we learn. I learn a lot! James and I start WW3. We sue for peace. Somehow the first issue gets done. Far from perfect, it's a good start. I can do better, but I believe in what we have.

Kurt Busiek calls. How's that mystery proposal? Jim Lee's starting a creator-owned line.

With the able assistance of the Homage gang, Jeff Mariotte singing the gospel, Amie Grenier lettering (thanks also to Richard Starkings and J.D.Gaushell for turning my handwriting into a font,) colors by Jeromy Cox, and Jonathan Peterson on editorial, Chance comes out. She wins a Harvey and two Eisners, but loses the Lulu. Three for four ain't bad. Jack was right, do what you believe in.

So, here we are. Chance's second trade, reprinting issues #5-8. George Freeman joins us as inker with our opening story. John Layman has taken over editorial with issue 11. It's been a rough year for many of us, but Chance has survived. She hasn't made that billion dollars yet. Maybe she never will. In all honesty, that's not why I signed on, and I'm having too much fun to care. I hope you will too.

Smitty

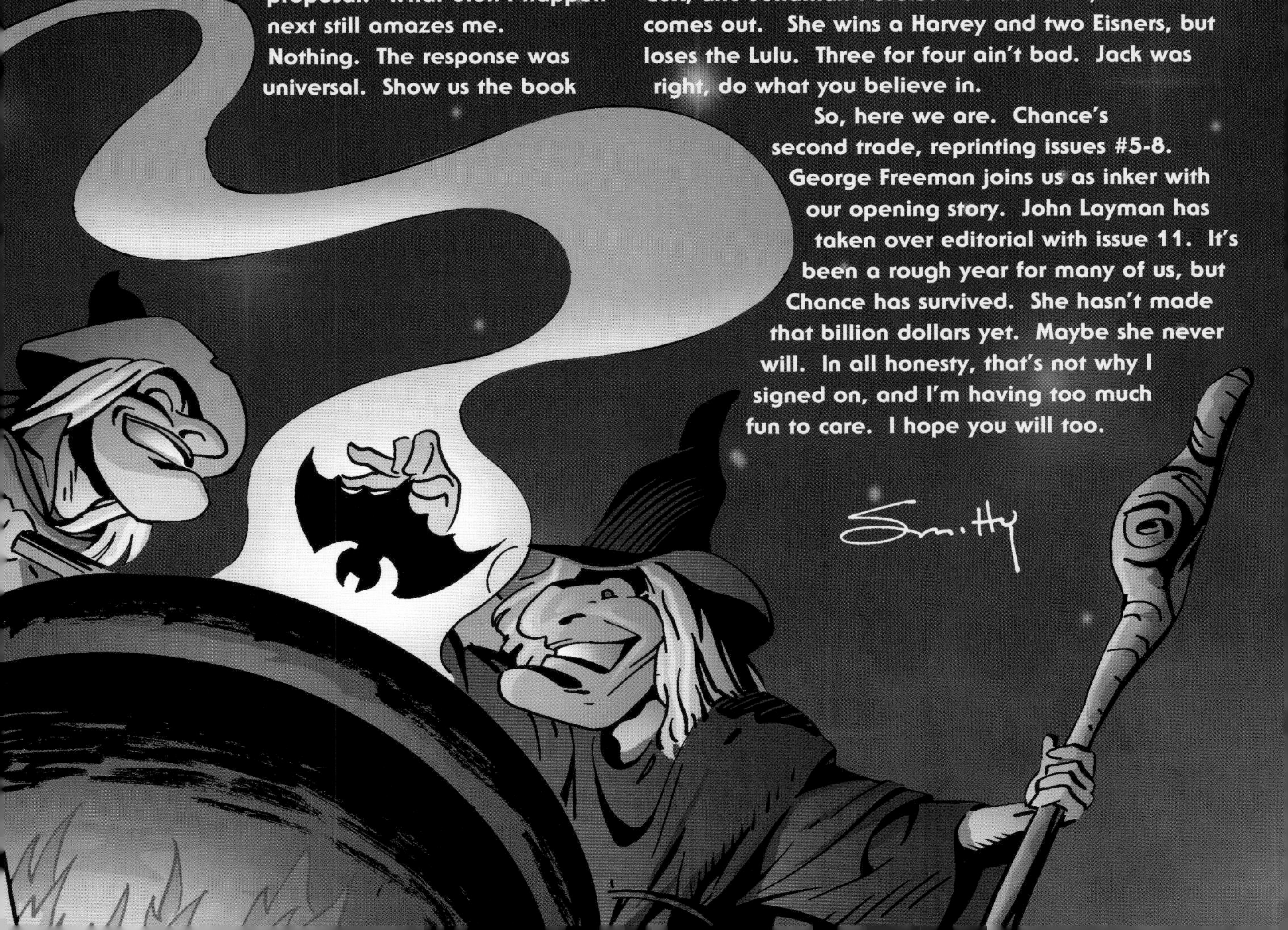

DEDICATIONS

To Ajo and Luli.
– James

In Memoriam:
For William Allen "Willi" Smith.
The best big brother a guy ever
had. I promise not to be a deckie.
See you on the other side.
– Paul

To the two most important women
in my life: My mom, Sylvia
Freeman, who always supported
my dreams. My wife, Laurie, who
gave me new dreams.
– George

To my Mother,
Judy Emerson,
I love you.
– Jeromy

CHAPTER 1

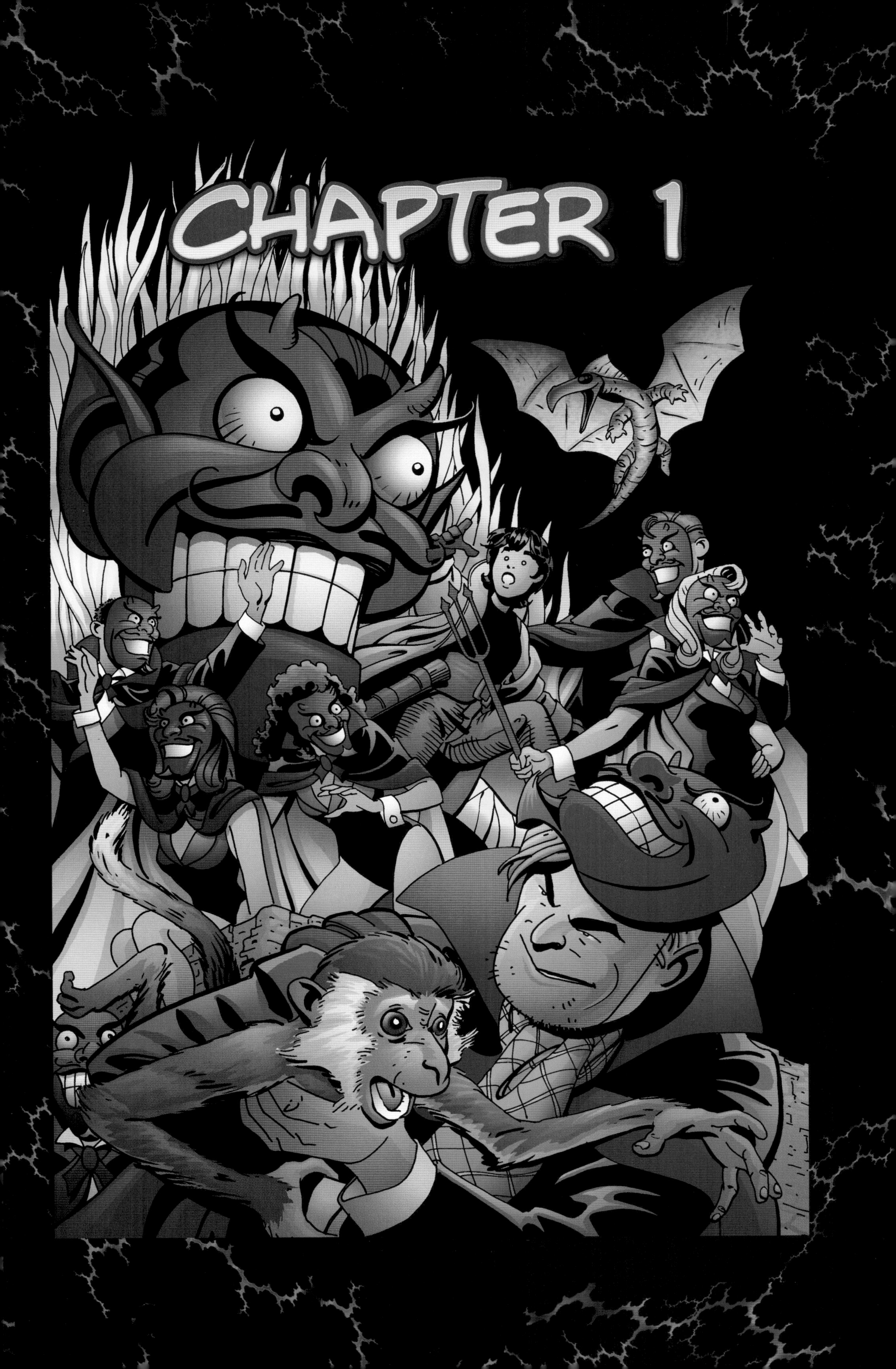

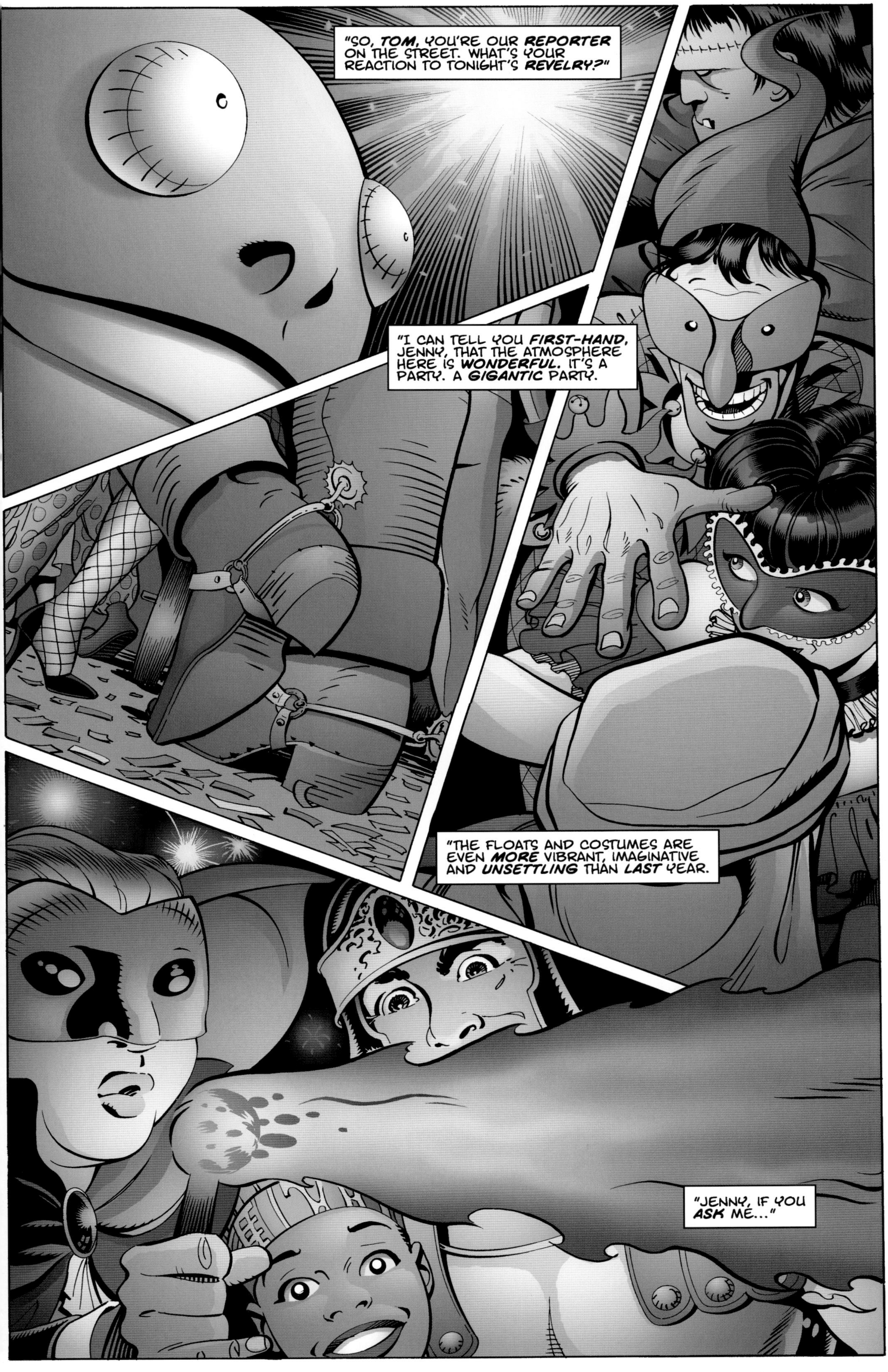
"SO, TOM, YOU'RE OUR REPORTER ON THE STREET. WHAT'S YOUR REACTION TO TONIGHT'S REVELRY?"
"I CAN TELL YOU FIRST-HAND, JENNY, THAT THE ATMOSPHERE HERE IS WONDERFUL. IT'S A PARTY. A GIGANTIC PARTY.
"THE FLOATS AND COSTUMES ARE EVEN MORE VIBRANT, IMAGINATIVE AND UNSETTLING THAN LAST YEAR.
"JENNY, IF YOU ASK ME..."

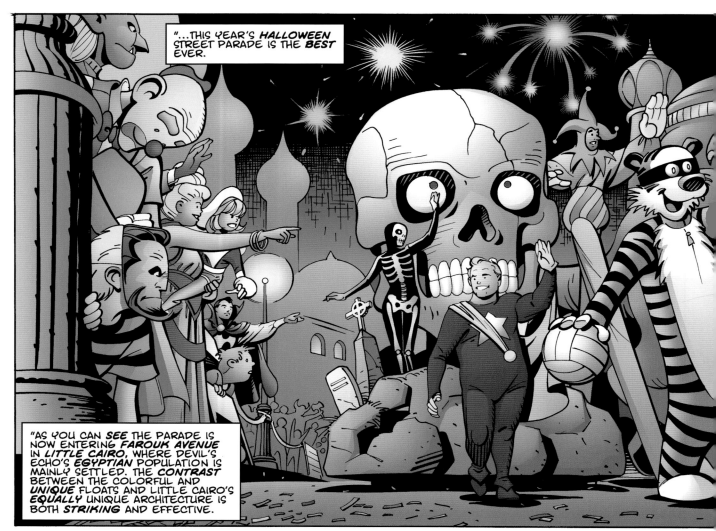

"...THIS YEAR'S *HALLOWEEN* STREET PARADE IS THE *BEST* EVER.

"AS YOU CAN *SEE* THE PARADE IS NOW ENTERING *FAROUK AVENUE* IN *LITTLE CAIRO*, WHERE DEVIL'S ECHO'S *EGYPTIAN* POPULATION IS MAINLY SETTLED. THE *CONTRAST* BETWEEN THE COLORFUL AND *UNIQUE* FLOATS AND LITTLE CAIRO'S *EQUALLY* UNIQUE ARCHITECTURE IS BOTH *STRIKING* AND EFFECTIVE.

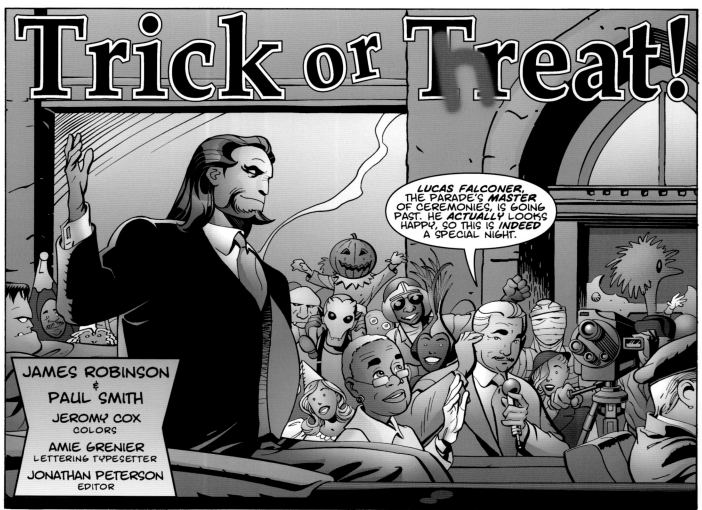

Trick or Treat!

LUCAS FALCONER, THE PARADE'S *MASTER* OF CEREMONIES, IS GOING PAST. HE *ACTUALLY* LOOKS HAPPY, SO THIS IS *INDEED* A SPECIAL NIGHT.

JAMES ROBINSON
&
PAUL SMITH

JEROMY COX
COLORS

AMIE GRENIER
LETTERING TYPESETTER

JONATHAN PETERSON
EDITOR

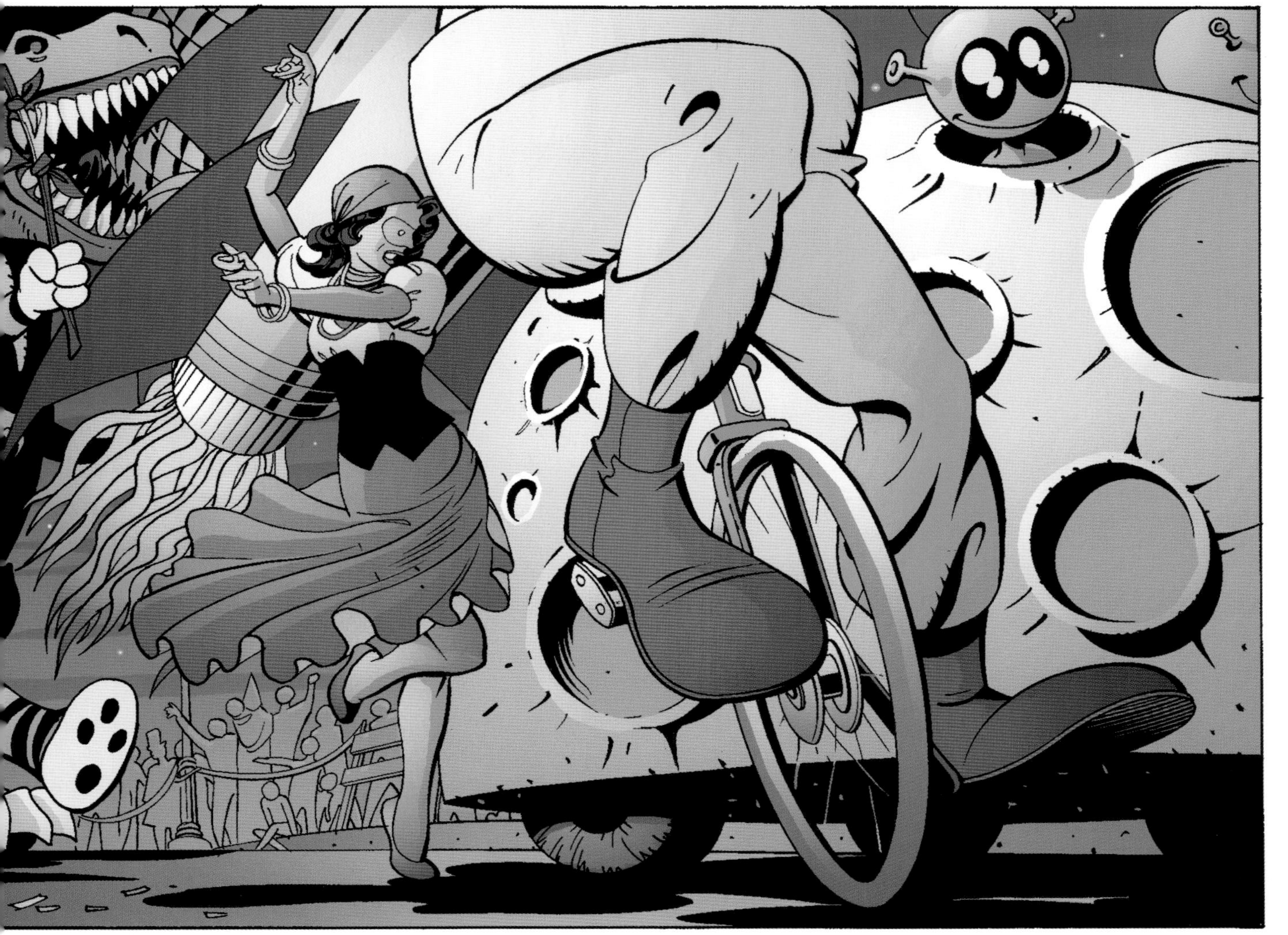

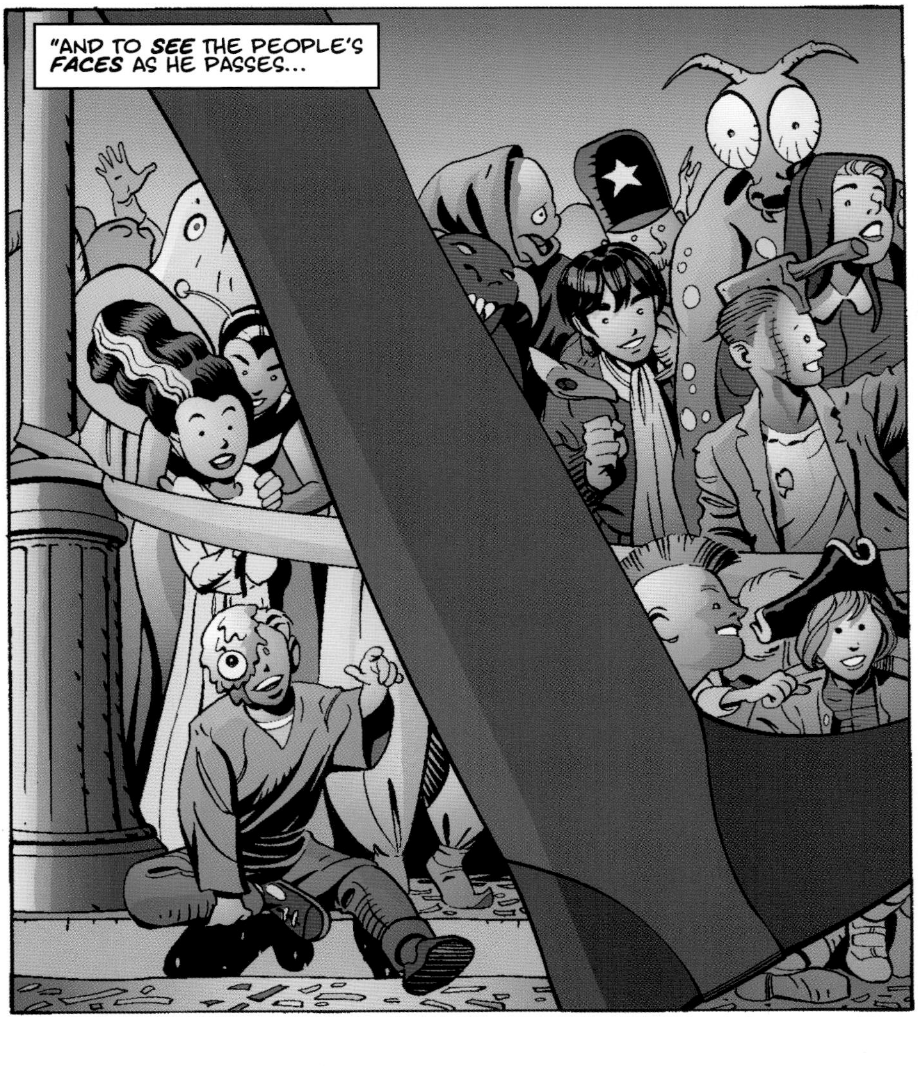
"AND TO SEE THE PEOPLE'S FACES AS HE PASSES...

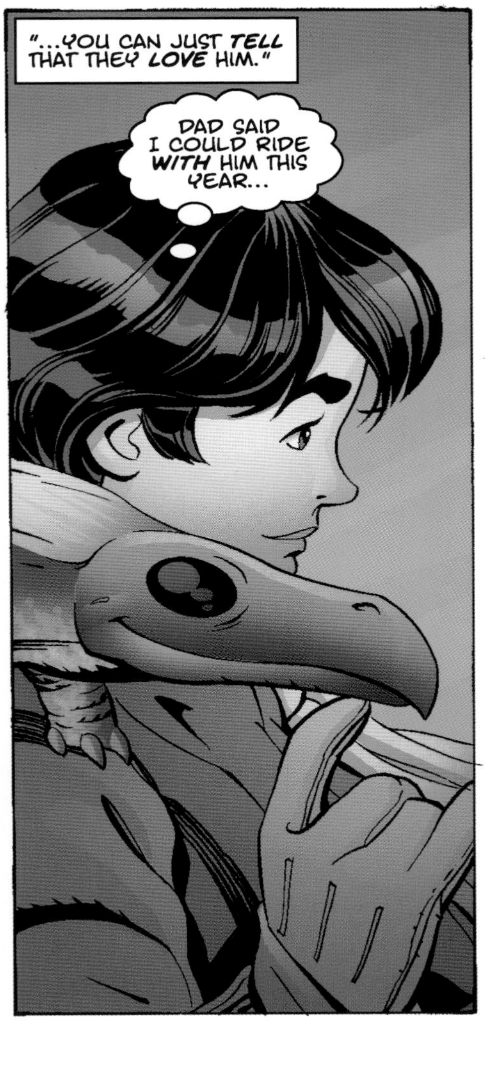
"...YOU CAN JUST TELL THAT THEY LOVE HIM."
DAD SAID I COULD RIDE WITH HIM THIS YEAR...

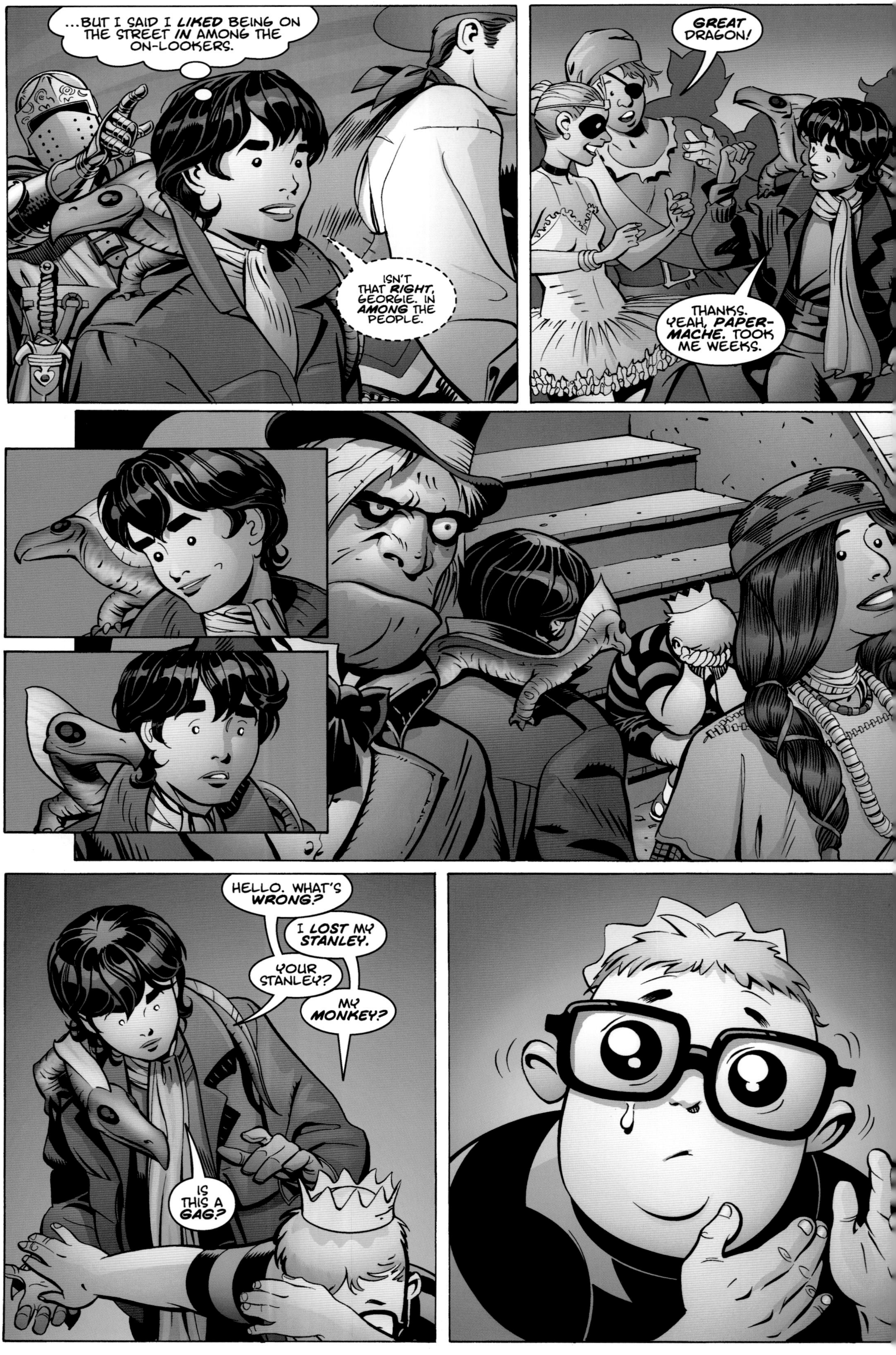
...BUT I SAID I LIKED BEING ON THE STREET IN AMONG THE ON-LOOKERS.
ISN'T THAT RIGHT, GEORGIE. IN AMONG THE PEOPLE.
GREAT DRAGON!
THANKS. YEAH, PAPER-MACHE. TOOK ME WEEKS.
HELLO. WHAT'S WRONG?
I LOST MY STANLEY.
YOUR STANLEY?
MY MONKEY?
IS THIS A GAG?

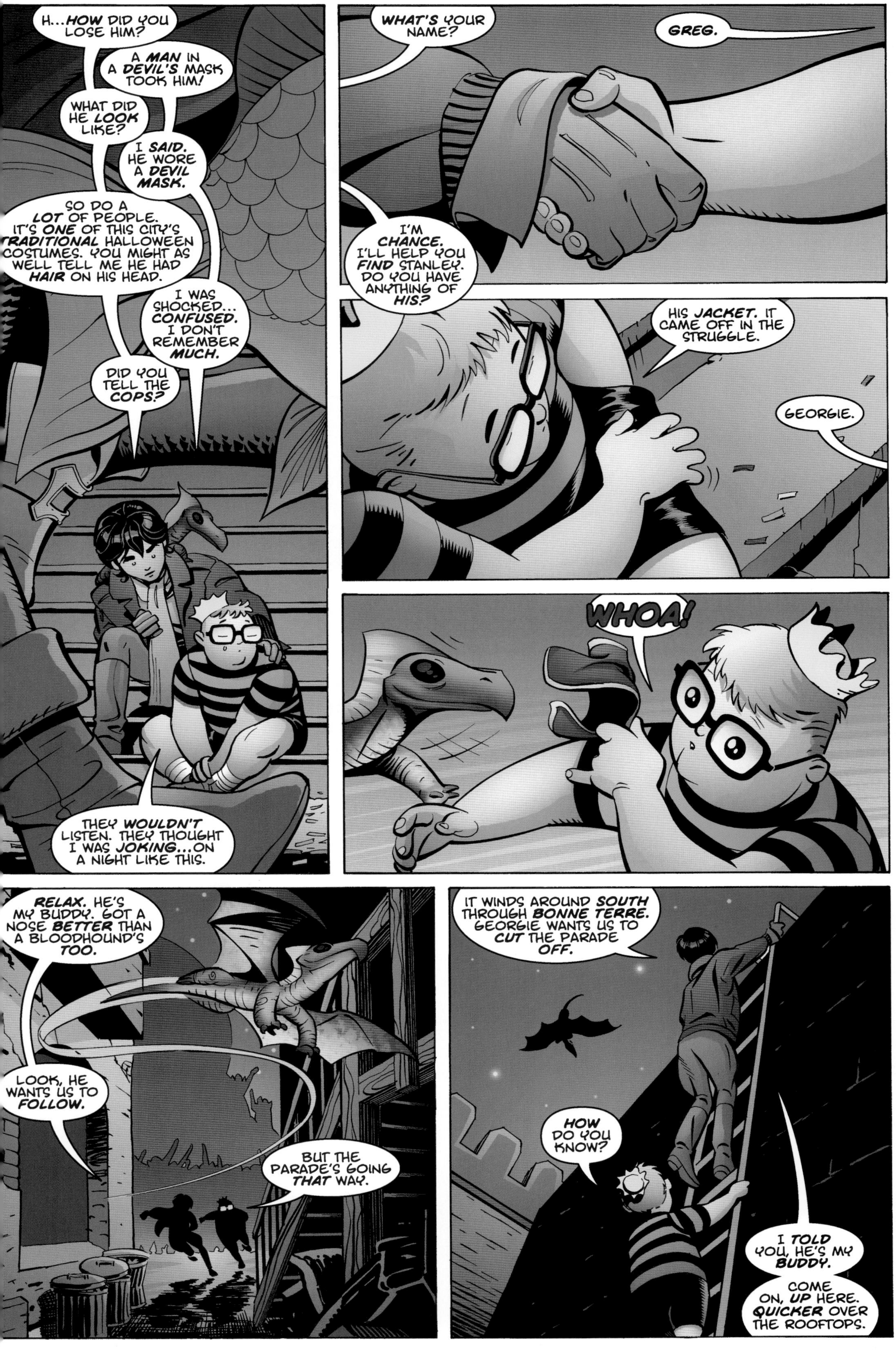
H...HOW DID YOU LOSE HIM?
A MAN IN A DEVIL'S MASK TOOK HIM!
WHAT DID HE LOOK LIKE?
I SAID. HE WORE A DEVIL MASK.
SO DO A LOT OF PEOPLE. IT'S ONE OF THIS CITY'S TRADITIONAL HALLOWEEN COSTUMES. YOU MIGHT AS WELL TELL ME HE HAD HAIR ON HIS HEAD.
I WAS SHOCKED... CONFUSED. I DON'T REMEMBER MUCH.
DID YOU TELL THE COPS?
THEY WOULDN'T LISTEN. THEY THOUGHT I WAS JOKING...ON A NIGHT LIKE THIS.
WHAT'S YOUR NAME?
GREG.
I'M CHANCE. I'LL HELP YOU FIND STANLEY. DO YOU HAVE ANYTHING OF HIS?
HIS JACKET. IT CAME OFF IN THE STRUGGLE.
GEORGIE.
WHOA!
RELAX. HE'S MY BUDDY. GOT A NOSE BETTER THAN A BLOODHOUND'S TOO.
LOOK, HE WANTS US TO FOLLOW.
BUT THE PARADE'S GOING THAT WAY.
IT WINDS AROUND SOUTH THROUGH BONNE TERRE. GEORGIE WANTS US TO CUT THE PARADE OFF.
HOW DO YOU KNOW?
I TOLD YOU, HE'S MY BUDDY.
COME ON, UP HERE. QUICKER OVER THE ROOFTOPS.

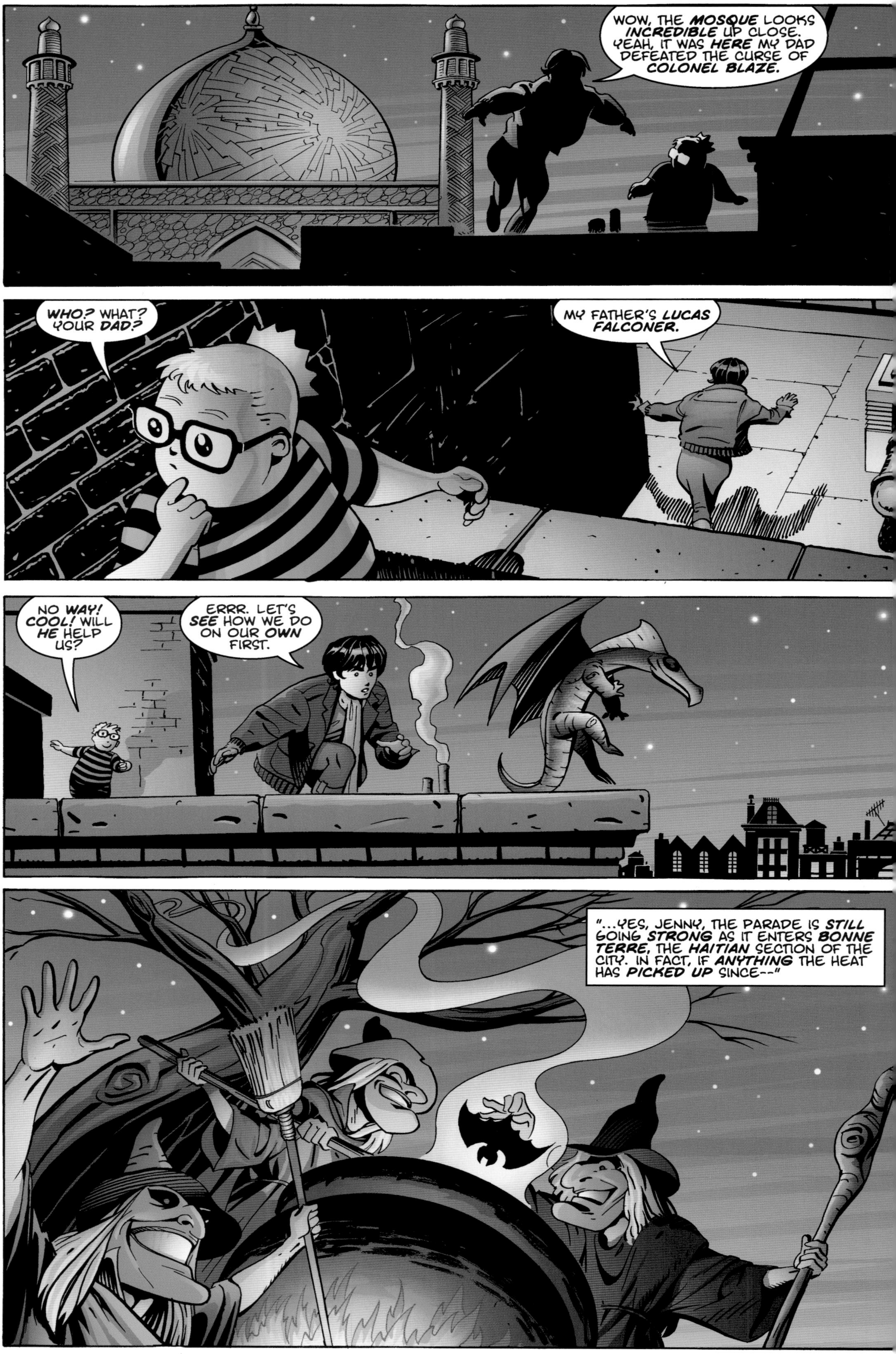
WOW, THE MOSQUE LOOKS INCREDIBLE UP CLOSE. YEAH, IT WAS HERE MY DAD DEFEATED THE CURSE OF COLONEL BLAZE.
WHO? WHAT? YOUR DAD?
MY FATHER'S LUCAS FALCONER.
NO WAY! COOL! WILL HE HELP US?
ERRR. LET'S SEE HOW WE DO ON OUR OWN FIRST.
"...YES, JENNY, THE PARADE IS STILL GOING STRONG AS IT ENTERS BONNE TERRE, THE HAITIAN SECTION OF THE CITY. IN FACT, IF ANYTHING THE HEAT HAS PICKED UP SINCE--"

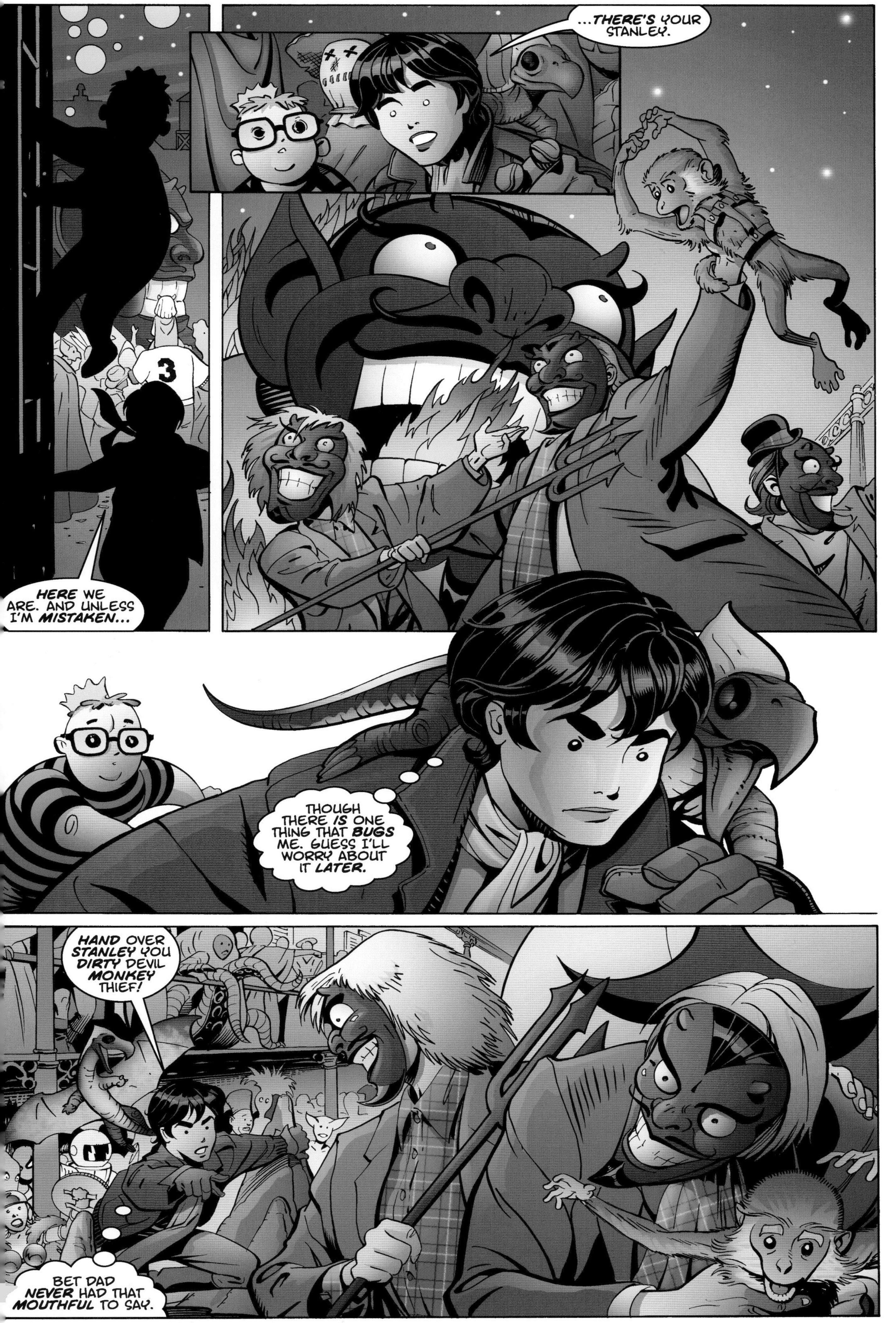
HERE WE ARE. AND UNLESS I'M MISTAKEN...
...THERE'S YOUR STANLEY.
THOUGH THERE IS ONE THING THAT BUGS ME. GUESS I'LL WORRY ABOUT IT LATER.
HAND OVER STANLEY YOU DIRTY DEVIL MONKEY THIEF!
BET DAD NEVER HAD THAT MOUTHFUL TO SAY.
3

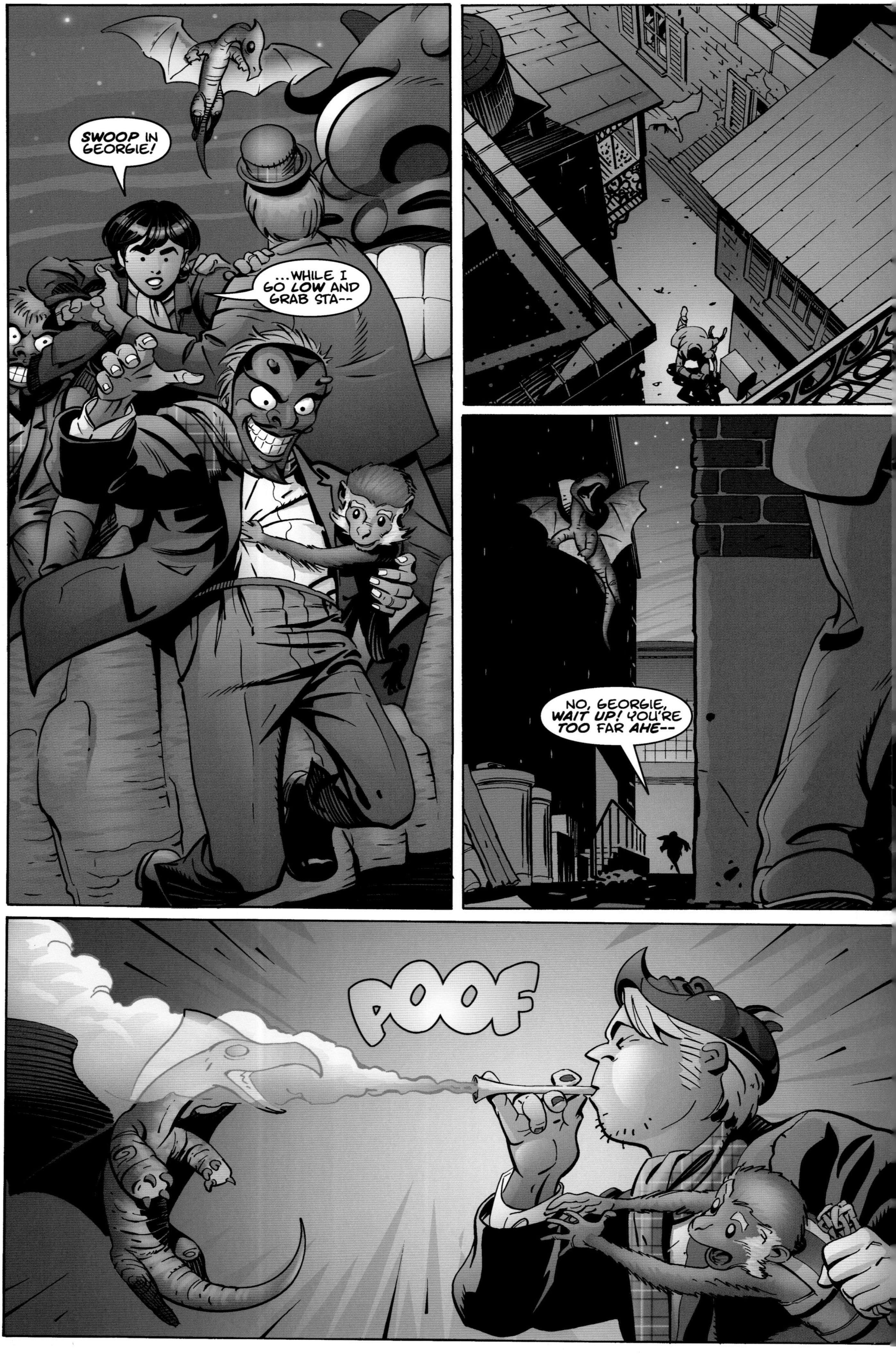
SWOOP IN GEORGIE!
...WHILE I GO LOW AND GRAB STA--
NO, GEORGIE, WAIT UP! YOU'RE TOO FAR AHE--
POOF

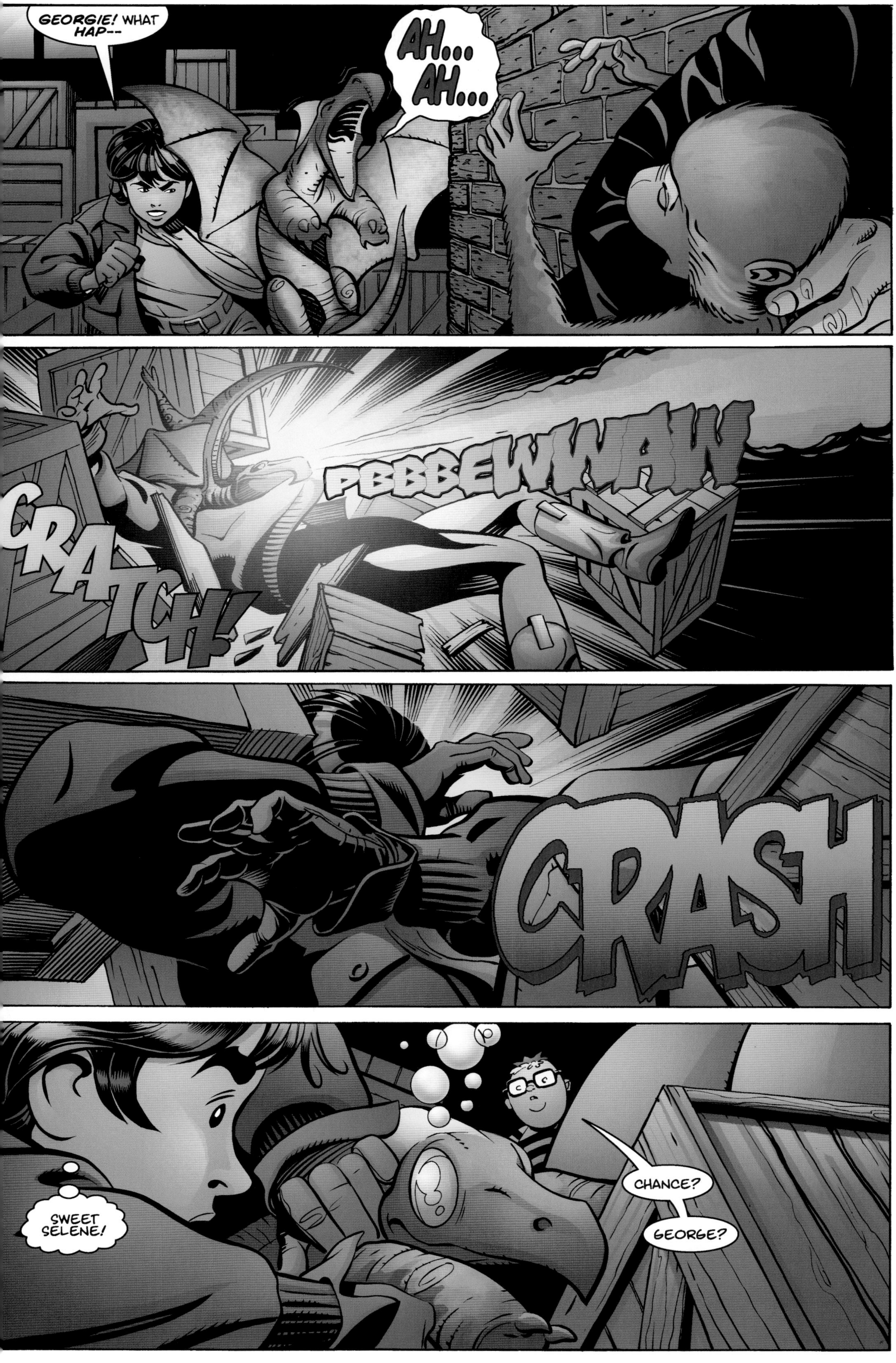
GEORGIE! WHAT HAP--
AH... AH...
CRATCH!
PBBBEWWAW
CRASH
SWEET SELENE!
CHANCE?
GEORGE?

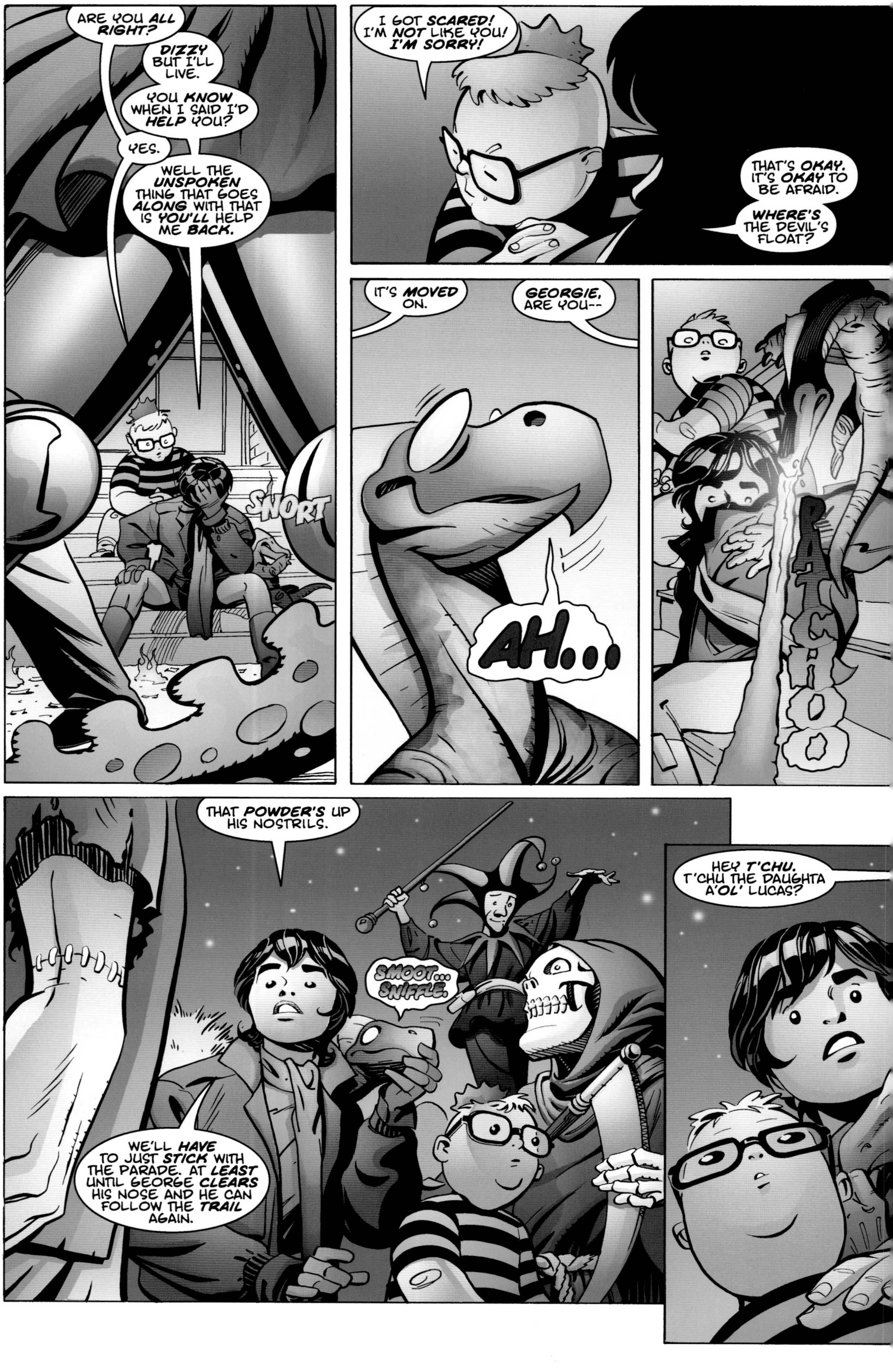

ARE YOU ALL RIGHT?
DIZZY BUT I'LL LIVE.
YOU KNOW WHEN I SAID I'D HELP YOU?
YES.
WELL THE UNSPOKEN THING THAT GOES ALONG WITH THAT IS YOU'LL HELP ME BACK.
SNORT
I GOT SCARED! I'M NOT LIKE YOU! I'M SORRY!
THAT'S OKAY. IT'S OKAY TO BE AFRAID.
WHERE'S THE DEVIL'S FLOAT?
IT'S MOVED ON.
GEORGIE, ARE YOU--
AH...
RACHOO
THAT POWDER'S UP HIS NOSTRILS.
SMOOT... SNIFFLE.
WE'LL HAVE TO JUST STICK WITH THE PARADE. AT LEAST UNTIL GEORGE CLEARS HIS NOSE AND HE CAN FOLLOW THE TRAIL AGAIN.
HEY T'CHU. T'CHU THE DAUGHTA A'OL' LUCAS?

LUCAS FALCONER. THAT'S *RIGHT*.

M'NAME'S *JEAN-PIERRE*.

ME'N LUCAS KNOW EACHO'THA O'OLD.

TOKENS, HEXES AND CONJERS
FORTUNES READ
CURSES PLACED, CURSES LIFTED
(All Prices Negotiable)

I DON'T... I DON'T...

CORS Y'DON KNOW ME, CHILD. IT WAS BACK *LONG* TIME WHEN I *LAS'*SAW YO'PAPA. LONG TIME. YO'*MOMMA* WAS ALIVE. *PRETTY* YOUNG T'ING. T'CHU TAKE *AFTA* HER.

I SEE T'CHU *FIGHTIN'*. WHAT'S THE SCENE?

THIS IS *GREG*. ONE OF THE *DEVILS* ON A PARADE FLOAT STOLE HIS *PET MONKEY*, STANLEY. WE'RE *FOLLOWING* THEM.

THING THAT *PUZZLES* ME THOUGH...

YEAH?

...IF THE DEVIL WANTS THE MONKEY *BAD* ENOUGH TO *STEAL* IT...WHY HANG *AROUND* IN THE PARADE? *WHY* HASN'T HE *RUN?*

PARADE...ITS *ROUTE*. NO'JUST RANDOM.

WHAT'S SO *SPECIAL* ABOUT IT?

NO'MANY PEOPLE KNOW... YO'PAPA N'MAYBE A *FEW* HISTORIANS. *ME*, O'COURSE.

N'*MAYBE* SANDERS...HIM D'AT RUNS THE *ACU*. HE KNOWS *MORE* 'BOUT THE *DARK* SIDE N'HE LETS ON.

WHAT ABOUT THE *ROUTE?*

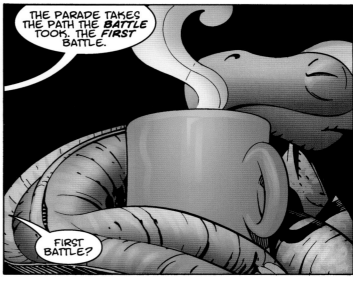

THE PARADE TAKES THE PATH THE *BATTLE* TOOK. THE *FIRST* BATTLE.

FIRST BATTLE?

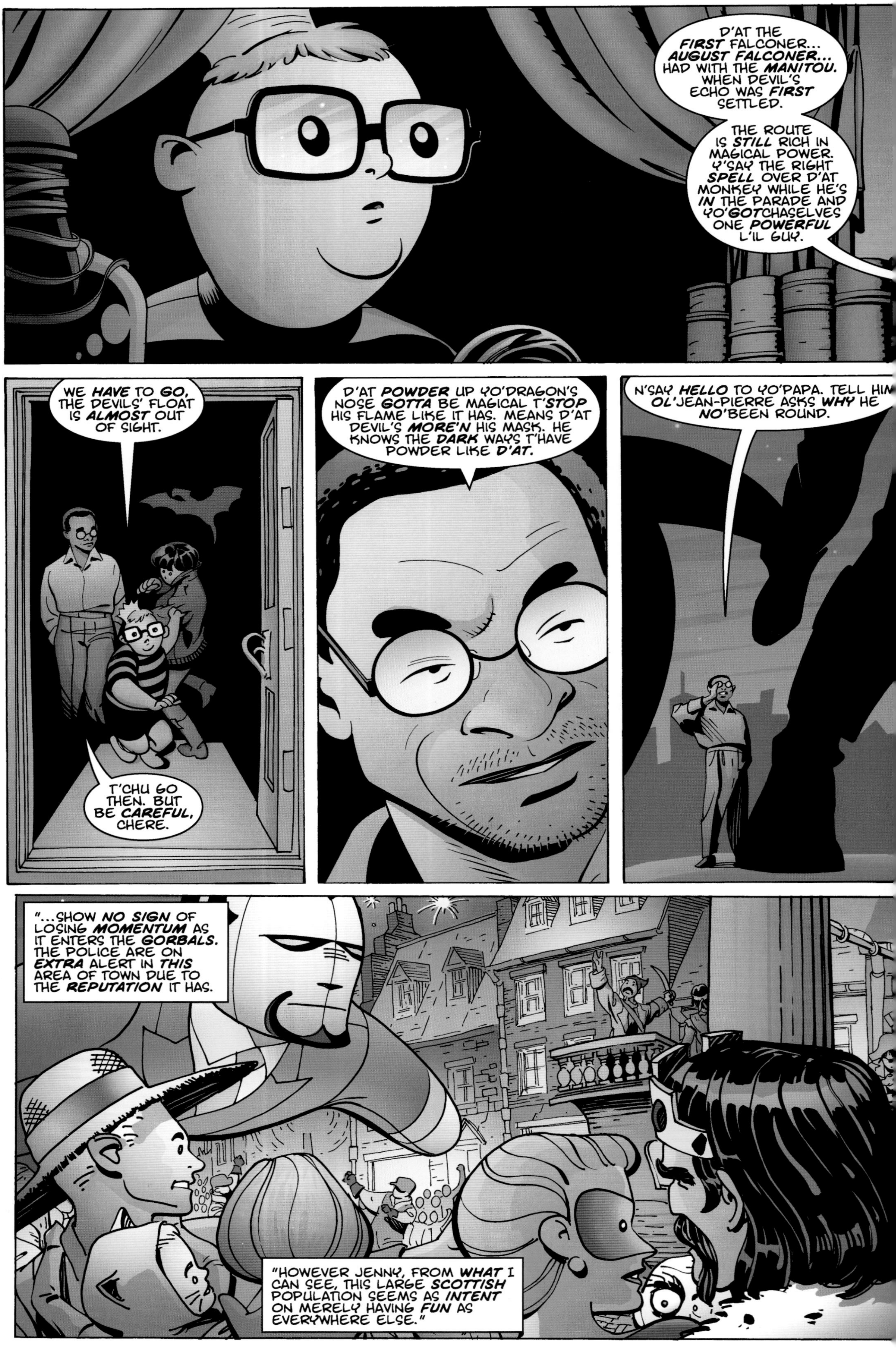
D'AT THE FIRST FALCONER... AUGUST FALCONER... HAD WITH THE MANITOU. WHEN DEVIL'S ECHO WAS FIRST SETTLED.
THE ROUTE IS STILL RICH IN MAGICAL POWER. Y'SAY THE RIGHT SPELL OVER D'AT MONKEY WHILE HE'S IN THE PARADE AND YO'GOTCHASELVES ONE POWERFUL L'IL GUY.
WE HAVE TO GO, THE DEVILS' FLOAT IS ALMOST OUT OF SIGHT.
T'CHU GO THEN. BUT BE CAREFUL, CHERE.
D'AT POWDER UP YO'DRAGON'S NOSE GOTTA BE MAGICAL T'STOP HIS FLAME LIKE IT HAS. MEANS D'AT DEVIL'S MORE'N HIS MASK. HE KNOWS THE DARK WAYS T'HAVE POWDER LIKE D'AT.
N'SAY HELLO TO YO'PAPA. TELL HIM OL'JEAN-PIERRE ASKS WHY HE NO'BEEN ROUND.
"...SHOW NO SIGN OF LOSING MOMENTUM AS IT ENTERS THE GORBALS. THE POLICE ARE ON EXTRA ALERT IN THIS AREA OF TOWN DUE TO THE REPUTATION IT HAS.
"HOWEVER JENNY, FROM WHAT I CAN SEE, THIS LARGE SCOTTISH POPULATION SEEMS AS INTENT ON MERELY HAVING FUN AS EVERYWHERE ELSE."

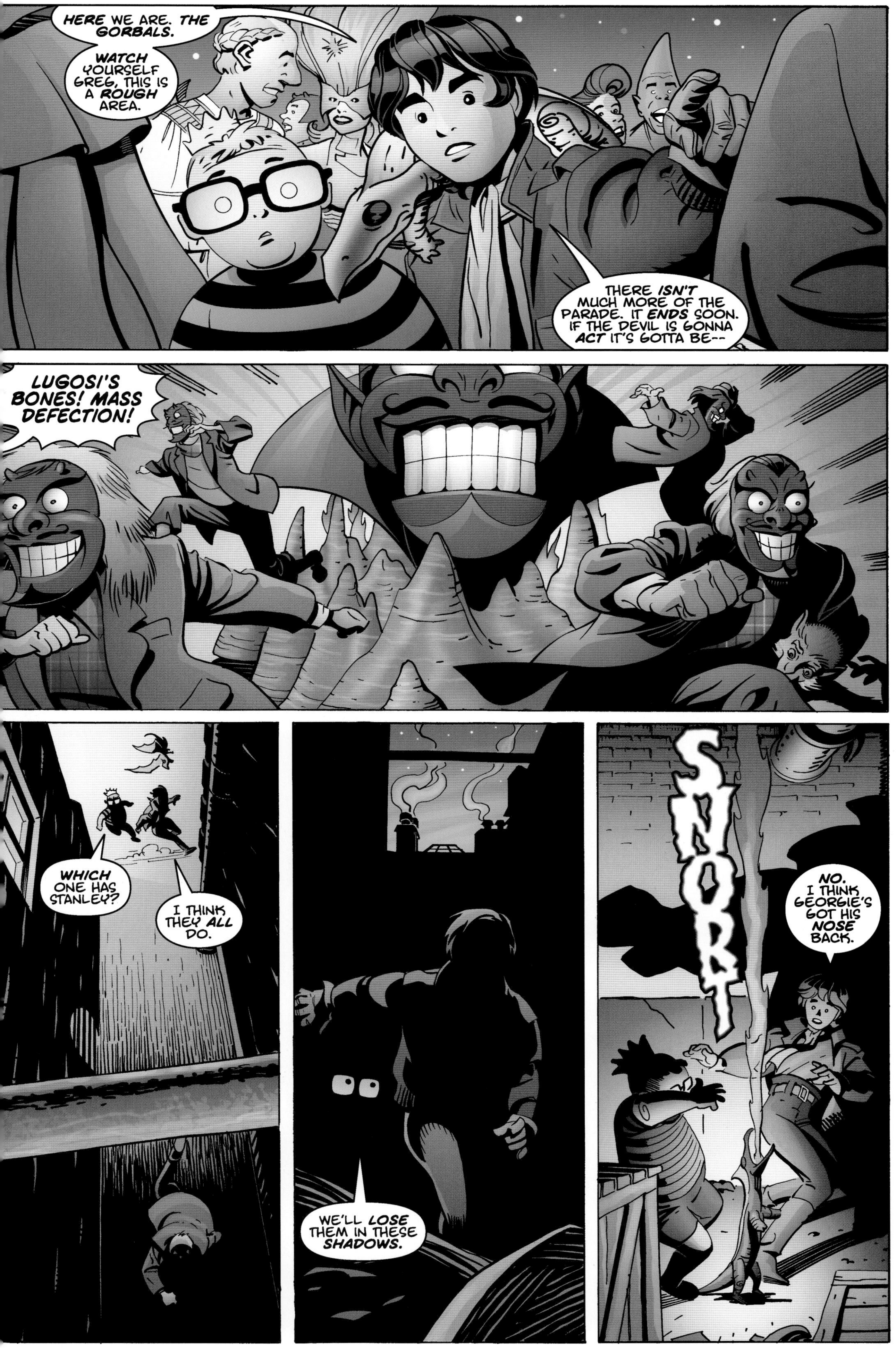
HERE WE ARE. THE GORBALS.
WATCH YOURSELF GREG, THIS IS A ROUGH AREA.
THERE ISN'T MUCH MORE OF THE PARADE. IT ENDS SOON. IF THE DEVIL IS GONNA ACT IT'S GOTTA BE--
LUGOSI'S BONES! MASS DEFECTION!
WHICH ONE HAS STANLEY?
I THINK THEY ALL DO.
WE'LL LOSE THEM IN THESE SHADOWS.
SNORT
NO. I THINK GEORGIE'S GOT HIS NOSE BACK.

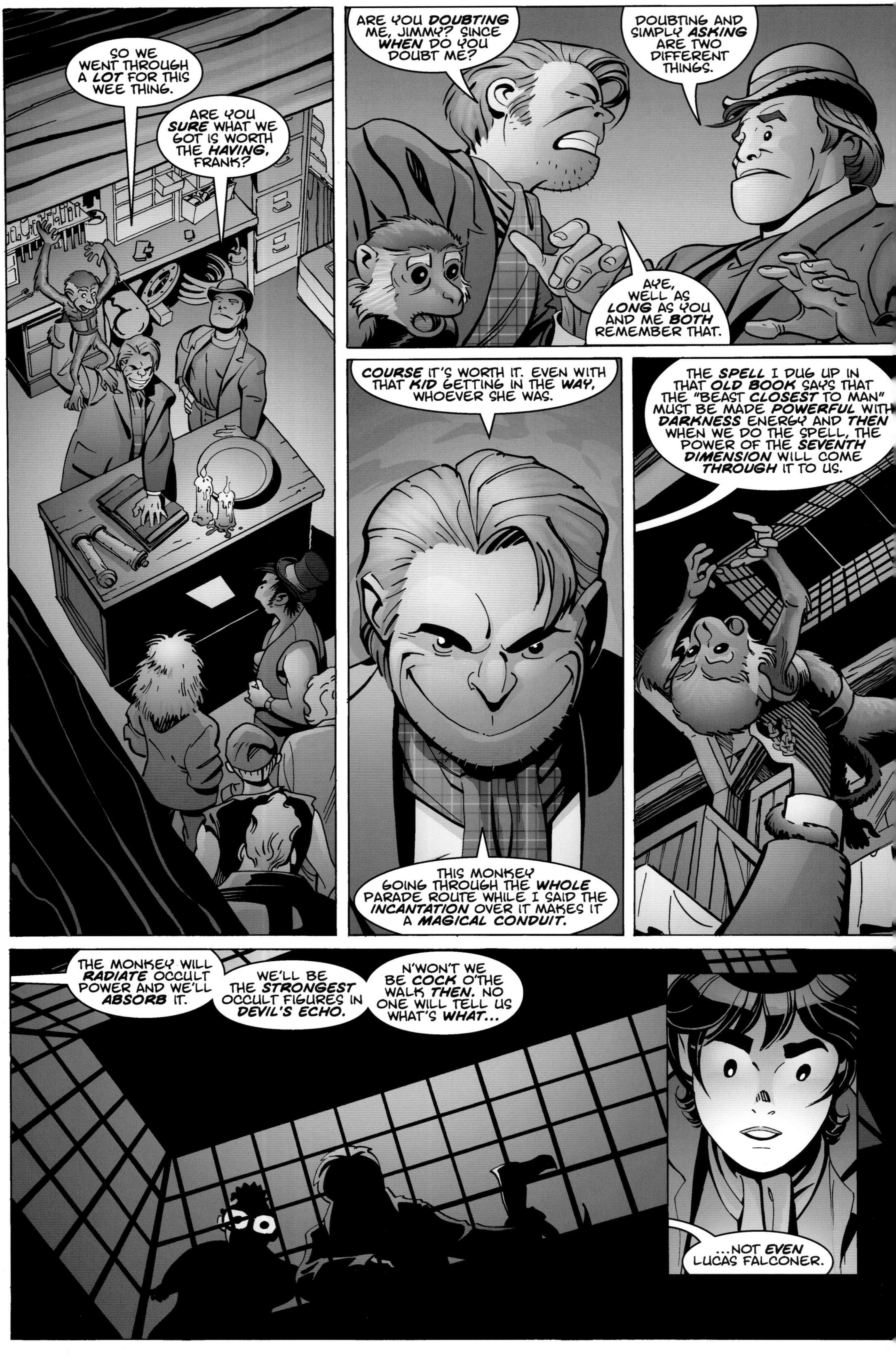
SO WE WENT THROUGH A LOT FOR THIS WEE THING.
ARE YOU SURE WHAT WE GOT IS WORTH THE HAVING, FRANK?
ARE YOU DOUBTING ME, JIMMY? SINCE WHEN DO YOU DOUBT ME?
DOUBTING AND SIMPLY ASKING ARE TWO DIFFERENT THINGS.
AYE, WELL AS LONG AS YOU AND ME BOTH REMEMBER THAT.
COURSE IT'S WORTH IT. EVEN WITH THAT KID GETTING IN THE WAY, WHOEVER SHE WAS.
THIS MONKEY GOING THROUGH THE WHOLE PARADE ROUTE WHILE I SAID THE INCANTATION OVER IT MAKES IT A MAGICAL CONDUIT.
THE SPELL I DUG UP IN THAT OLD BOOK SAYS THAT THE "BEAST CLOSEST TO MAN" MUST BE MADE POWERFUL WITH DARKNESS ENERGY AND THEN WHEN WE DO THE SPELL, THE POWER OF THE SEVENTH DIMENSION WILL COME THROUGH IT TO US.
THE MONKEY WILL RADIATE OCCULT POWER AND WE'LL ABSORB IT.
WE'LL BE THE STRONGEST OCCULT FIGURES IN DEVIL'S ECHO.
N'WON'T WE BE COCK O'THE WALK THEN. NO ONE WILL TELL US WHAT'S WHAT...
...NOT EVEN LUCAS FALCONER.

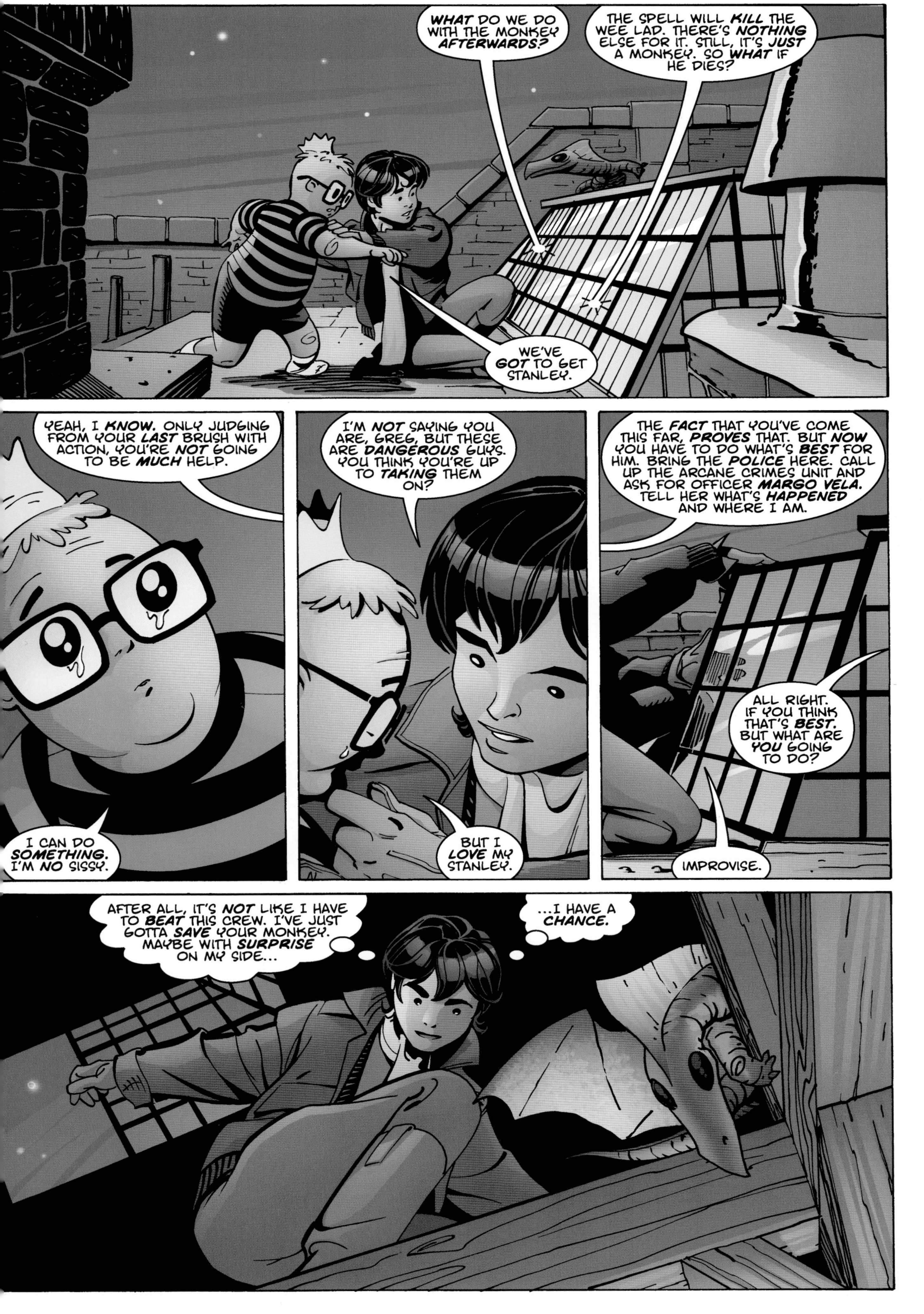
WHAT DO WE DO WITH THE MONKEY AFTERWARDS?
THE SPELL WILL KILL THE WEE LAD. THERE'S NOTHING ELSE FOR IT. STILL, IT'S JUST A MONKEY. SO WHAT IF HE DIES?
WE'VE GOT TO GET STANLEY.
YEAH, I KNOW. ONLY JUDGING FROM YOUR LAST BRUSH WITH ACTION, YOU'RE NOT GOING TO BE MUCH HELP.
I CAN DO SOMETHING. I'M NO SISSY.
I'M NOT SAYING YOU ARE, GREG, BUT THESE ARE DANGEROUS GUYS. YOU THINK YOU'RE UP TO TAKING THEM ON?
BUT I LOVE MY STANLEY.
THE FACT THAT YOU'VE COME THIS FAR, PROVES THAT. BUT NOW YOU HAVE TO DO WHAT'S BEST FOR HIM. BRING THE POLICE HERE. CALL UP THE ARCANE CRIMES UNIT AND ASK FOR OFFICER MARGO VELA. TELL HER WHAT'S HAPPENED AND WHERE I AM.
ALL RIGHT. IF YOU THINK THAT'S BEST. BUT WHAT ARE YOU GOING TO DO?
IMPROVISE.
AFTER ALL, IT'S NOT LIKE I HAVE TO BEAT THIS CREW. I'VE JUST GOTTA SAVE YOUR MONKEY. MAYBE WITH SURPRISE ON MY SIDE...
...I HAVE A CHANCE.

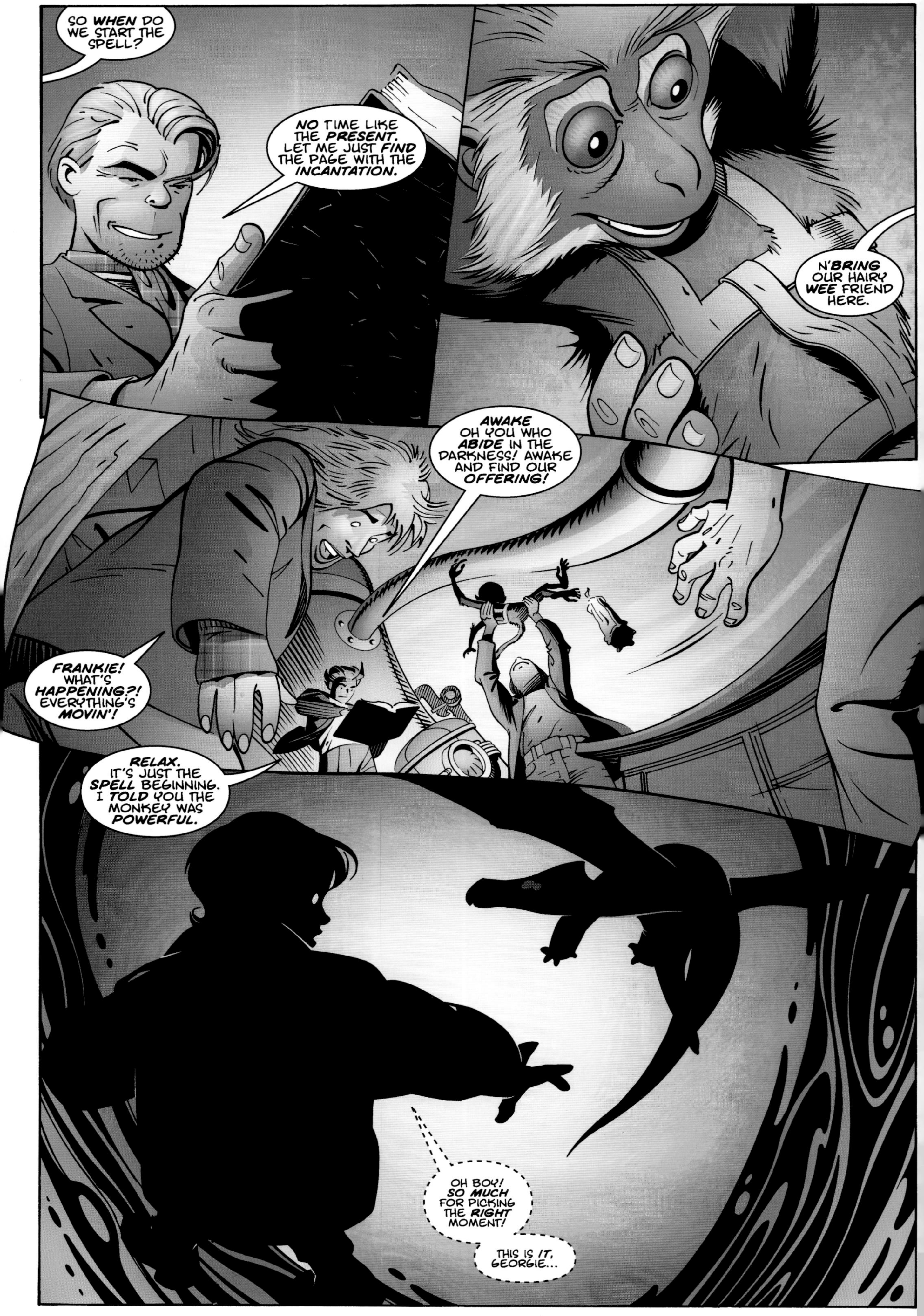
SO WHEN DO WE START THE SPELL?
NO TIME LIKE THE PRESENT. LET ME JUST FIND THE PAGE WITH THE INCANTATION.
N'BRING OUR HAIRY WEE FRIEND HERE.
AWAKE OH YOU WHO ABIDE IN THE DARKNESS! AWAKE AND FIND OUR OFFERING!
FRANKIE! WHAT'S HAPPENING?! EVERYTHING'S MOVIN'!
RELAX. IT'S JUST THE SPELL BEGINNING. I TOLD YOU THE MONKEY WAS POWERFUL.
OH BOY! SO MUCH FOR PICKING THE RIGHT MOMENT!
THIS IS IT, GEORGIE...

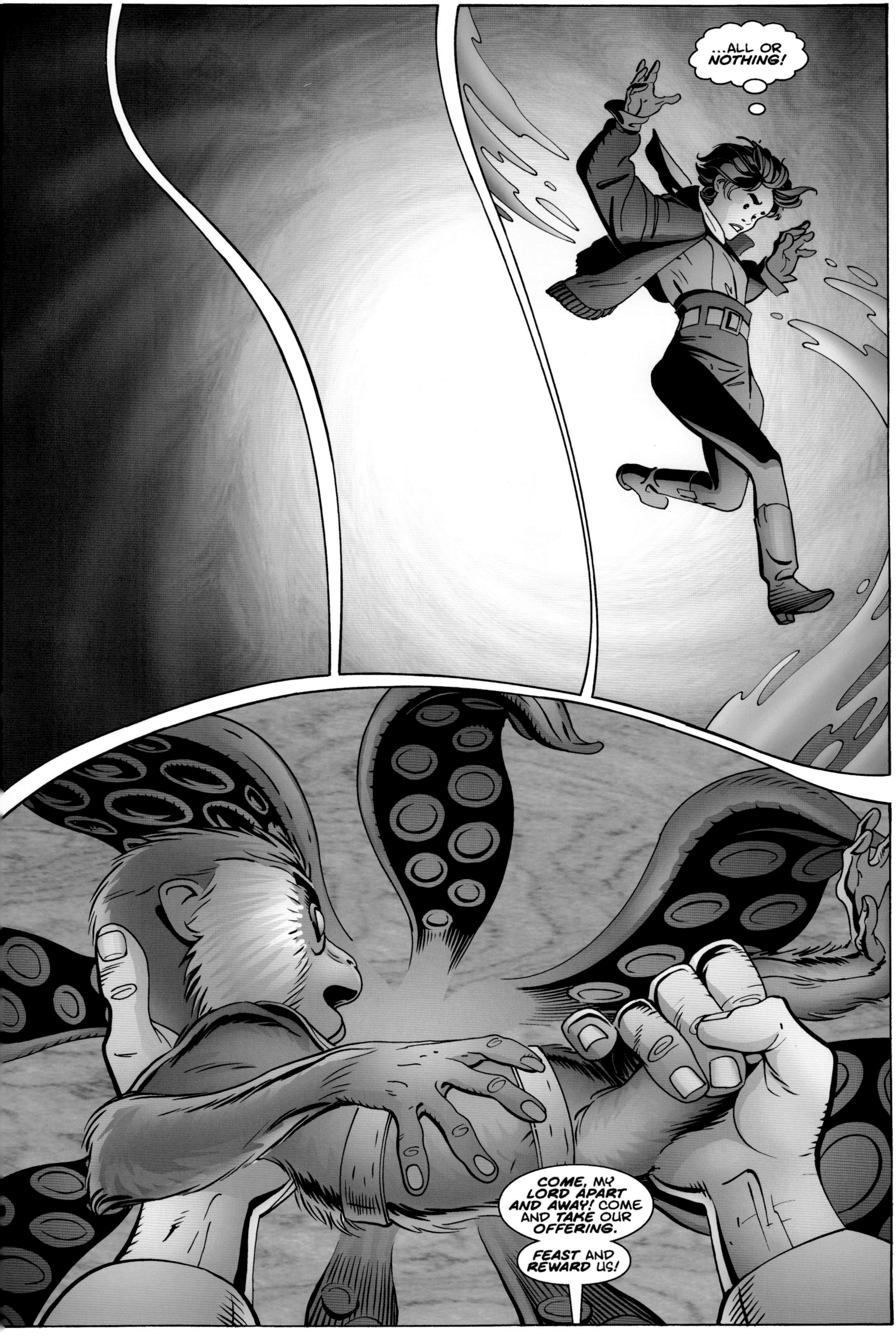
...ALL OR NOTHING!
COME, MY LORD APART AND AWAY! COME AND TAKE OUR OFFERING.
FEAST AND REWARD US!

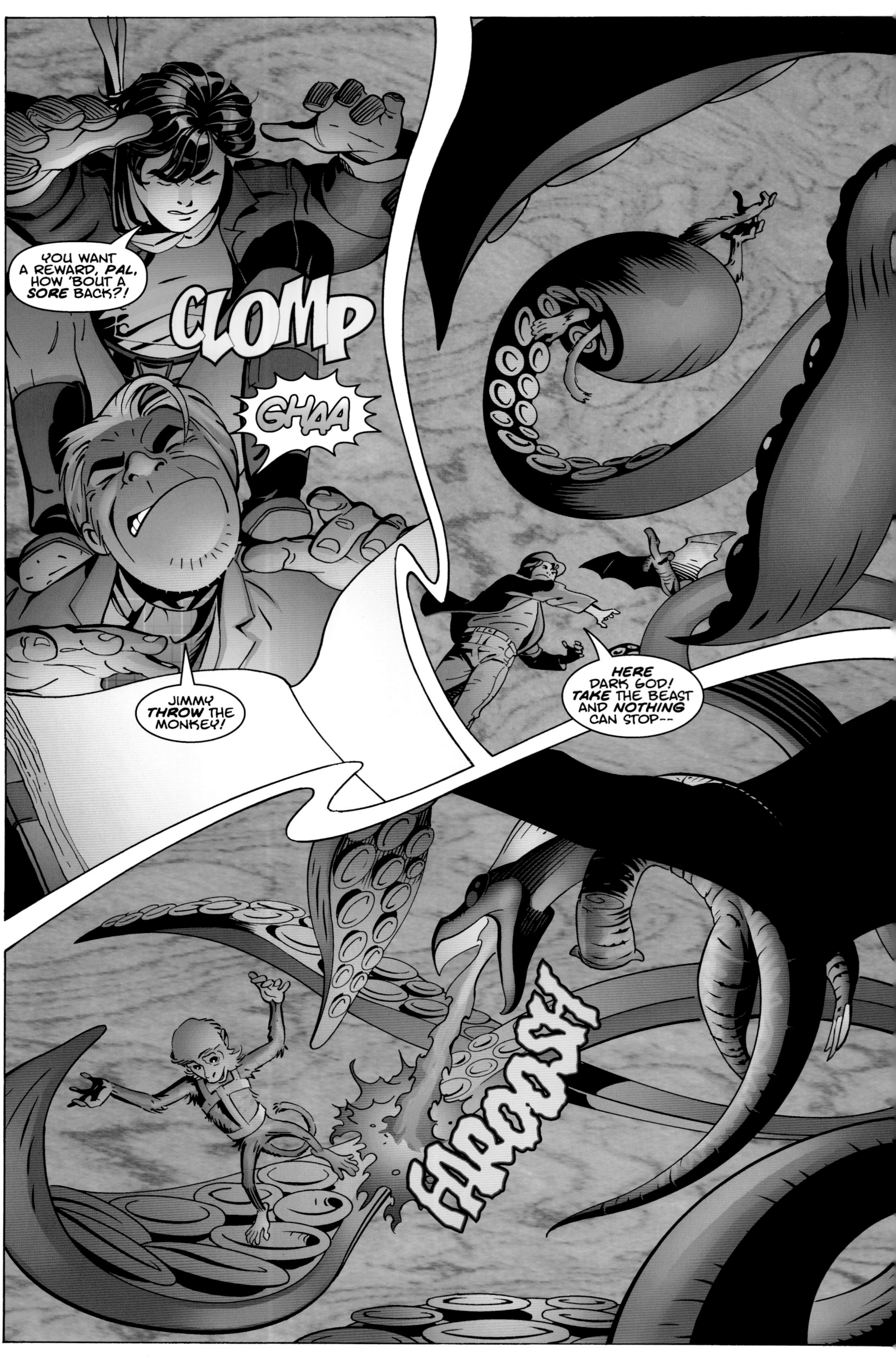
YOU WANT A REWARD, PAL, HOW 'BOUT A SORE BACK?!
CLOMP
GHAA
JIMMY THROW THE MONKEY!
HERE DARK GOD! TAKE THE BEAST AND NOTHING CAN STOP--
FROOSH

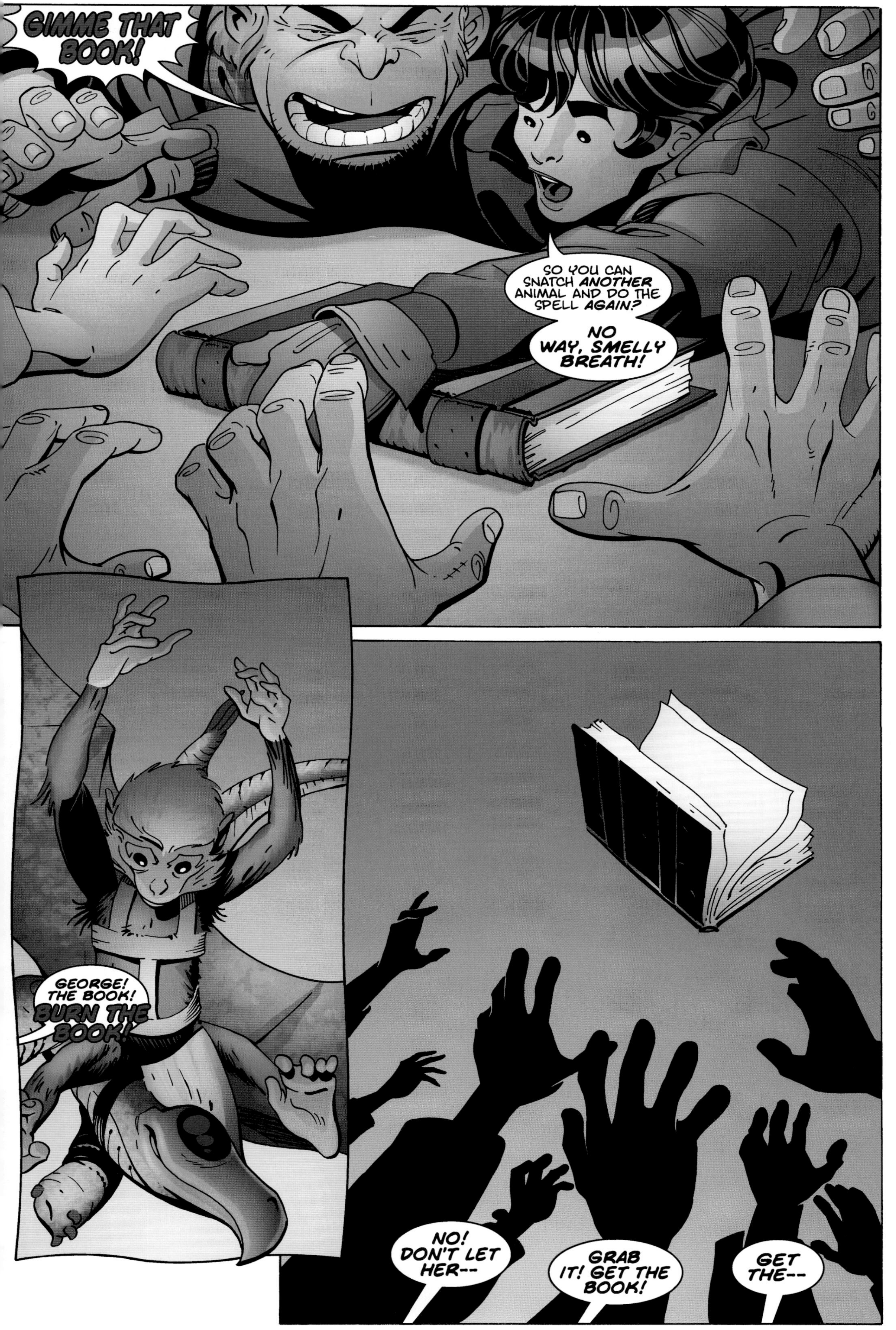
GIMME THAT BOOK!
SO YOU CAN SNATCH ANOTHER ANIMAL AND DO THE SPELL AGAIN?
NO WAY, SMELLY BREATH!
GEORGE! THE BOOK! BURN THE BOOK!
NO! DON'T LET HER--
GRAB IT! GET THE BOOK!
GET THE--

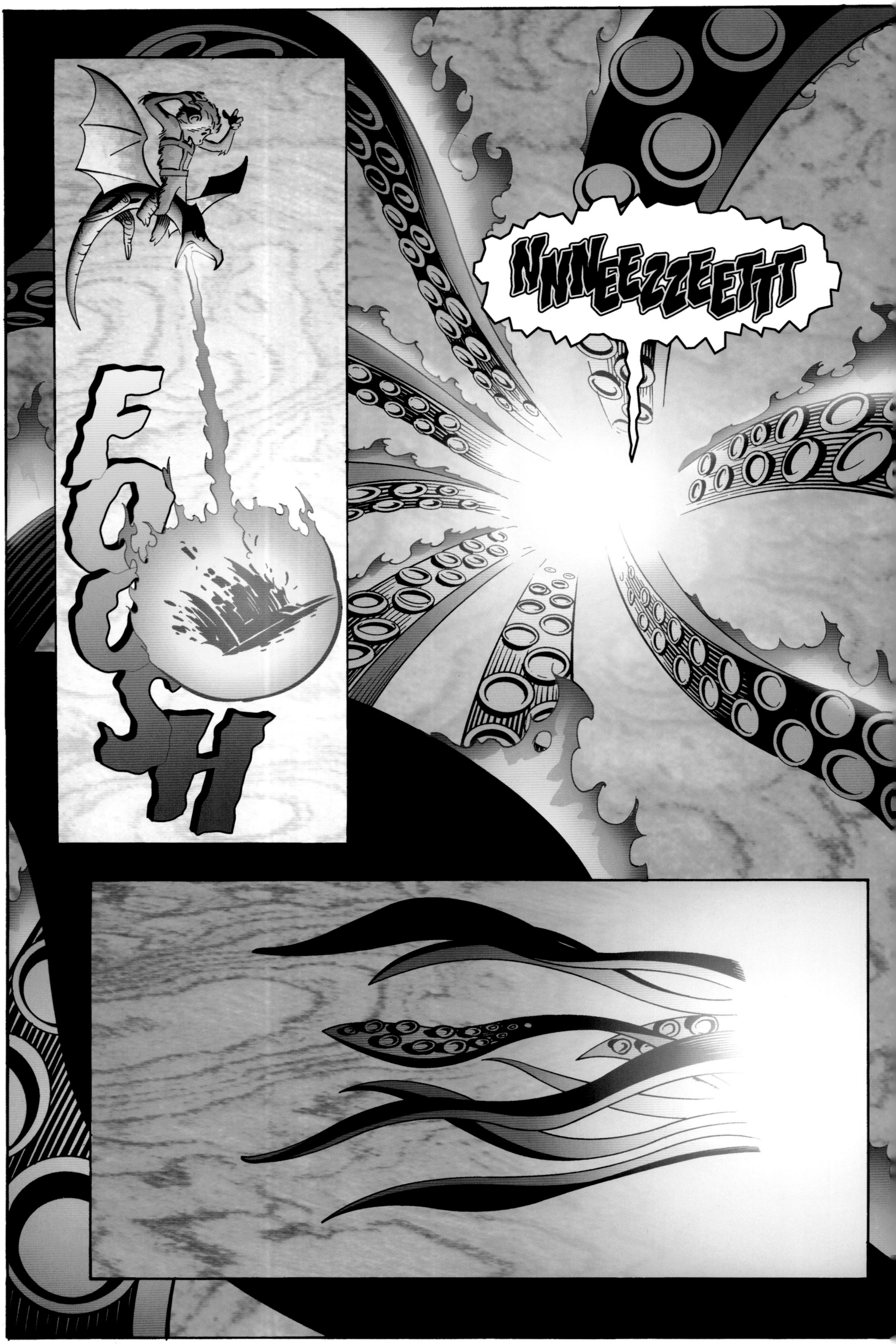
FOOSH
NNNEEZZEETTT

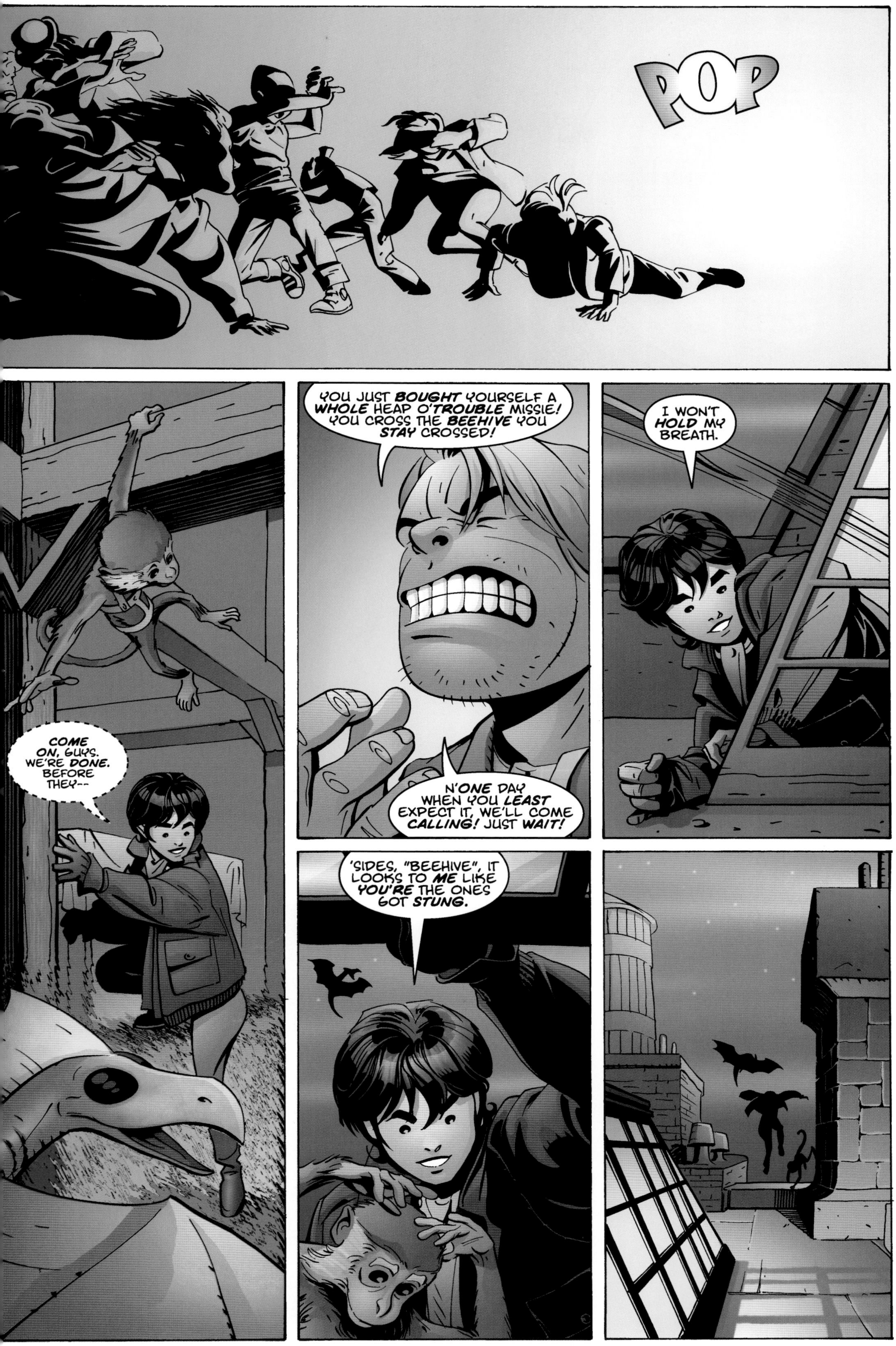
POP
YOU JUST BOUGHT YOURSELF A WHOLE HEAP O'TROUBLE MISSIE! YOU CROSS THE BEEHIVE YOU STAY CROSSED!
N'ONE DAY WHEN YOU LEAST EXPECT IT, WE'LL COME CALLING! JUST WAIT!
I WON'T HOLD MY BREATH.
COME ON, GUYS. WE'RE DONE. BEFORE THEY--
'SIDES, "BEEHIVE", IT LOOKS TO ME LIKE YOU'RE THE ONES GOT STUNG.

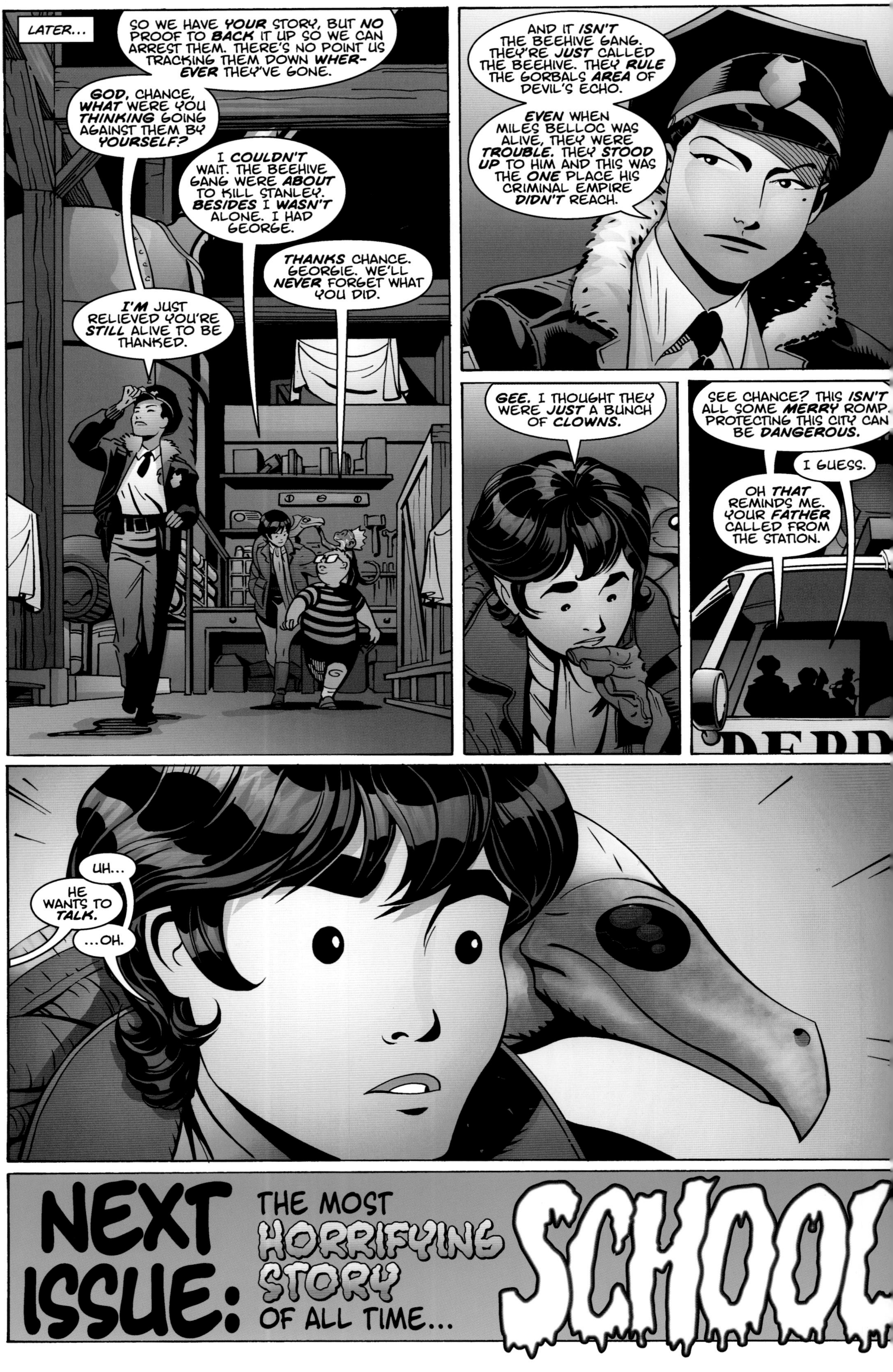
LATER...
SO WE HAVE YOUR STORY, BUT NO PROOF TO BACK IT UP SO WE CAN ARREST THEM. THERE'S NO POINT US TRACKING THEM DOWN WHEREVER THEY'VE GONE.
GOD, CHANCE, WHAT WERE YOU THINKING GOING AGAINST THEM BY YOURSELF?
I COULDN'T WAIT. THE BEEHIVE GANG WERE ABOUT TO KILL STANLEY. BESIDES I WASN'T ALONE. I HAD GEORGE.
THANKS CHANCE. GEORGIE. WE'LL NEVER FORGET WHAT YOU DID.
I'M JUST RELIEVED YOU'RE STILL ALIVE TO BE THANKED.
AND IT ISN'T THE BEEHIVE GANG. THEY'RE JUST CALLED THE BEEHIVE. THEY RULE THE GORBALS AREA OF DEVIL'S ECHO.
EVEN WHEN MILES BELLOC WAS ALIVE, THEY WERE TROUBLE. THEY STOOD UP TO HIM AND THIS WAS THE ONE PLACE HIS CRIMINAL EMPIRE DIDN'T REACH.
GEE. I THOUGHT THEY WERE JUST A BUNCH OF CLOWNS.
SEE CHANCE? THIS ISN'T ALL SOME MERRY ROMP. PROTECTING THIS CITY CAN BE DANGEROUS.
I GUESS.
OH THAT REMINDS ME. YOUR FATHER CALLED FROM THE STATION.
UH...
HE WANTS TO TALK.
...OH.
NEXT ISSUE: THE MOST HORRIFYING STORY OF ALL TIME... SCHOOL

CHAPTER 2

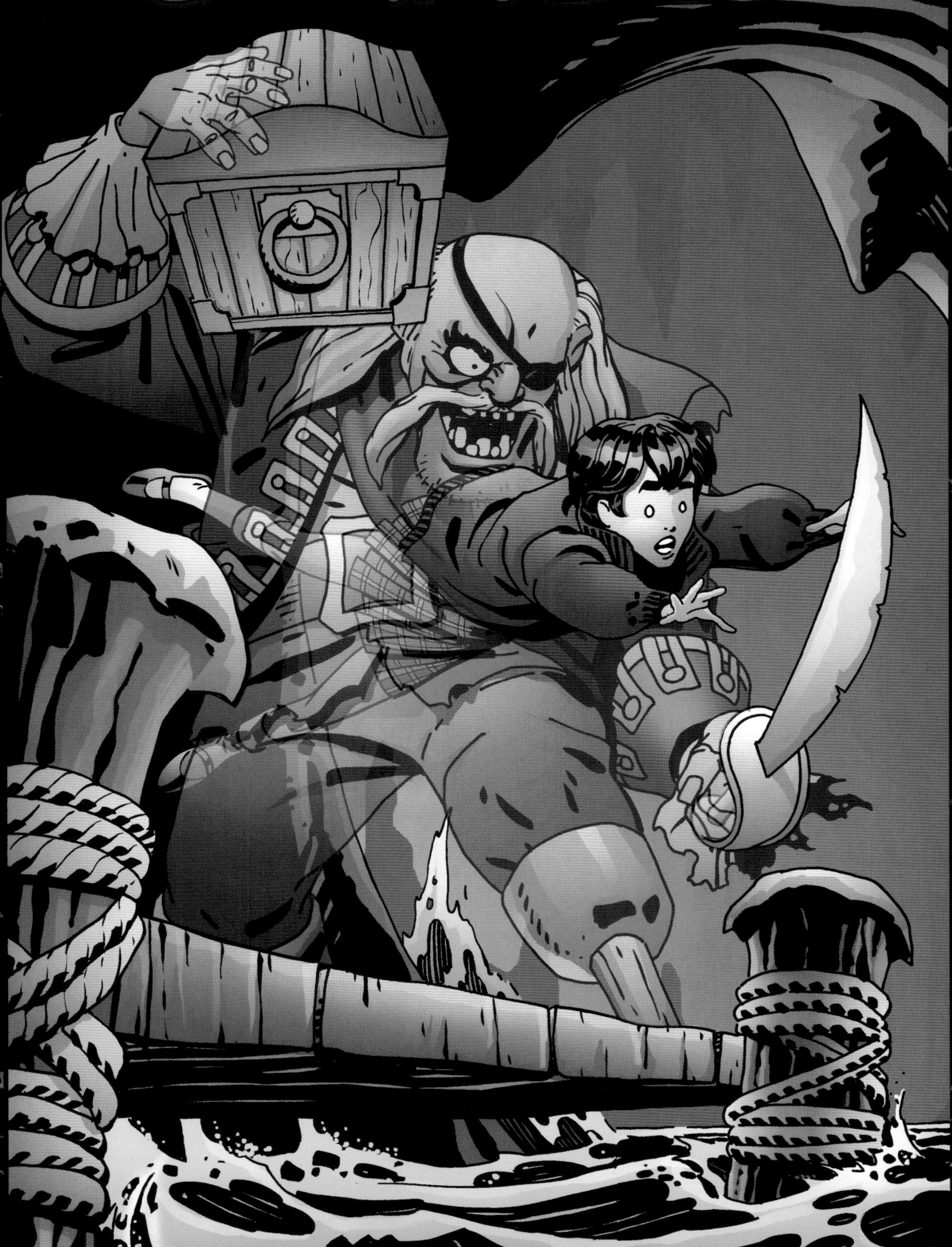

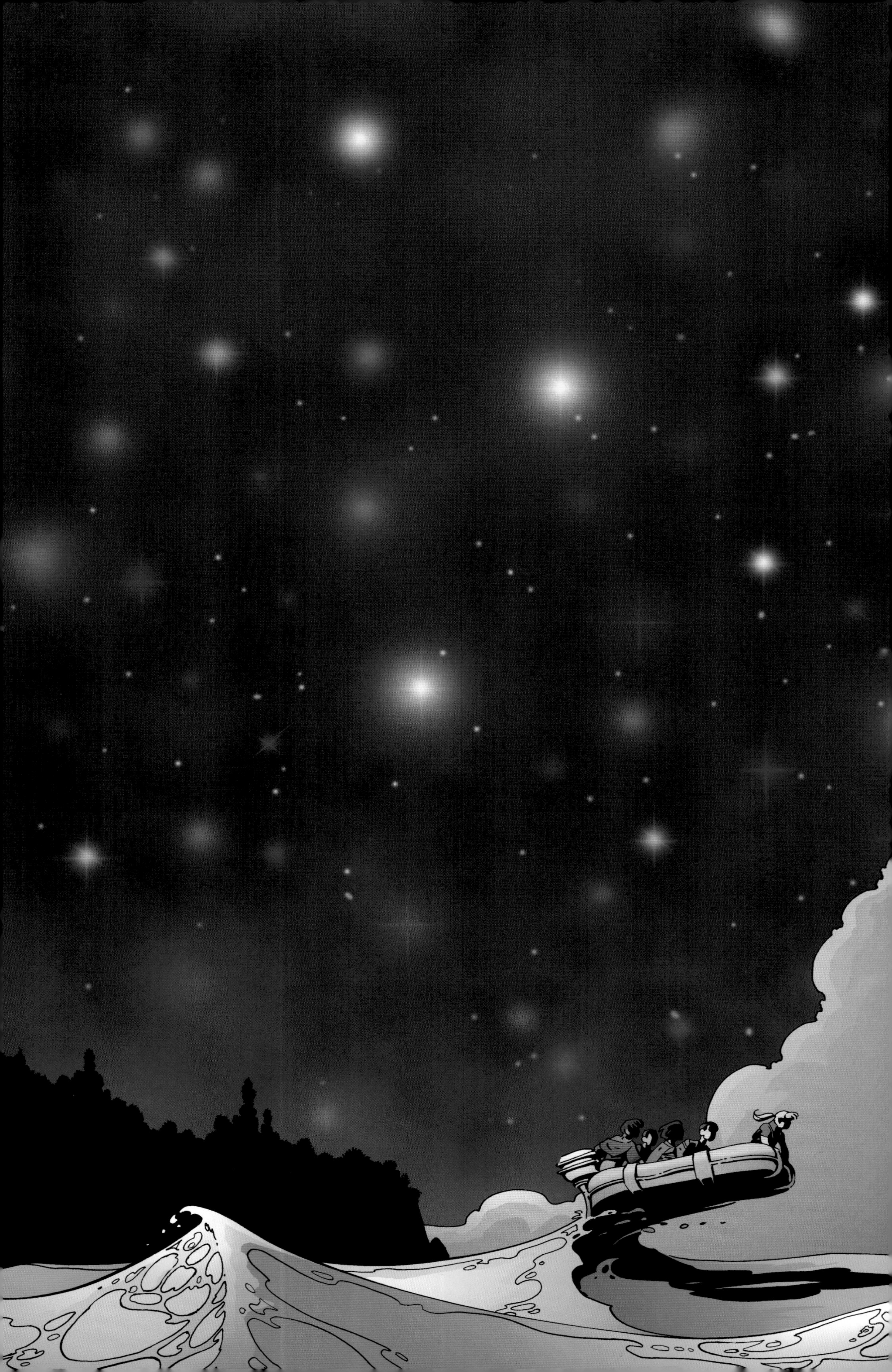

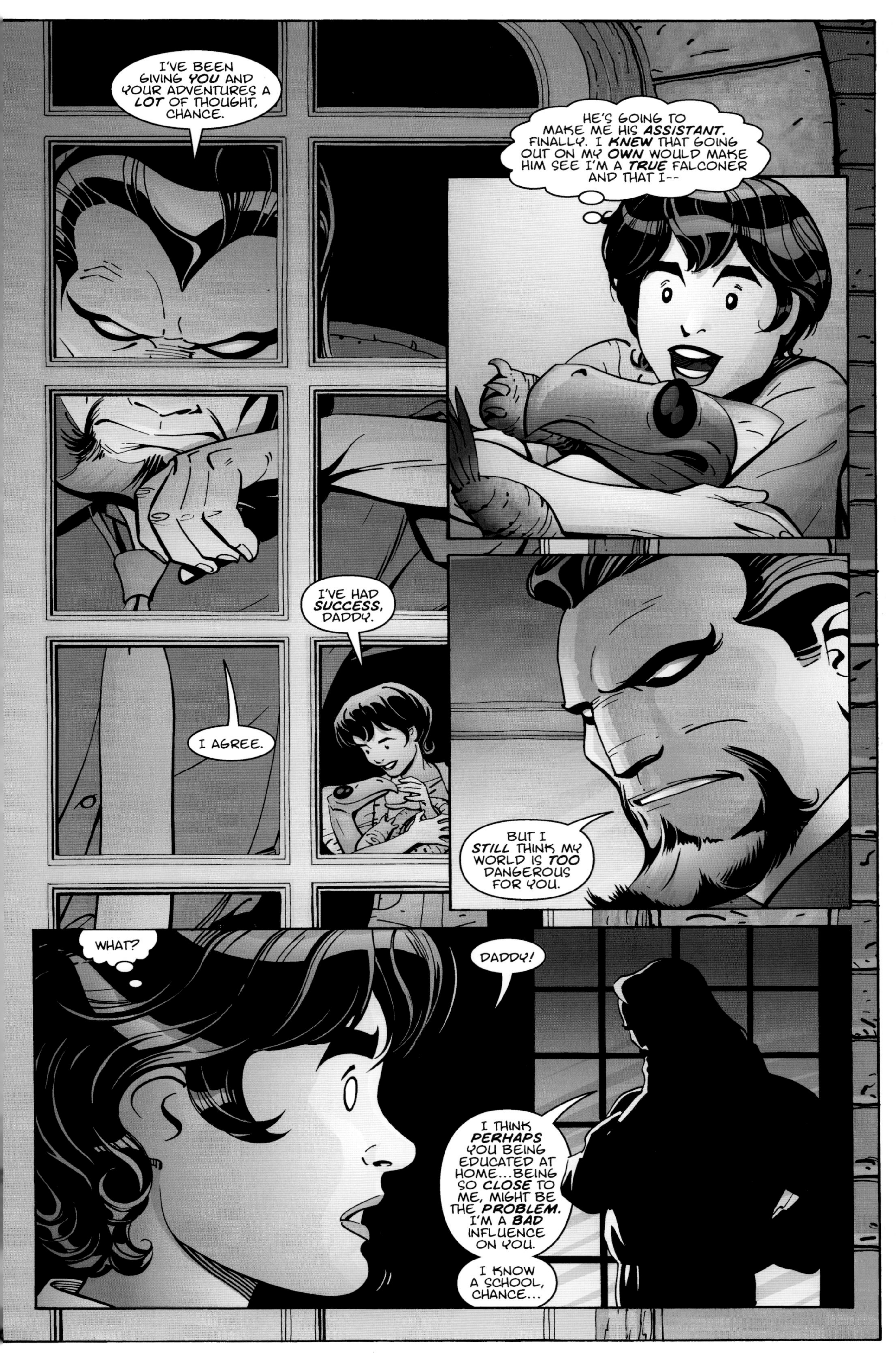

I'VE BEEN GIVING YOU AND YOUR ADVENTURES A LOT OF THOUGHT, CHANCE.
HE'S GOING TO MAKE ME HIS ASSISTANT. FINALLY. I KNEW THAT GOING OUT ON MY OWN WOULD MAKE HIM SEE I'M A TRUE FALCONER AND THAT I--
I'VE HAD SUCCESS, DADDY.
I AGREE.
BUT I STILL THINK MY WORLD IS TOO DANGEROUS FOR YOU.
WHAT?
DADDY!
I THINK PERHAPS YOU BEING EDUCATED AT HOME...BEING SO CLOSE TO ME, MIGHT BE THE PROBLEM. I'M A BAD INFLUENCE ON YOU.
I KNOW A SCHOOL, CHANCE...

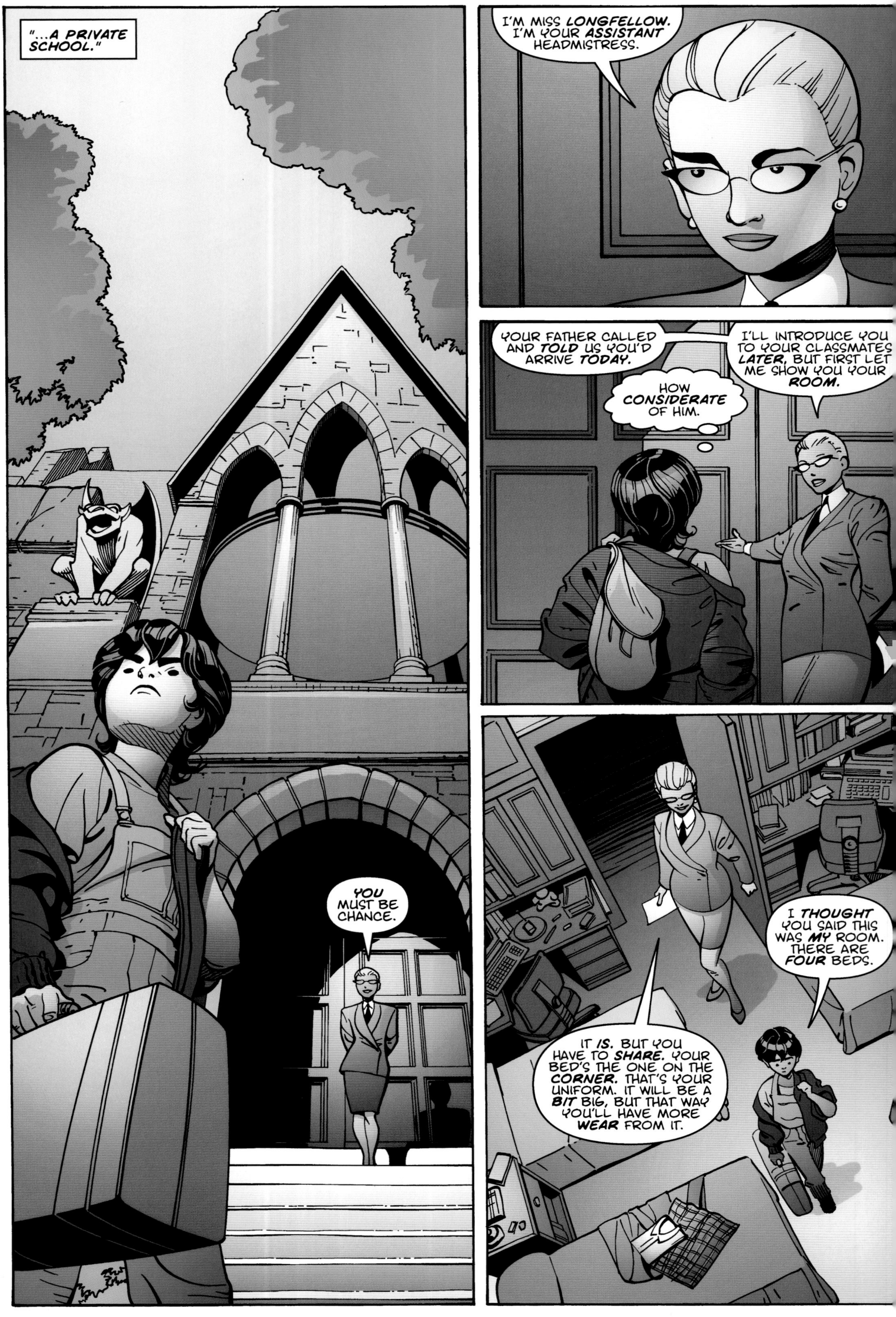
"...A PRIVATE SCHOOL."
YOU MUST BE CHANCE.
I'M MISS LONGFELLOW. I'M YOUR ASSISTANT HEADMISTRESS.
YOUR FATHER CALLED AND TOLD US YOU'D ARRIVE TODAY.
HOW CONSIDERATE OF HIM.
I'LL INTRODUCE YOU TO YOUR CLASSMATES LATER, BUT FIRST LET ME SHOW YOU YOUR ROOM.
I THOUGHT YOU SAID THIS WAS MY ROOM. THERE ARE FOUR BEDS.
IT IS. BUT YOU HAVE TO SHARE. YOUR BED'S THE ONE ON THE CORNER. THAT'S YOUR UNIFORM. IT WILL BE A BIT BIG, BUT THAT WAY YOU'LL HAVE MORE WEAR FROM IT.

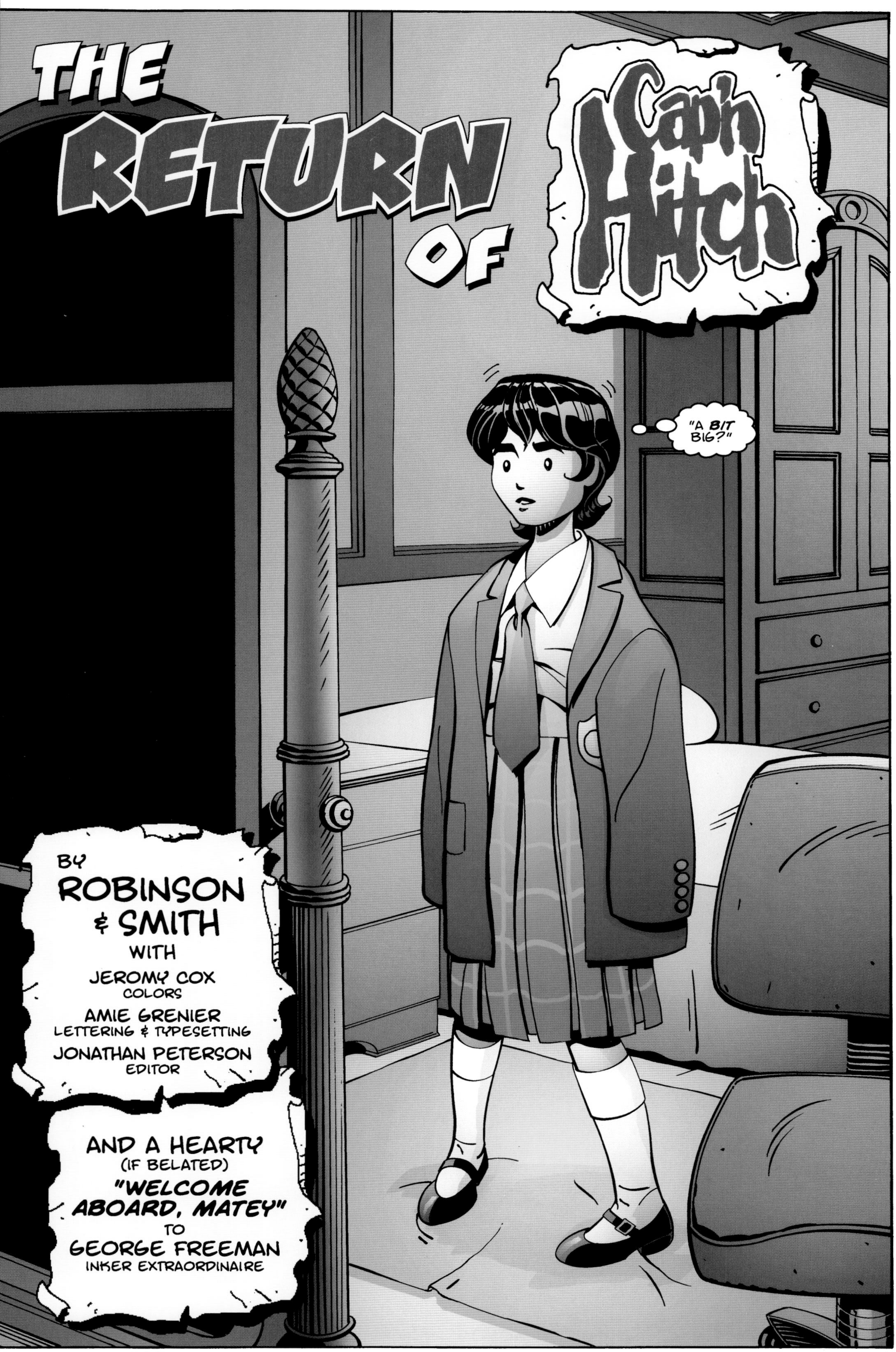
THE RETURN OF
Cap'n Hitch
"A BIT BIG?"
BY
ROBINSON & SMITH
WITH
JEROMY COX
COLORS
AMIE GRENIER
LETTERING & TYPESETTING
JONATHAN PETERSON
EDITOR
AND A HEARTY (IF BELATED) "WELCOME ABOARD, MATEY" TO GEORGE FREEMAN
INKER EXTRAORDINAIRE

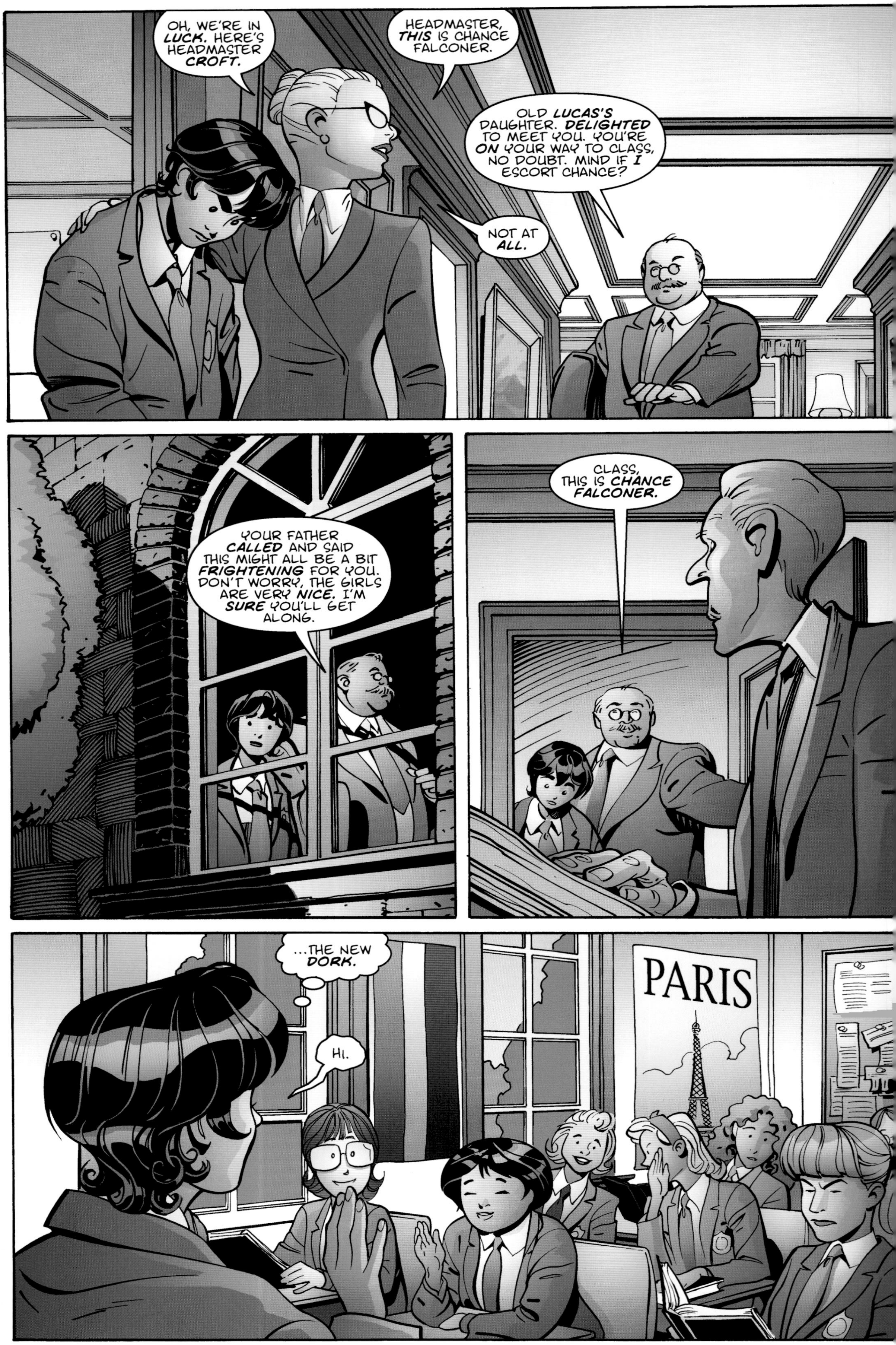
OH, WE'RE IN LUCK. HERE'S HEADMASTER CROFT.
HEADMASTER, THIS IS CHANCE FALCONER.
OLD LUCAS'S DAUGHTER. DELIGHTED TO MEET YOU. YOU'RE ON YOUR WAY TO CLASS, NO DOUBT. MIND IF I ESCORT CHANCE?
NOT AT ALL.
YOUR FATHER CALLED AND SAID THIS MIGHT ALL BE A BIT FRIGHTENING FOR YOU. DON'T WORRY, THE GIRLS ARE VERY NICE. I'M SURE YOU'LL GET ALONG.
CLASS, THIS IS CHANCE FALCONER.
...THE NEW DORK.
HI.
PARIS

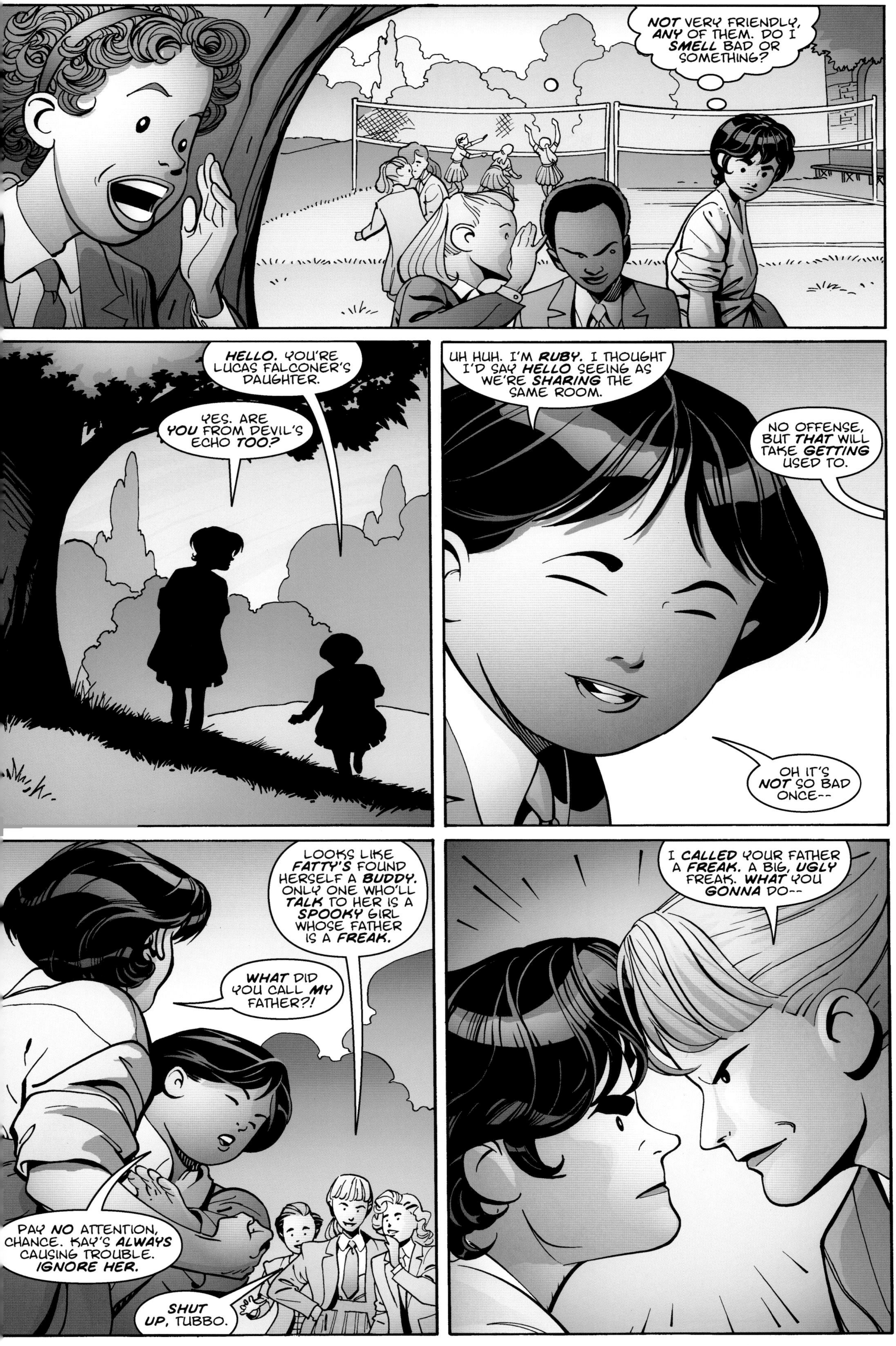
NOT VERY FRIENDLY, ANY OF THEM. DO I SMELL BAD OR SOMETHING?
HELLO. YOU'RE LUCAS FALCONER'S DAUGHTER.
YES. ARE YOU FROM DEVIL'S ECHO TOO?
UH HUH. I'M RUBY. I THOUGHT I'D SAY HELLO SEEING AS WE'RE SHARING THE SAME ROOM.
NO OFFENSE, BUT THAT WILL TAKE GETTING USED TO.
OH IT'S NOT SO BAD ONCE--
LOOKS LIKE FATTY'S FOUND HERSELF A BUDDY. ONLY ONE WHO'LL TALK TO HER IS A SPOOKY GIRL WHOSE FATHER IS A FREAK.
WHAT DID YOU CALL MY FATHER?!
PAY NO ATTENTION, CHANCE. KAY'S ALWAYS CAUSING TROUBLE. IGNORE HER.
SHUT UP, TUBBO.
I CALLED YOUR FATHER A FREAK. A BIG, UGLY FREAK. WHAT YOU GONNA DO--

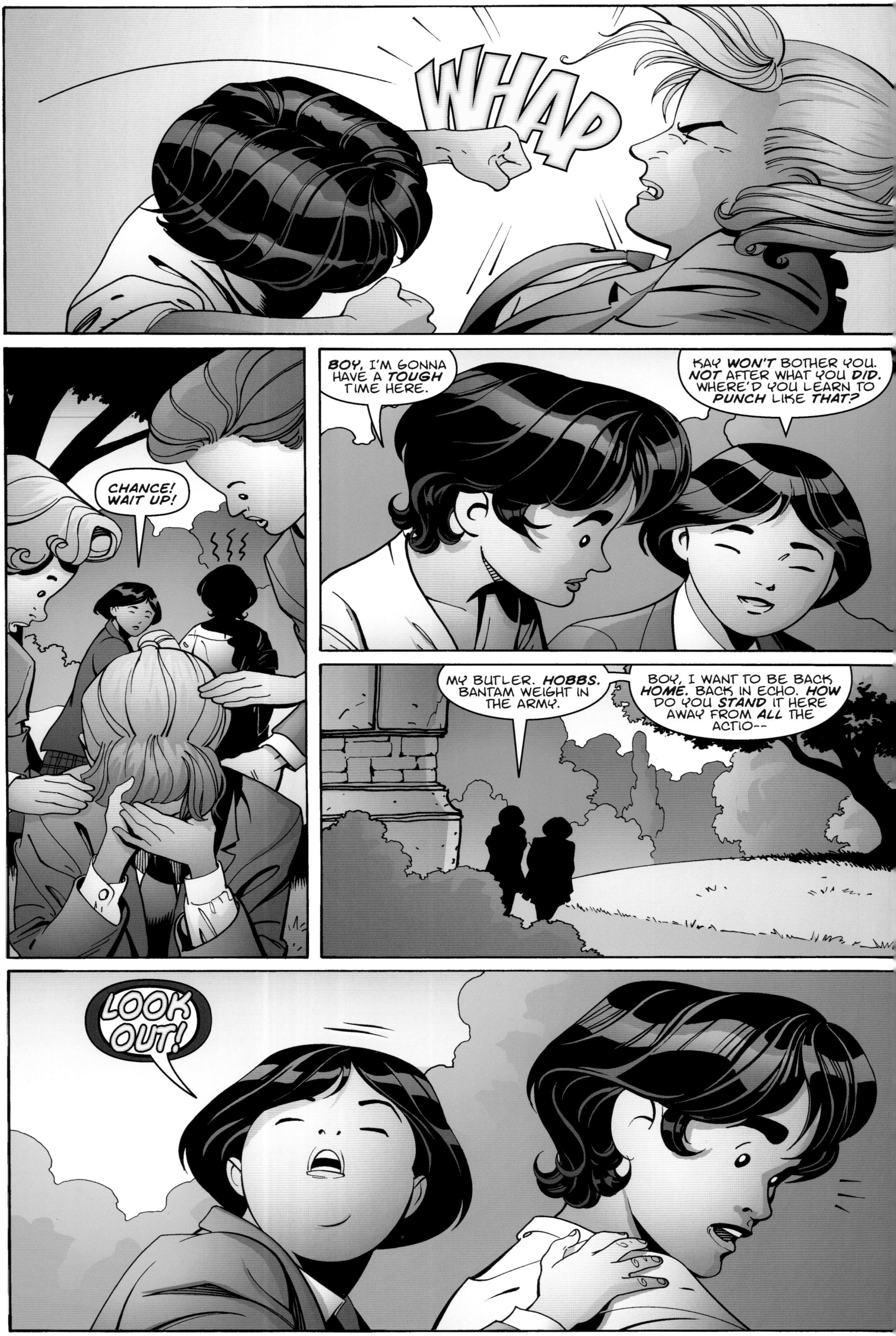
WHAP
CHANCE! WAIT UP!
BOY, I'M GONNA HAVE A TOUGH TIME HERE.
KAY WON'T BOTHER YOU. NOT AFTER WHAT YOU DID. WHERE'D YOU LEARN TO PUNCH LIKE THAT?
MY BUTLER. HOBBS. BANTAM WEIGHT IN THE ARMY.
BOY, I WANT TO BE BACK HOME. BACK IN ECHO. HOW DO YOU STAND IT HERE AWAY FROM ALL THE ACTIO--
LOOK OUT!

MUST HAVE **ROTTED** FREE.

IT'S **STONE.** IT **DOESN'T** ROT. AND LOOK, IT'S **SMOOTH** WHERE IT CAME AWAY. LIKE SOMEONE **CHISELED** INTO IT.

COULD **KAY** HAVE DONE THIS?

I THINK SHE'S **STILL** COUNTING STARS. BESIDES THIS TOOK A **WHILE.** MAYBE THE CHISEL MARKS ARE **OLD.** MAYBE IT **DID** JUST FALL FREE ON ITS **OWN** AND I'M TRYING TO FIND A MYSTERY WHERE THERE **ISN'T** ONE.

≥SIGH≤ I KNOW IT'S A GARGOYLE AND **NOT** A DRAGON. BUT IT **STILL** REMINDS ME OF **GEORGIE.** BOY, I **MISS** HIM. I HOPE HOBBS IS **FEEDING** HIM OKAY AND MAKING SURE HE GETS **EXERCISE.**

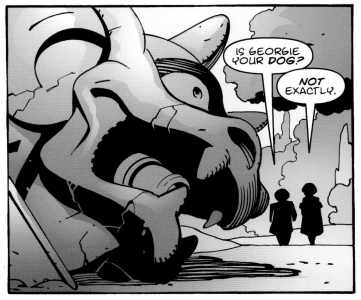

IS GEORGIE YOUR **DOG?**

NOT EXACTLY.

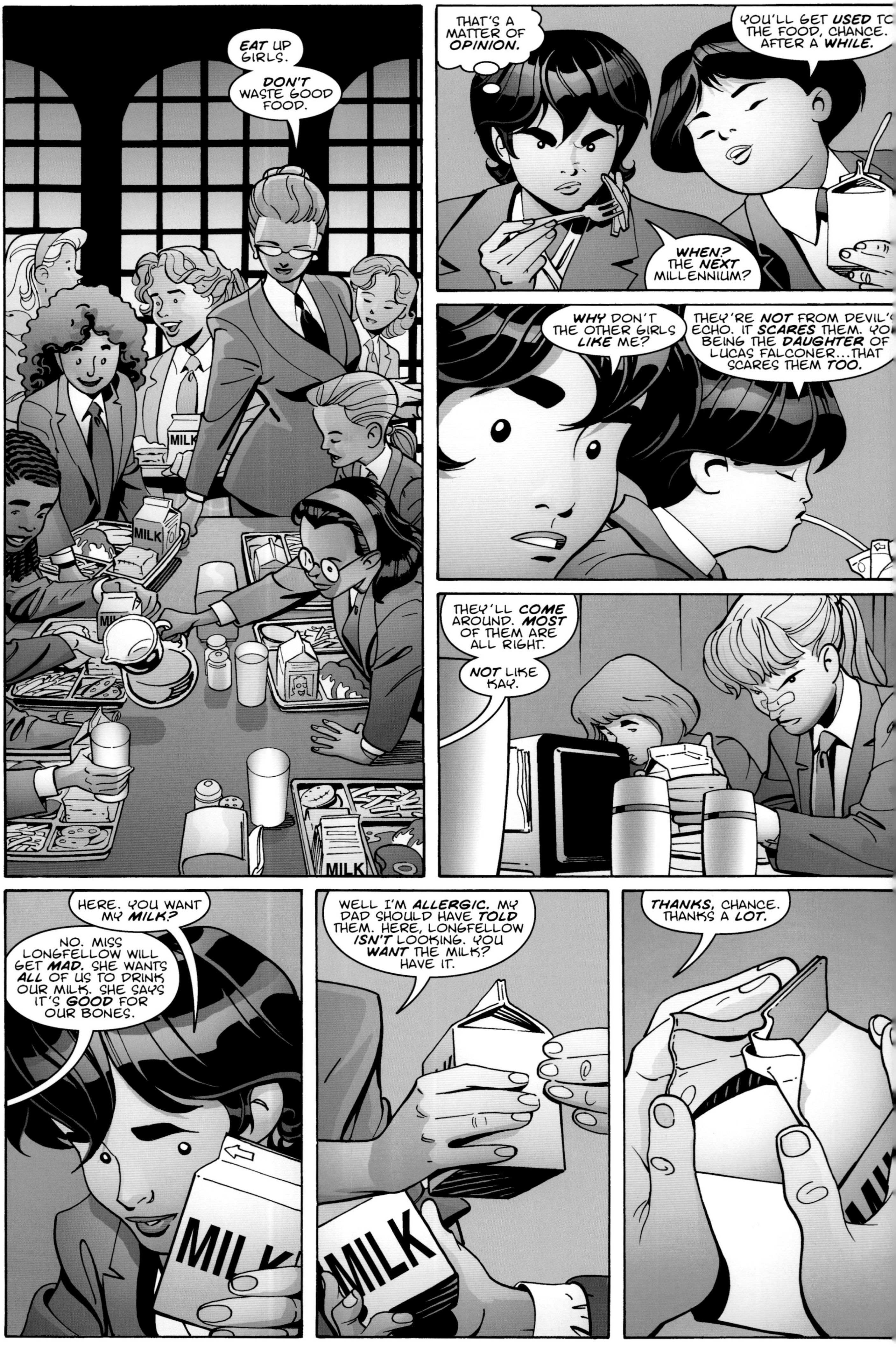
EAT UP GIRLS.
DON'T WASTE GOOD FOOD.
MILK
MILK
MILK
MILK
THAT'S A MATTER OF OPINION.
YOU'LL GET USED TO THE FOOD, CHANCE. AFTER A WHILE.
WHEN? THE NEXT MILLENNIUM?
WHY DON'T THE OTHER GIRLS LIKE ME?
THEY'RE NOT FROM DEVIL'S ECHO. IT SCARES THEM. YOU BEING THE DAUGHTER OF LUCAS FALCONER...THAT SCARES THEM TOO.
THEY'LL COME AROUND. MOST OF THEM ARE ALL RIGHT.
NOT LIKE KAY.
HERE. YOU WANT MY MILK?
NO. MISS LONGFELLOW WILL GET MAD. SHE WANTS ALL OF US TO DRINK OUR MILK. SHE SAYS IT'S GOOD FOR OUR BONES.
MILK
WELL I'M ALLERGIC. MY DAD SHOULD HAVE TOLD THEM. HERE, LONGFELLOW ISN'T LOOKING. YOU WANT THE MILK? HAVE IT.
MILK
THANKS, CHANCE. THANKS A LOT.

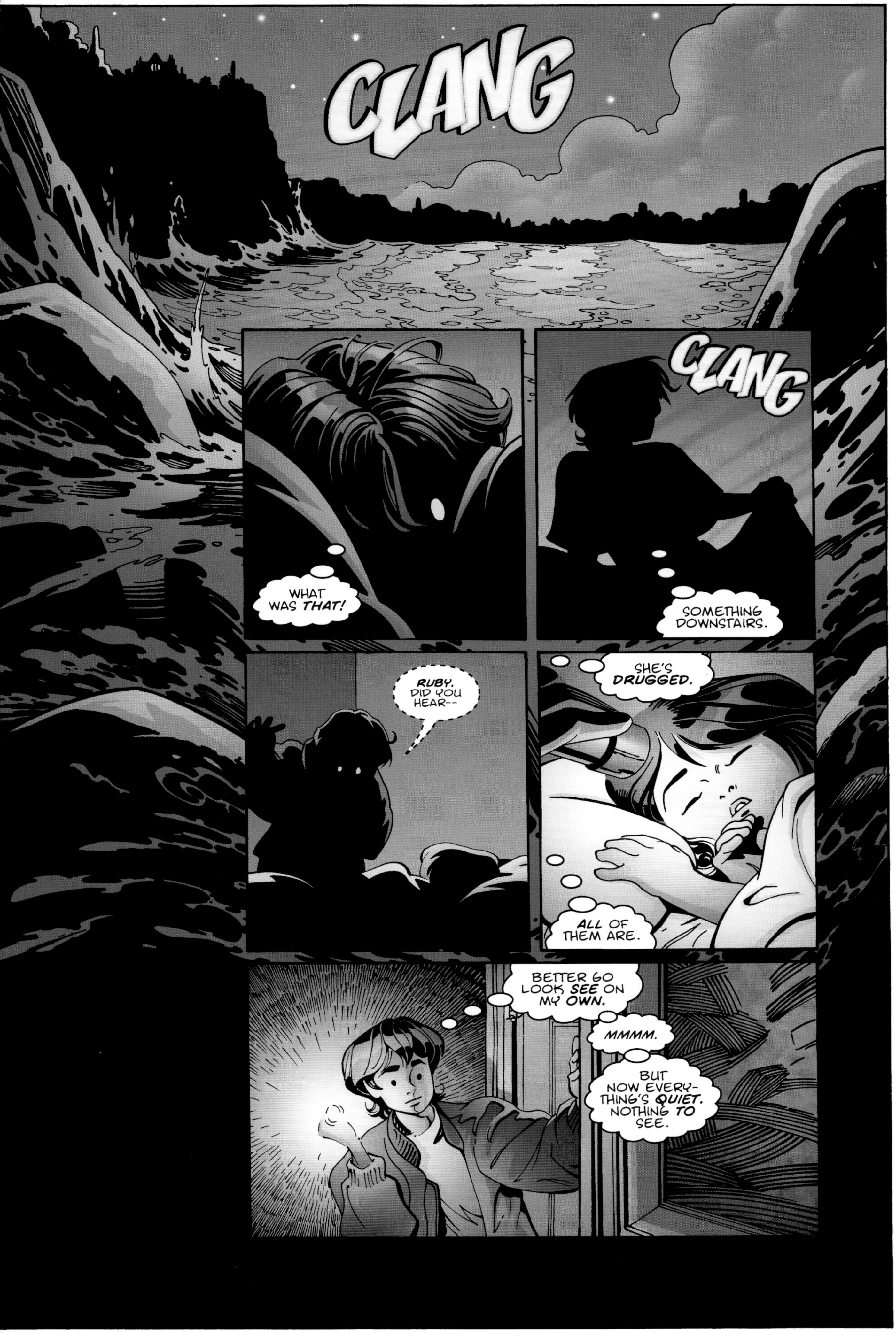
CLANG
WHAT WAS THAT!
CLANG
SOMETHING DOWNSTAIRS.
RUBY. DID YOU HEAR--
SHE'S DRUGGED.
ALL OF THEM ARE.
BETTER GO LOOK SEE ON MY OWN.
MMMM.
BUT NOW EVERY-THING'S QUIET. NOTHING TO SEE.

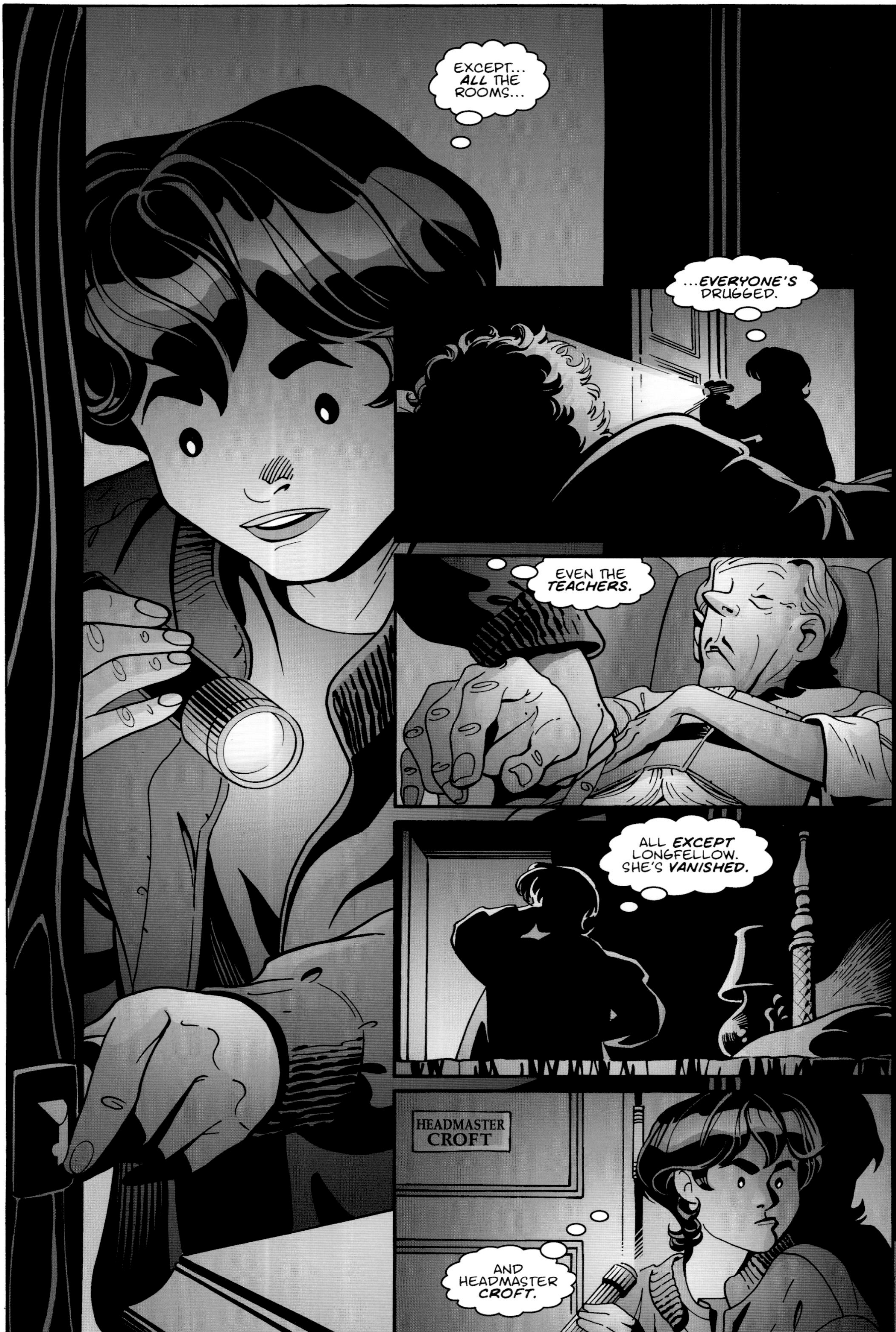
EXCEPT... ALL THE ROOMS...
...EVERYONE'S DRUGGED.
EVEN THE TEACHERS.
ALL EXCEPT LONGFELLOW. SHE'S VANISHED.
HEADMASTER CROFT
AND HEADMASTER CROFT.

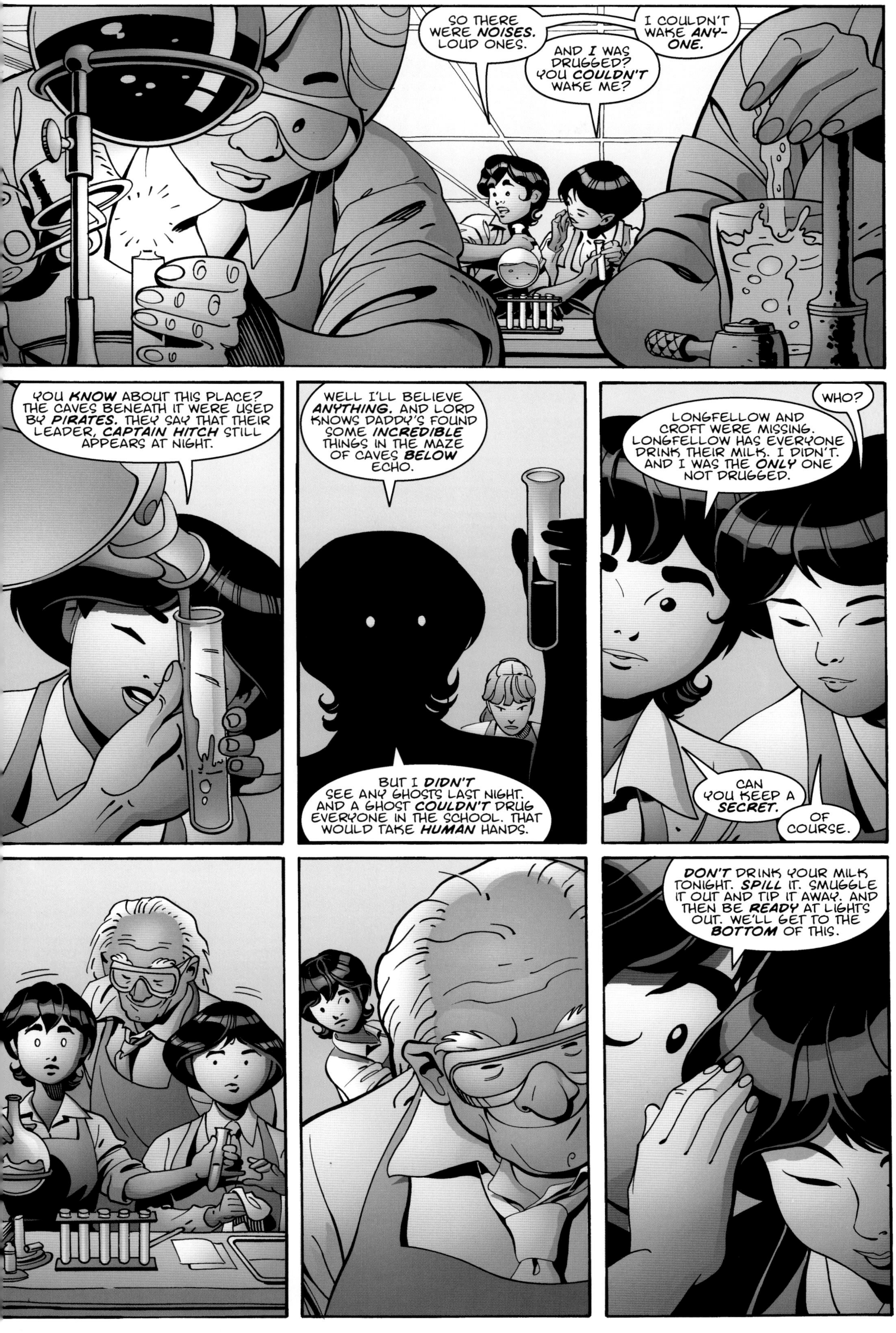
SO THERE WERE NOISES. LOUD ONES.
AND I WAS DRUGGED? YOU COULDN'T WAKE ME?
I COULDN'T WAKE ANY-ONE.
YOU KNOW ABOUT THIS PLACE? THE CAVES BENEATH IT WERE USED BY PIRATES. THEY SAY THAT THEIR LEADER, CAPTAIN HITCH STILL APPEARS AT NIGHT.
WELL I'LL BELIEVE ANYTHING. AND LORD KNOWS DADDY'S FOUND SOME INCREDIBLE THINGS IN THE MAZE OF CAVES BELOW ECHO.
BUT I DIDN'T SEE ANY GHOSTS LAST NIGHT. AND A GHOST COULDN'T DRUG EVERYONE IN THE SCHOOL. THAT WOULD TAKE HUMAN HANDS.
WHO?
LONGFELLOW AND CROFT WERE MISSING. LONGFELLOW HAS EVERYONE DRINK THEIR MILK. I DIDN'T. AND I WAS THE ONLY ONE NOT DRUGGED.
CAN YOU KEEP A SECRET.
OF COURSE.
DON'T DRINK YOUR MILK TONIGHT. SPILL IT. SMUGGLE IT OUT AND TIP IT AWAY. AND THEN BE READY AT LIGHTS OUT. WE'LL GET TO THE BOTTOM OF THIS.

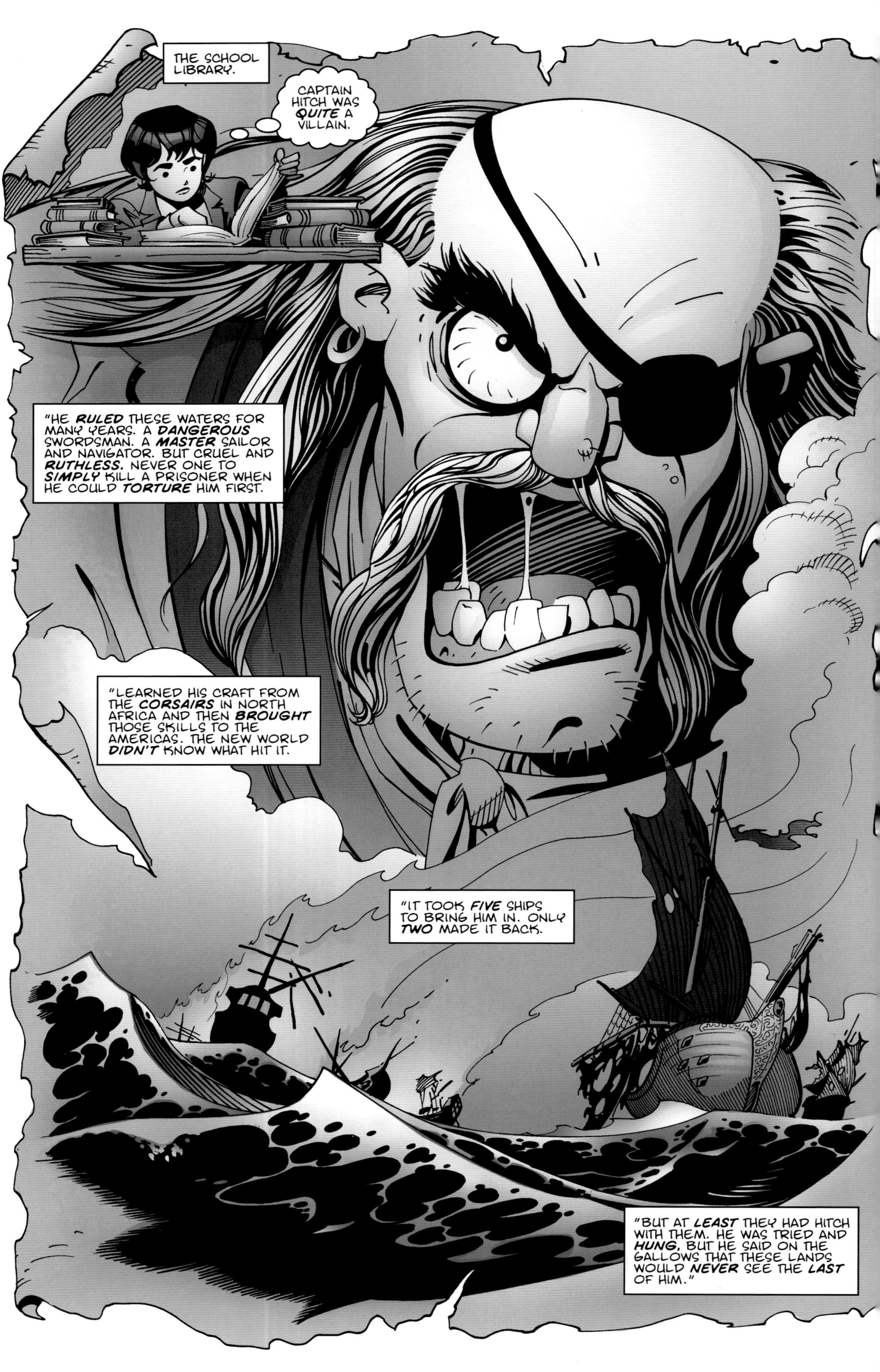
THE SCHOOL LIBRARY.
CAPTAIN HITCH WAS QUITE A VILLAIN.
"HE RULED THESE WATERS FOR MANY YEARS. A DANGEROUS SWORDSMAN. A MASTER SAILOR AND NAVIGATOR. BUT CRUEL AND RUTHLESS. NEVER ONE TO SIMPLY KILL A PRISONER WHEN HE COULD TORTURE HIM FIRST.
"LEARNED HIS CRAFT FROM THE CORSAIRS IN NORTH AFRICA AND THEN BROUGHT THOSE SKILLS TO THE AMERICAS. THE NEW WORLD DIDN'T KNOW WHAT HIT IT.
"IT TOOK FIVE SHIPS TO BRING HIM IN. ONLY TWO MADE IT BACK.
"BUT AT LEAST THEY HAD HITCH WITH THEM. HE WAS TRIED AND HUNG, BUT HE SAID ON THE GALLOWS THAT THESE LANDS WOULD NEVER SEE THE LAST OF HIM."

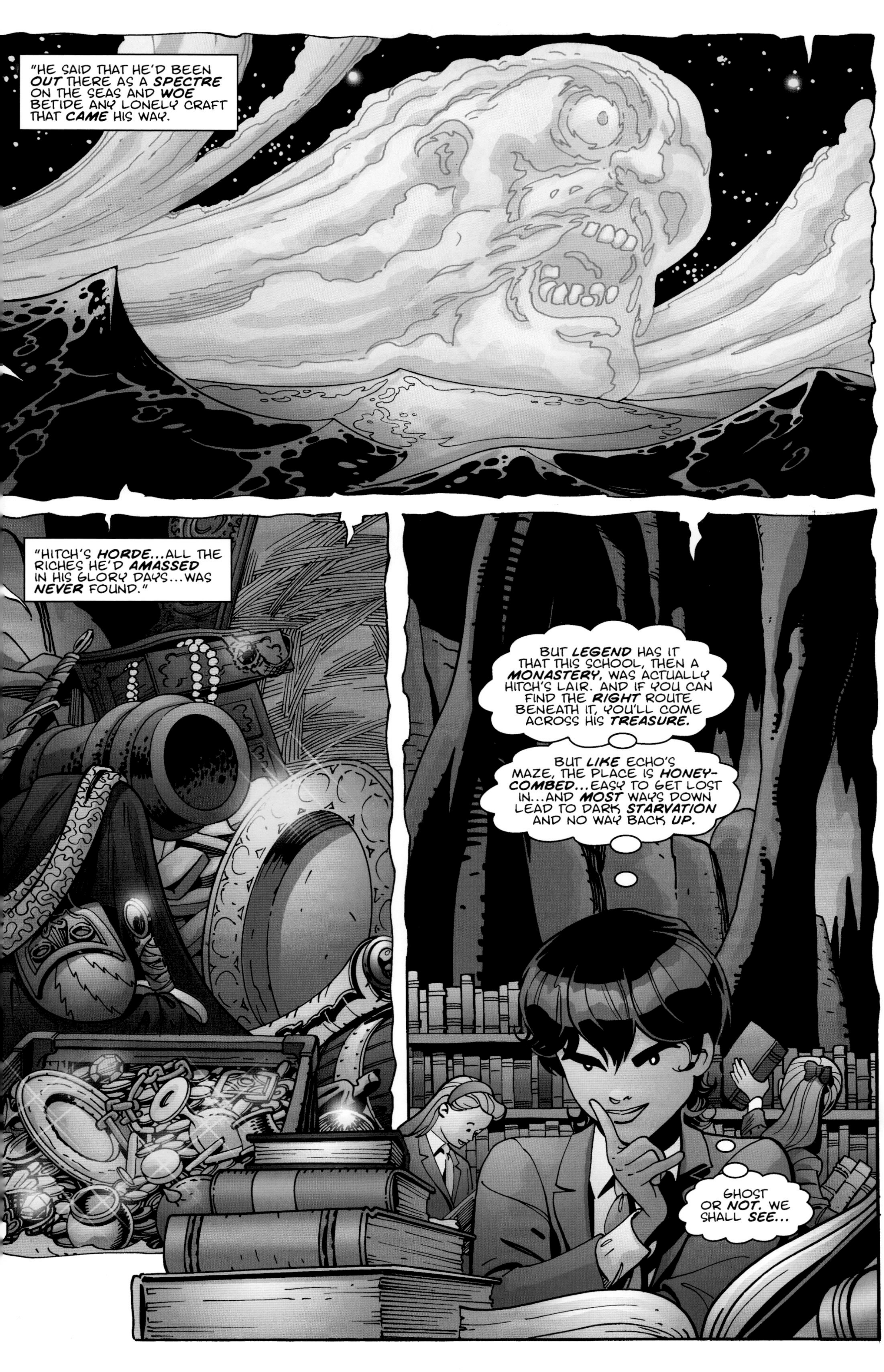
"HE SAID THAT HE'D BEEN OUT THERE AS A SPECTRE ON THE SEAS AND WOE BETIDE ANY LONELY CRAFT THAT CAME HIS WAY.
"HITCH'S HORDE...ALL THE RICHES HE'D AMASSED IN HIS GLORY DAYS...WAS NEVER FOUND."
BUT LEGEND HAS IT THAT THIS SCHOOL, THEN A MONASTERY, WAS ACTUALLY HITCH'S LAIR. AND IF YOU CAN FIND THE RIGHT ROUTE BENEATH IT, YOU'LL COME ACROSS HIS TREASURE.
BUT LIKE ECHO'S MAZE, THE PLACE IS HONEY-COMBED...EASY TO GET LOST IN...AND MOST WAYS DOWN LEAD TO DARK STARVATION AND NO WAY BACK UP.
GHOST OR NOT. WE SHALL SEE...

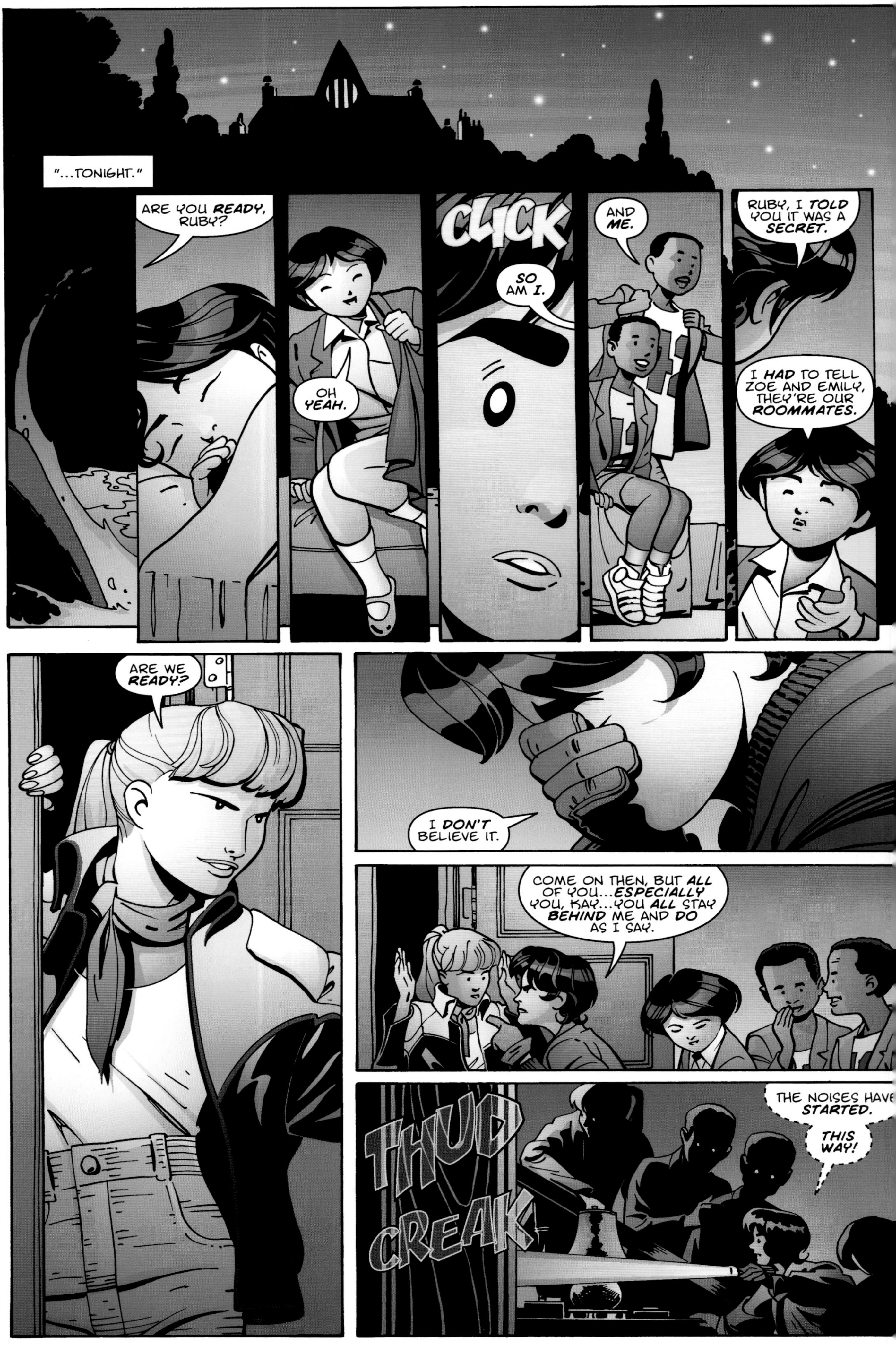
"...TONIGHT."
ARE YOU READY, RUBY?
OH YEAH.
CLICK
SO AM I.
AND ME.
RUBY, I TOLD YOU IT WAS A SECRET.
I HAD TO TELL ZOE AND EMILY, THEY'RE OUR ROOMMATES.
ARE WE READY?
I DON'T BELIEVE IT.
COME ON THEN, BUT ALL OF YOU...ESPECIALLY YOU, KAY...YOU ALL STAY BEHIND ME AND DO AS I SAY.
THUD
CREAK
THE NOISES HAVE STARTED.
THIS WAY!

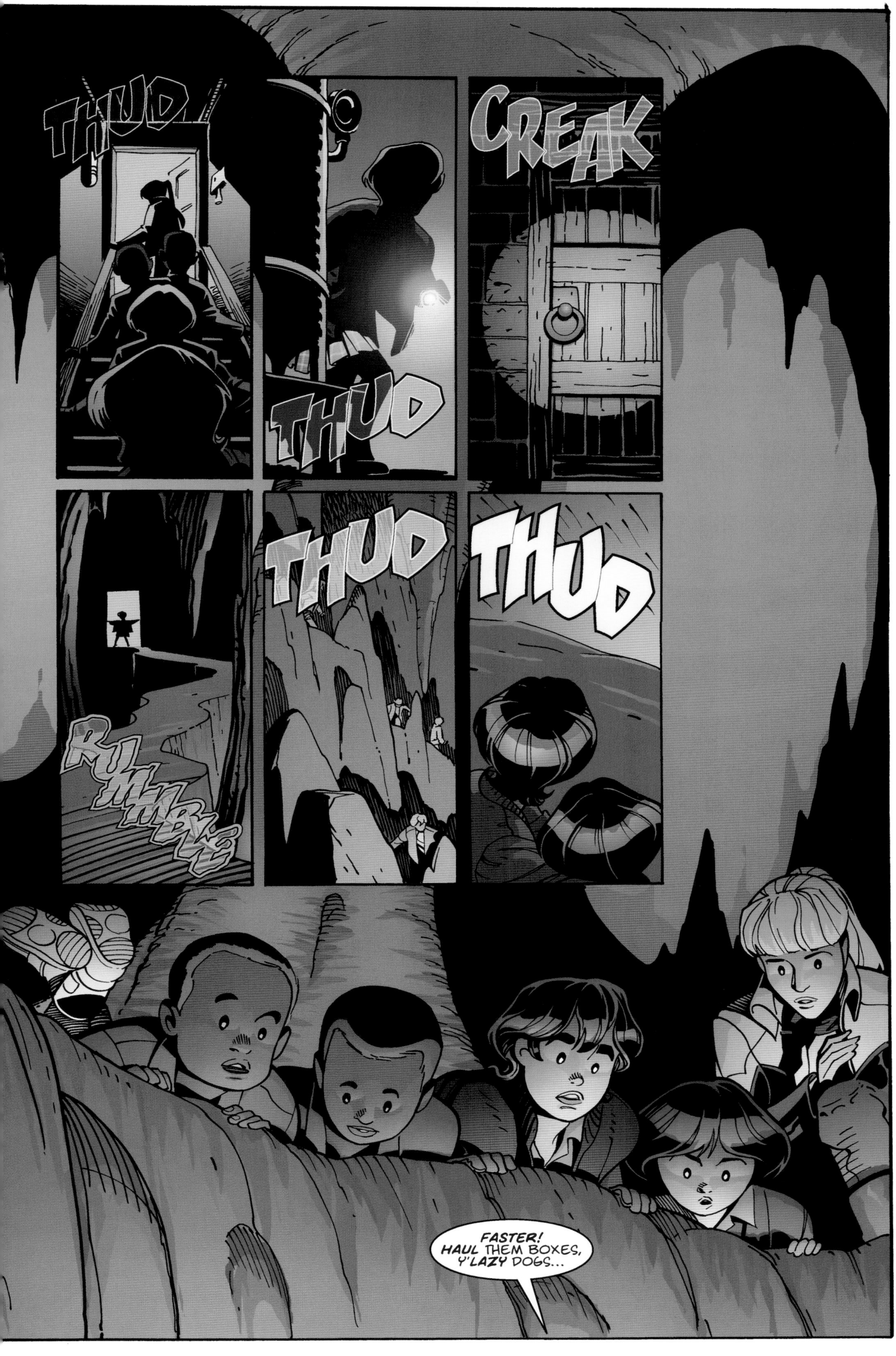
THUD
THUD
CREAK
RUMMBLE
THUD
THUD
FASTER! HAUL THEM BOXES, Y'LAZY DOGS...

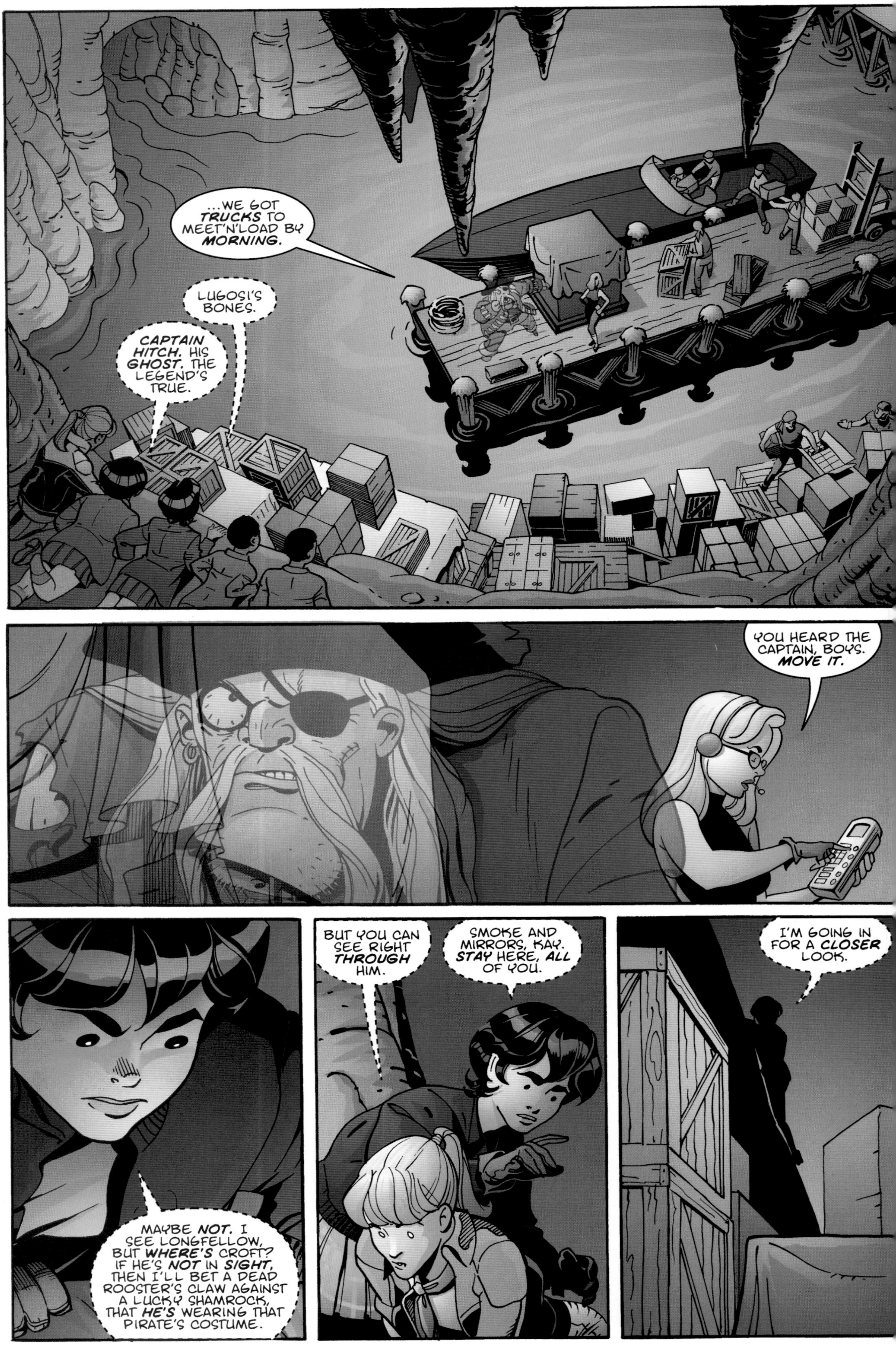
...WE GOT TRUCKS TO MEET'N'LOAD BY MORNING.
LUGOSI'S BONES.
CAPTAIN HITCH. HIS GHOST. THE LEGEND'S TRUE.
YOU HEARD THE CAPTAIN, BOYS. MOVE IT.
MAYBE NOT. I SEE LONGFELLOW, BUT WHERE'S CROFT? IF HE'S NOT IN SIGHT, THEN I'LL BET A DEAD ROOSTER'S CLAW AGAINST A LUCKY SHAMROCK, THAT HE'S WEARING THAT PIRATE'S COSTUME.
BUT YOU CAN SEE RIGHT THROUGH HIM.
SMOKE AND MIRRORS, KAY. STAY HERE, ALL OF YOU.
I'M GOING IN FOR A CLOSER LOOK.

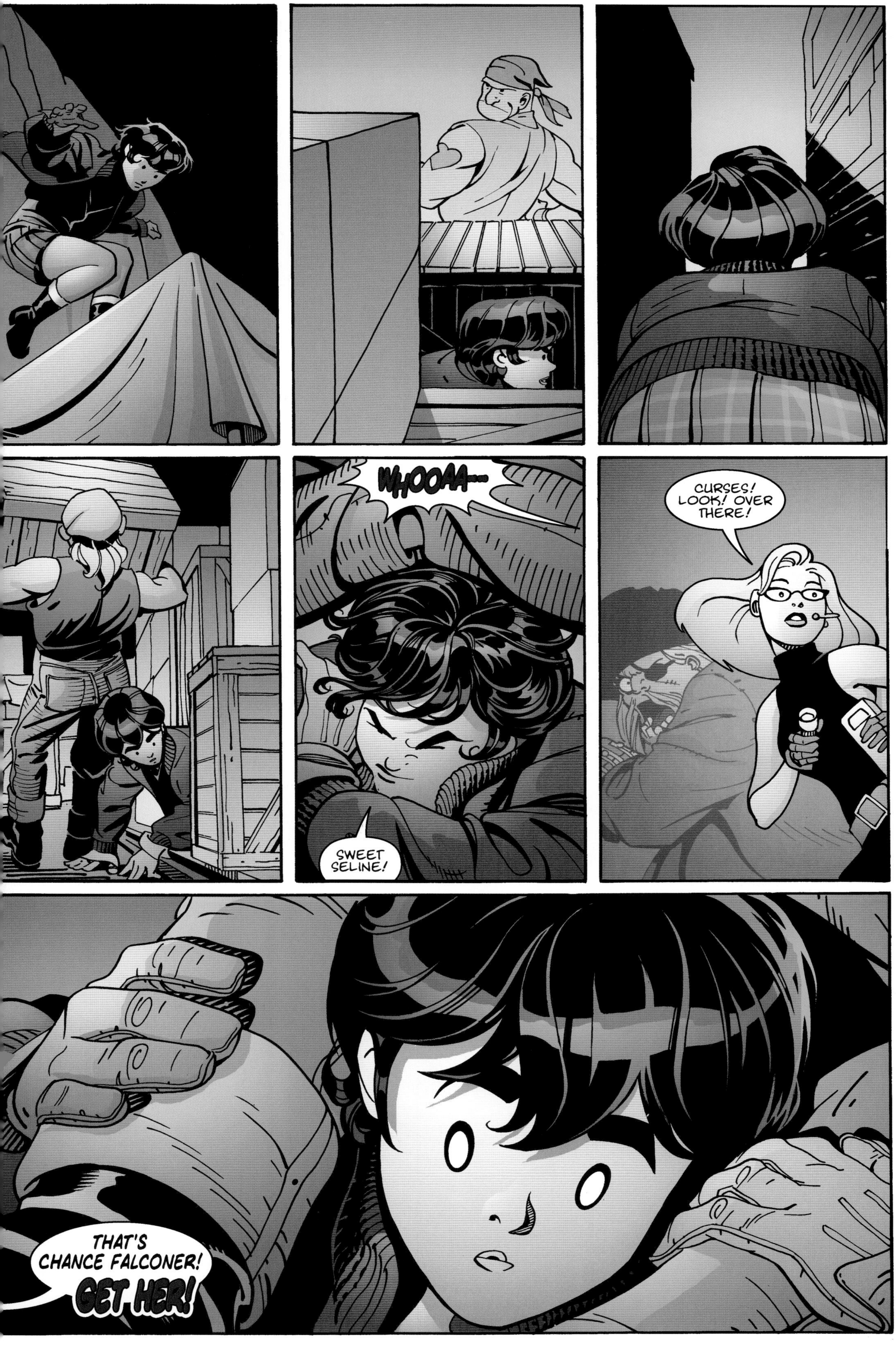
WHOOAA---
SWEET SELINE!
CURSES! LOOK! OVER THERE!
THAT'S CHANCE FALCONER! GET HER!

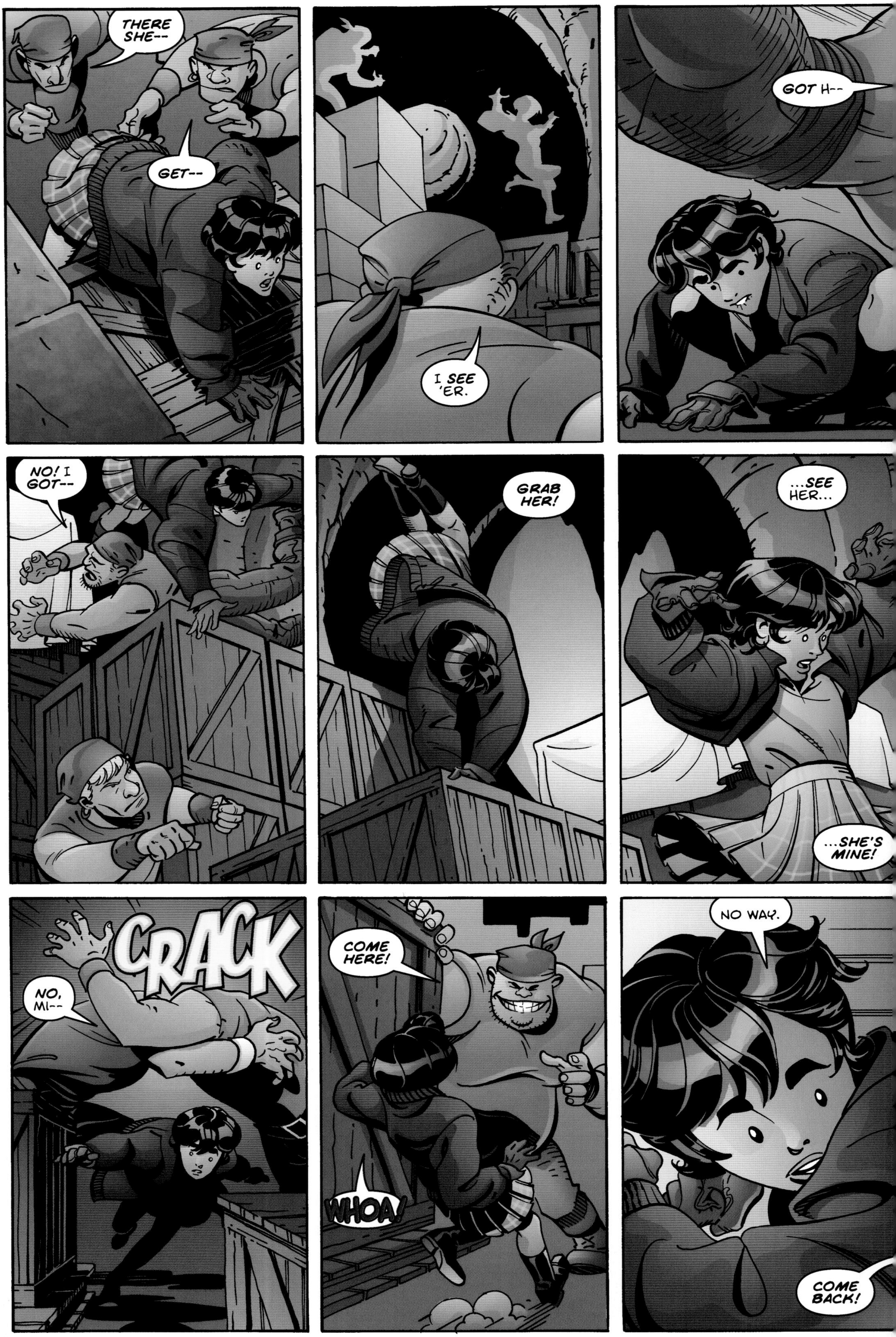
THERE SHE--
GET--
I SEE 'ER.
GOT H--
NO! I GOT--
GRAB HER!
...SEE HER...
...SHE'S MINE!
CRACK
NO, MI--
COME HERE!
WHOA!
NO WAY.
COME BACK!

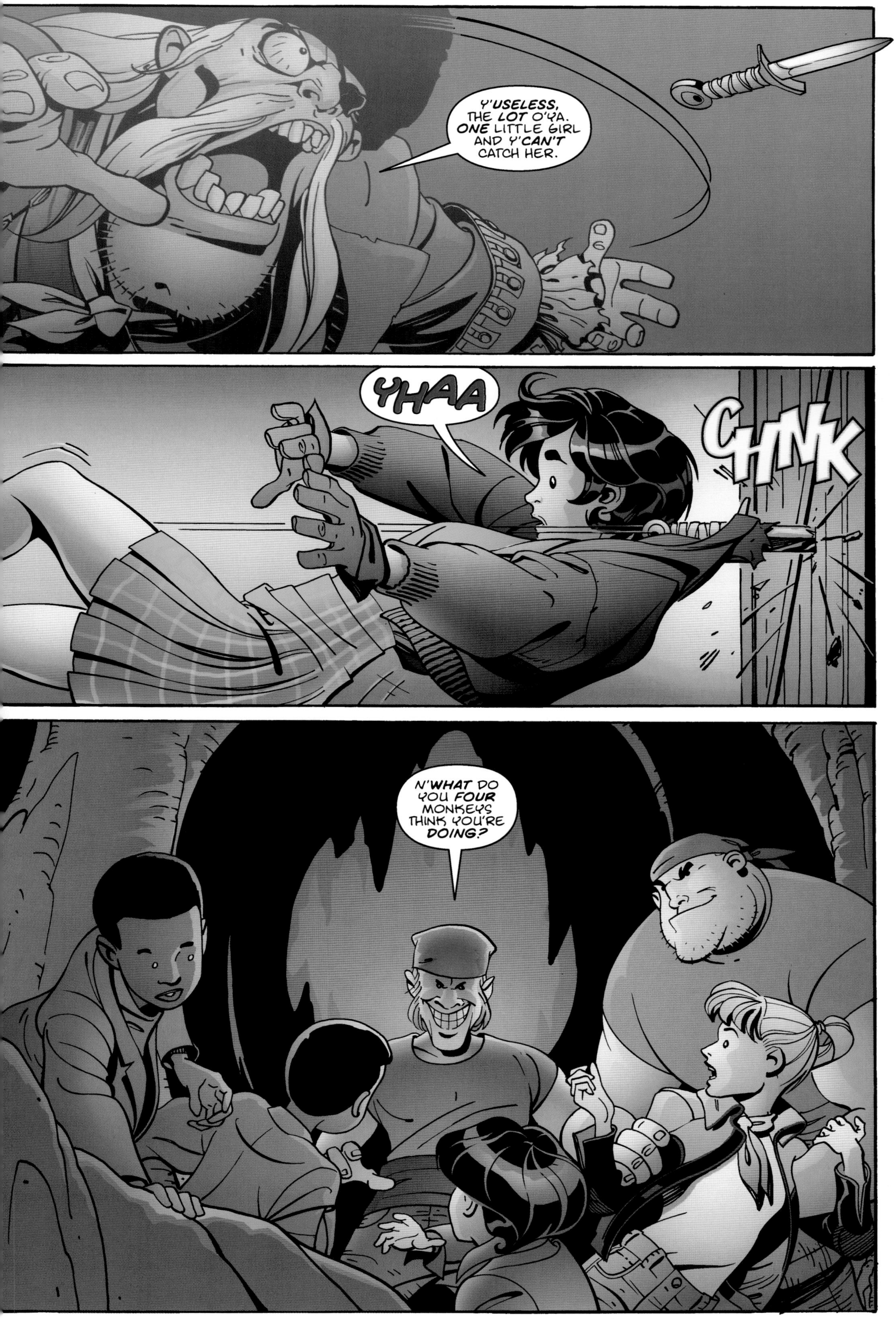

Y'USELESS, THE LOT O'YA. ONE LITTLE GIRL AND Y'CAN'T CATCH HER.
YHAA
CHINK
N'WHAT DO YOU FOUR MONKEYS THINK YOU'RE DOING?

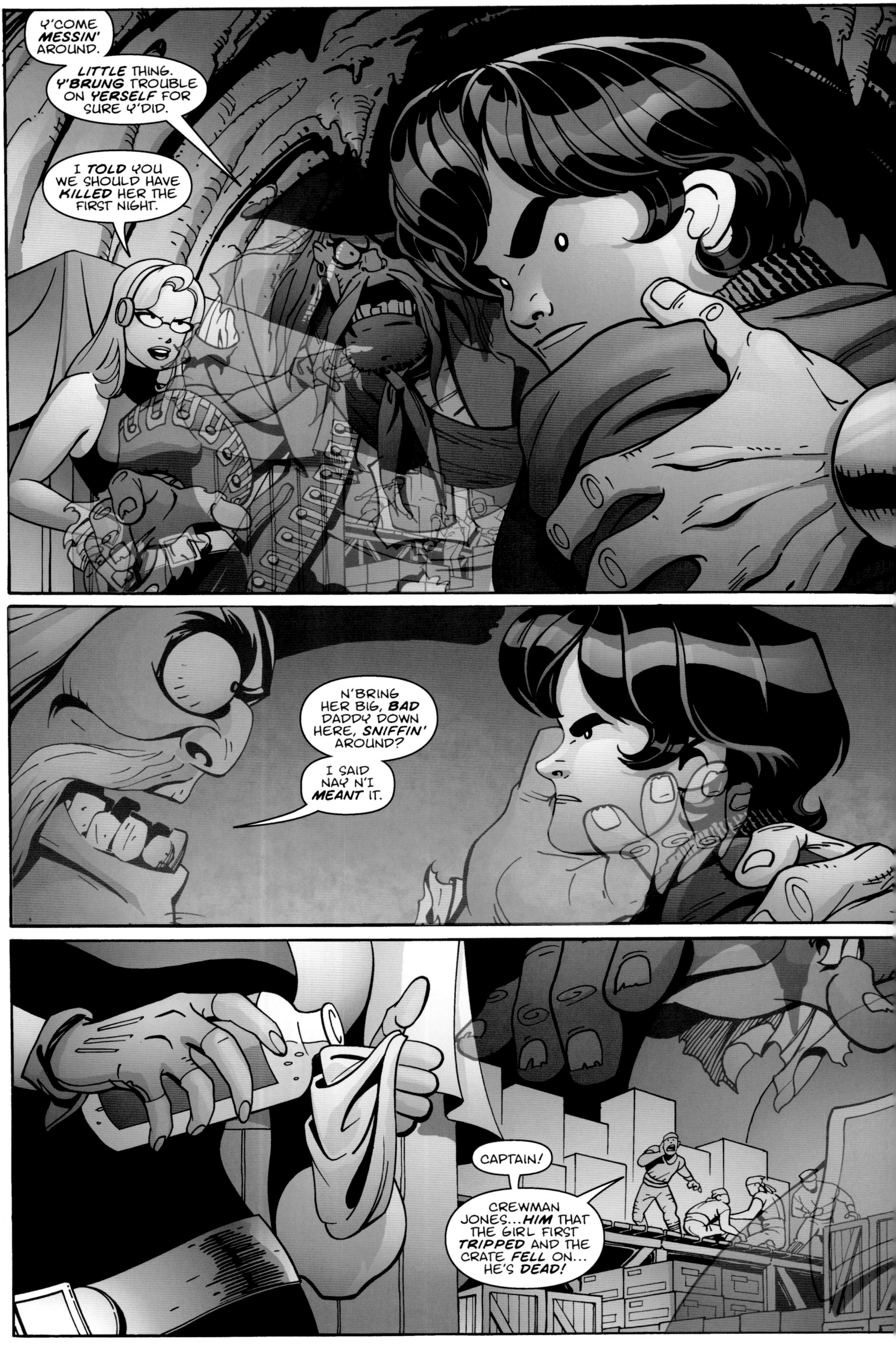
Y'COME MESSIN' AROUND.
LITTLE THING. Y'BRUNG TROUBLE ON YERSELF FOR SURE Y'DID.
I TOLD YOU WE SHOULD HAVE KILLED HER THE FIRST NIGHT.
N'BRING HER BIG, BAD DADDY DOWN HERE, SNIFFIN' AROUND?
I SAID NAY N'I MEANT IT.
CAPTAIN!
CREWMAN JONES...HIM THAT THE GIRL FIRST TRIPPED AND THE CRATE FELL ON... HE'S DEAD!

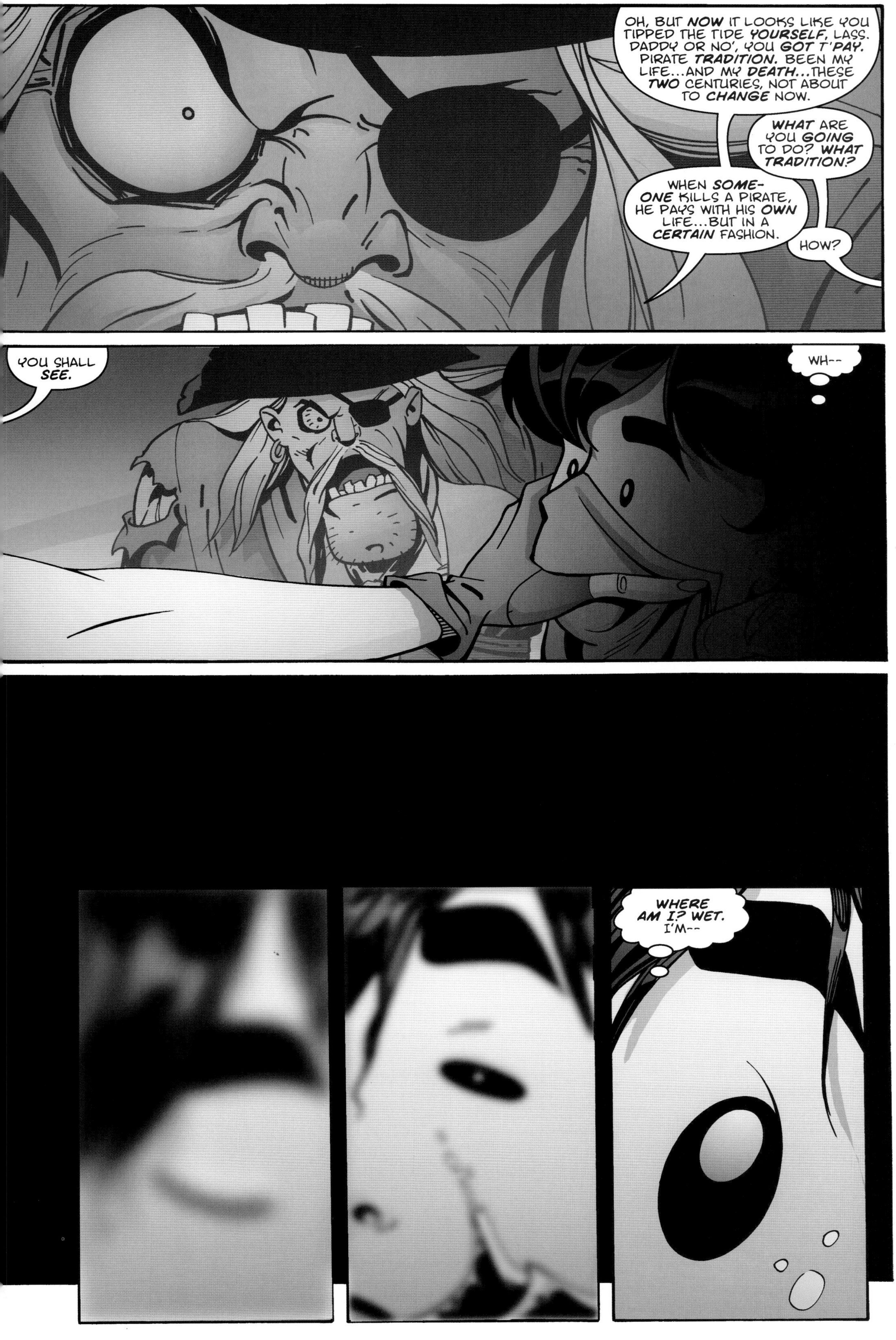
OH, BUT NOW IT LOOKS LIKE YOU TIPPED THE TIDE YOURSELF, LASS. DADDY OR NO', YOU GOT T'PAY. PIRATE TRADITION. BEEN MY LIFE...AND MY DEATH...THESE TWO CENTURIES, NOT ABOUT TO CHANGE NOW.
WHAT ARE YOU GOING TO DO? WHAT TRADITION?
WHEN SOMEONE KILLS A PIRATE, HE PAYS WITH HIS OWN LIFE...BUT IN A CERTAIN FASHION.
HOW?
YOU SHALL SEE.
WH--
WHERE AM I? WET. I'M--

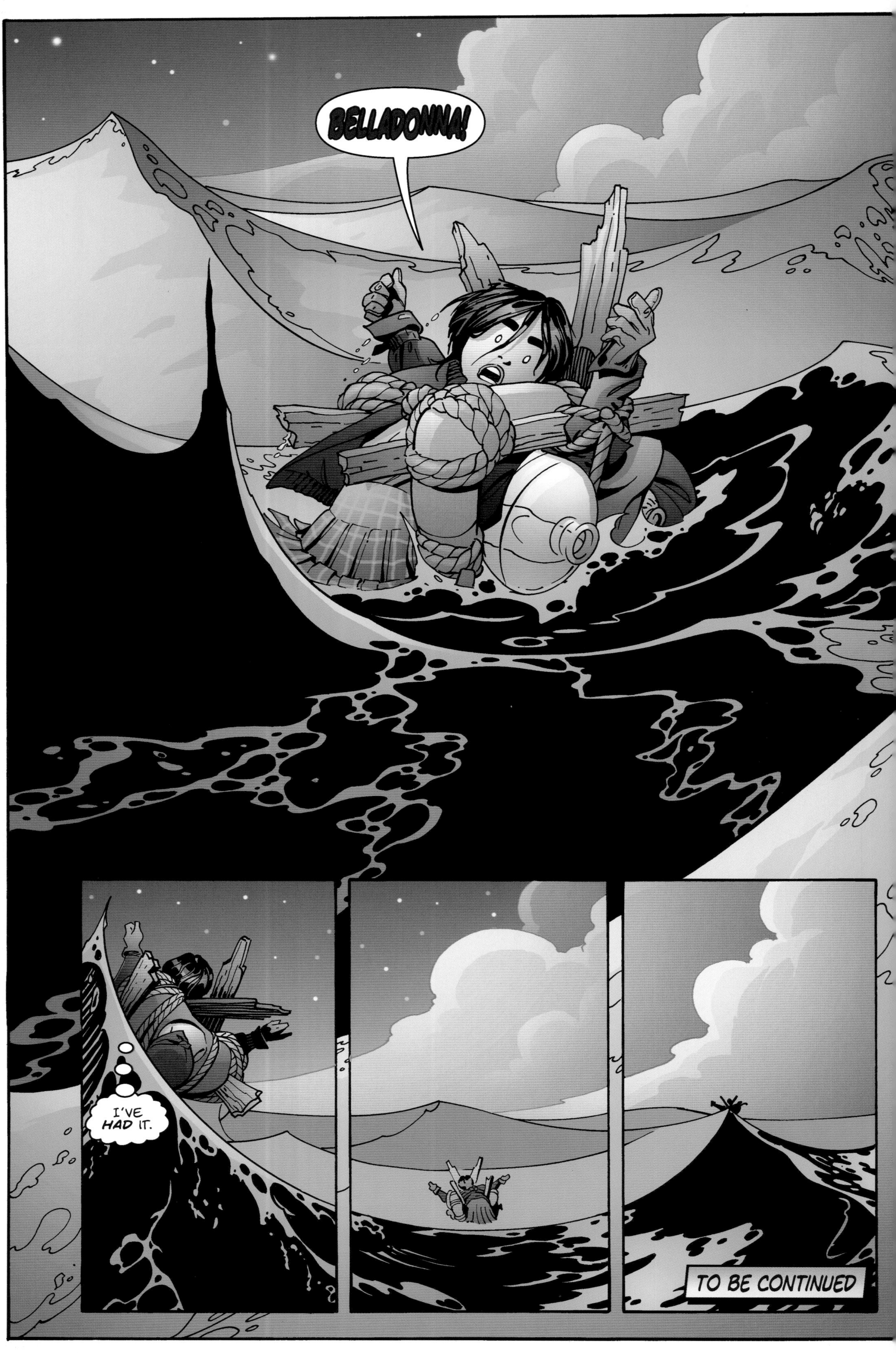
BELLADONNA!
I'VE HAD IT.
TO BE CONTINUED

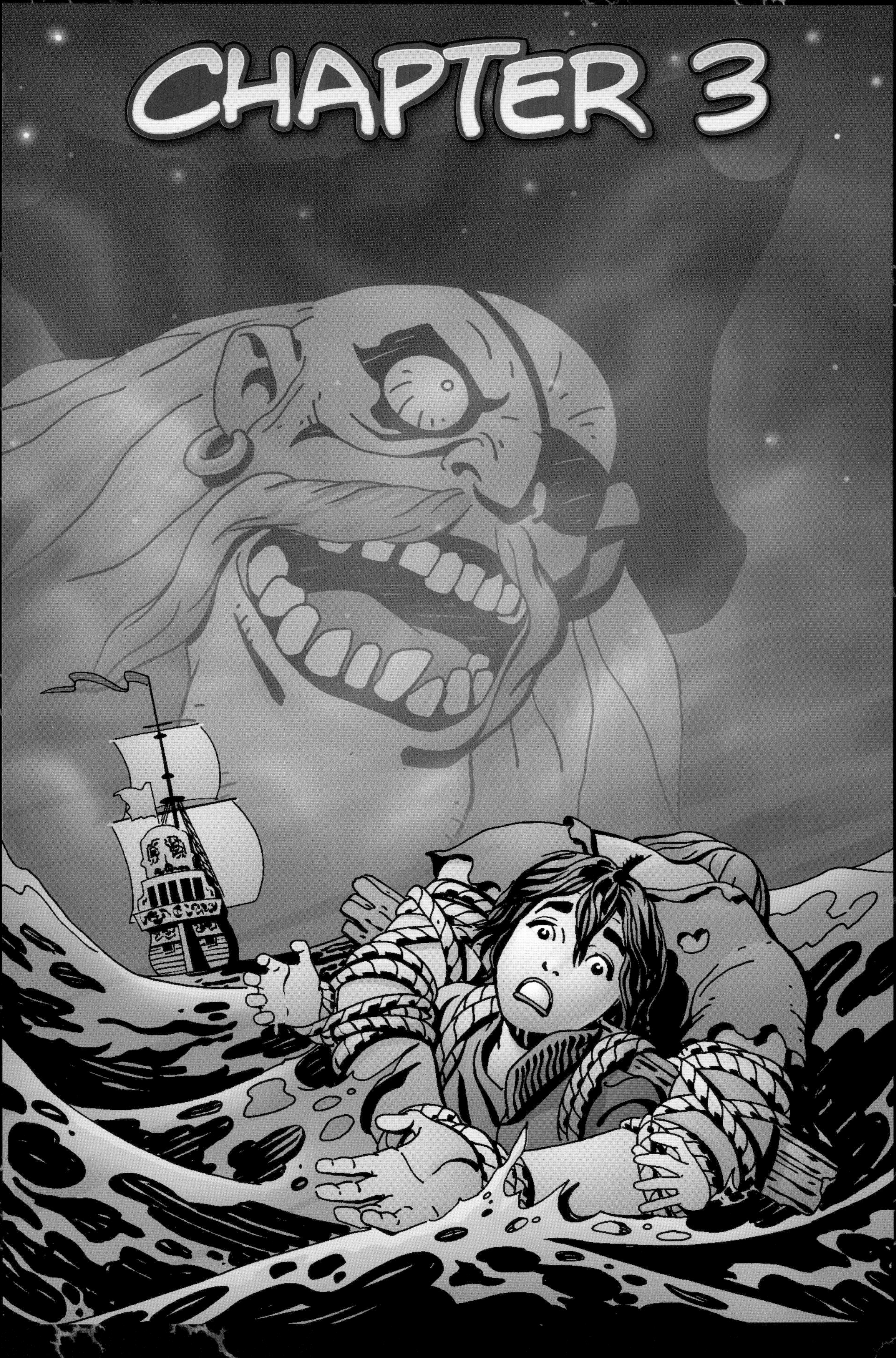
CHAPTER 3

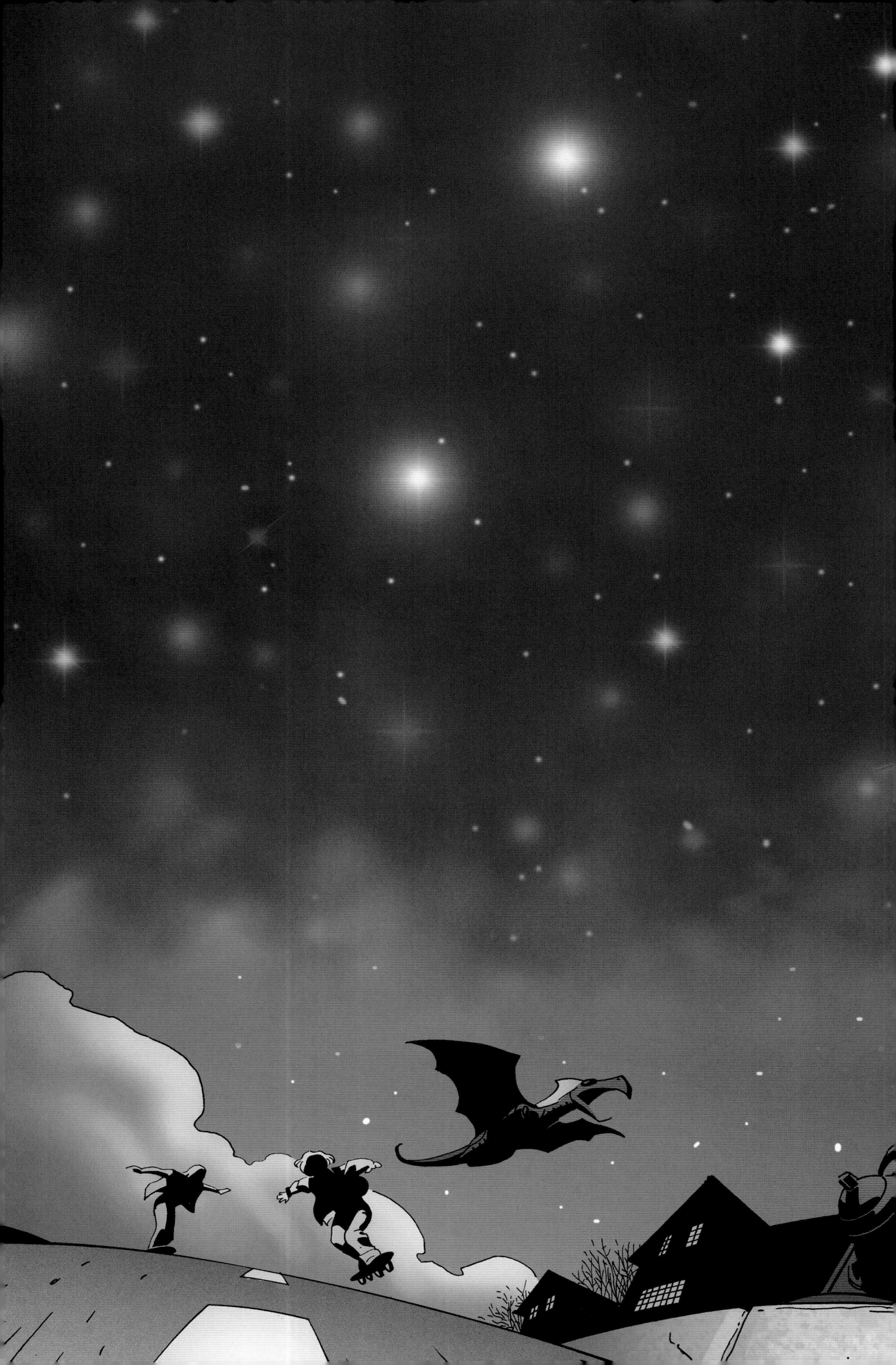

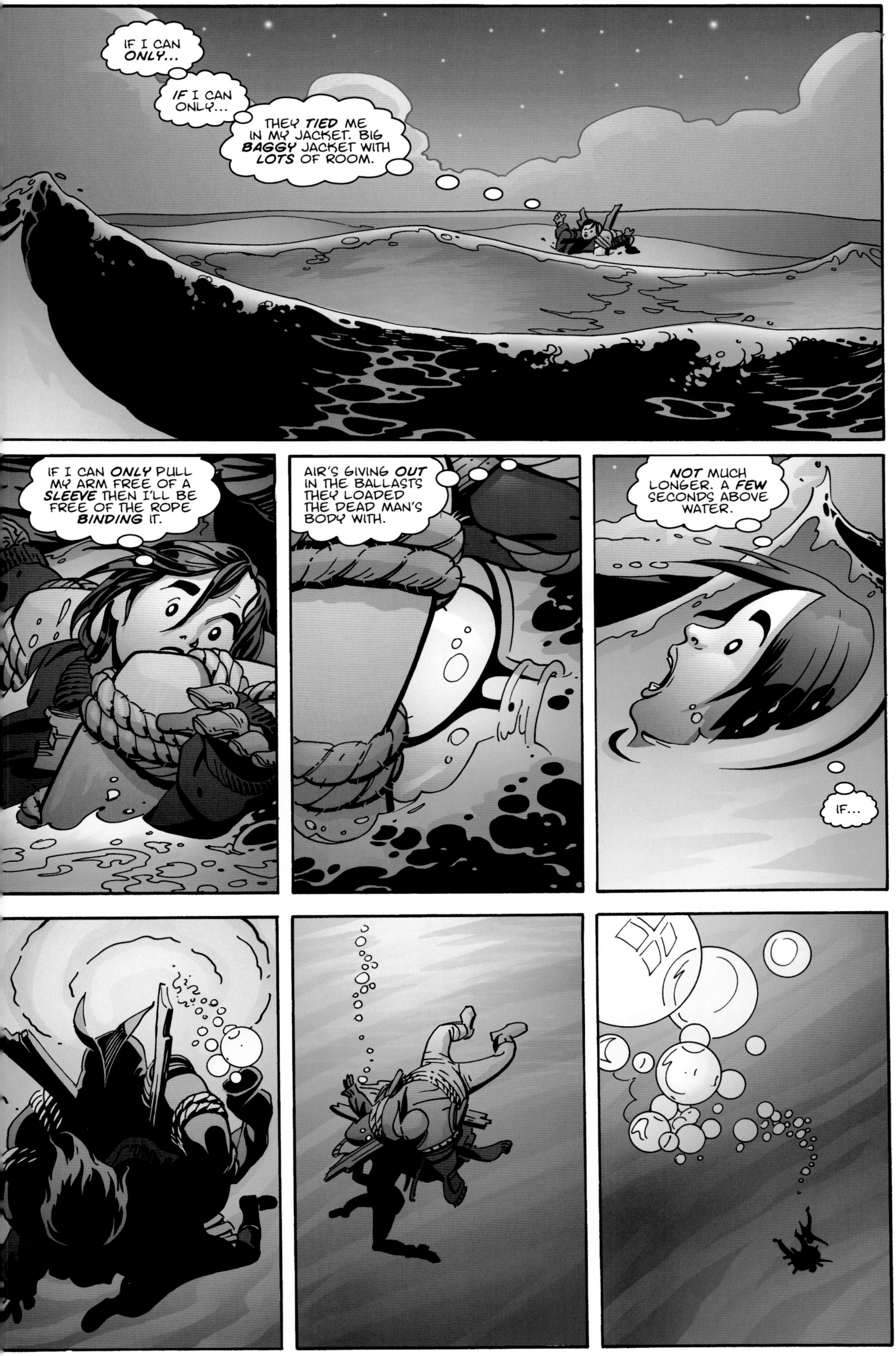

IF I CAN ONLY...
IF I CAN ONLY...
THEY TIED ME IN MY JACKET. BIG BAGGY JACKET WITH LOTS OF ROOM.
IF I CAN ONLY PULL MY ARM FREE OF A SLEEVE THEN I'LL BE FREE OF THE ROPE BINDING IT.
AIR'S GIVING OUT IN THE BALLASTS THEY LOADED THE DEAD MAN'S BODY WITH.
NOT MUCH LONGER. A FEW SECONDS ABOVE WATER.
IF...

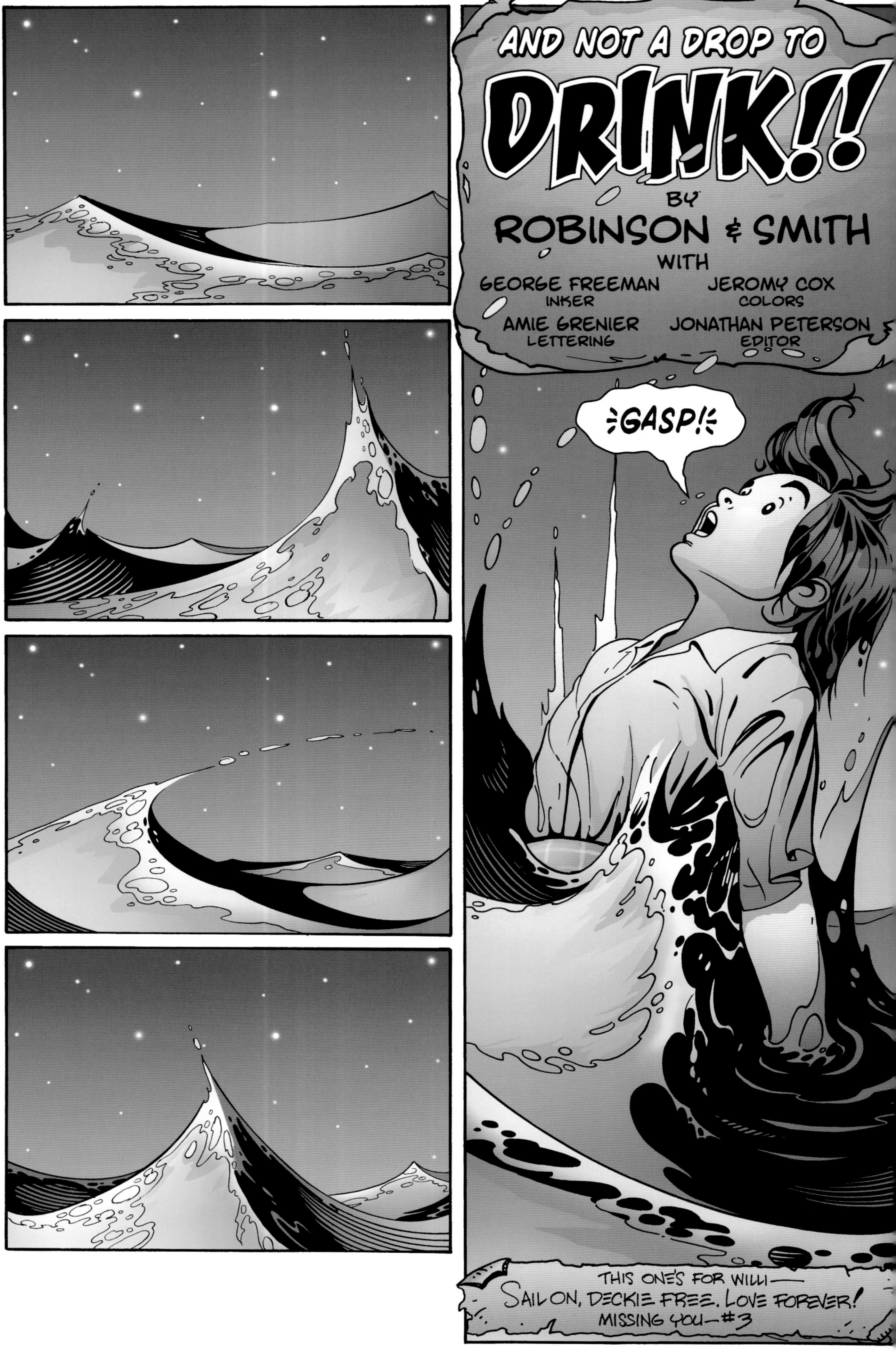
AND NOT A DROP TO
DRINK!!
BY
ROBINSON & SMITH
WITH
GEORGE FREEMAN
INKER
JEROMY COX
COLORS
AMIE GRENIER
LETTERING
JONATHAN PETERSON
EDITOR
GASP!
THIS ONE'S FOR WILLI—
SAIL ON, DECKIE FREE. LOVE FOREVER!
MISSING YOU—#3

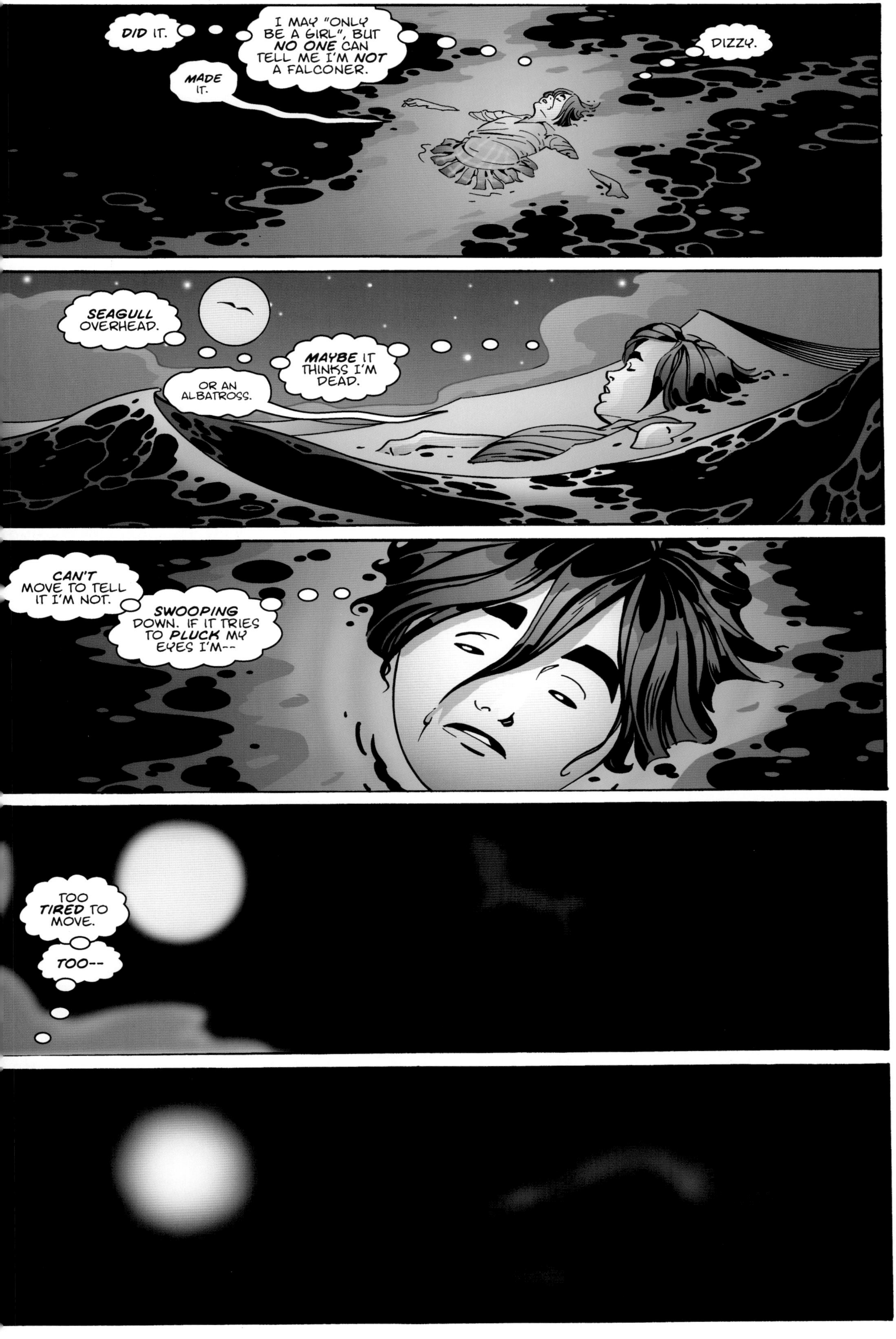

DID IT.
MADE IT.
I MAY "ONLY BE A GIRL", BUT NO ONE CAN TELL ME I'M NOT A FALCONER.
DIZZY.
SEAGULL OVERHEAD.
OR AN ALBATROSS.
MAYBE IT THINKS I'M DEAD.
CAN'T MOVE TO TELL IT I'M NOT.
SWOOPING DOWN. IF IT TRIES TO PLUCK MY EYES I'M--
TOO TIRED TO MOVE.
TOO--

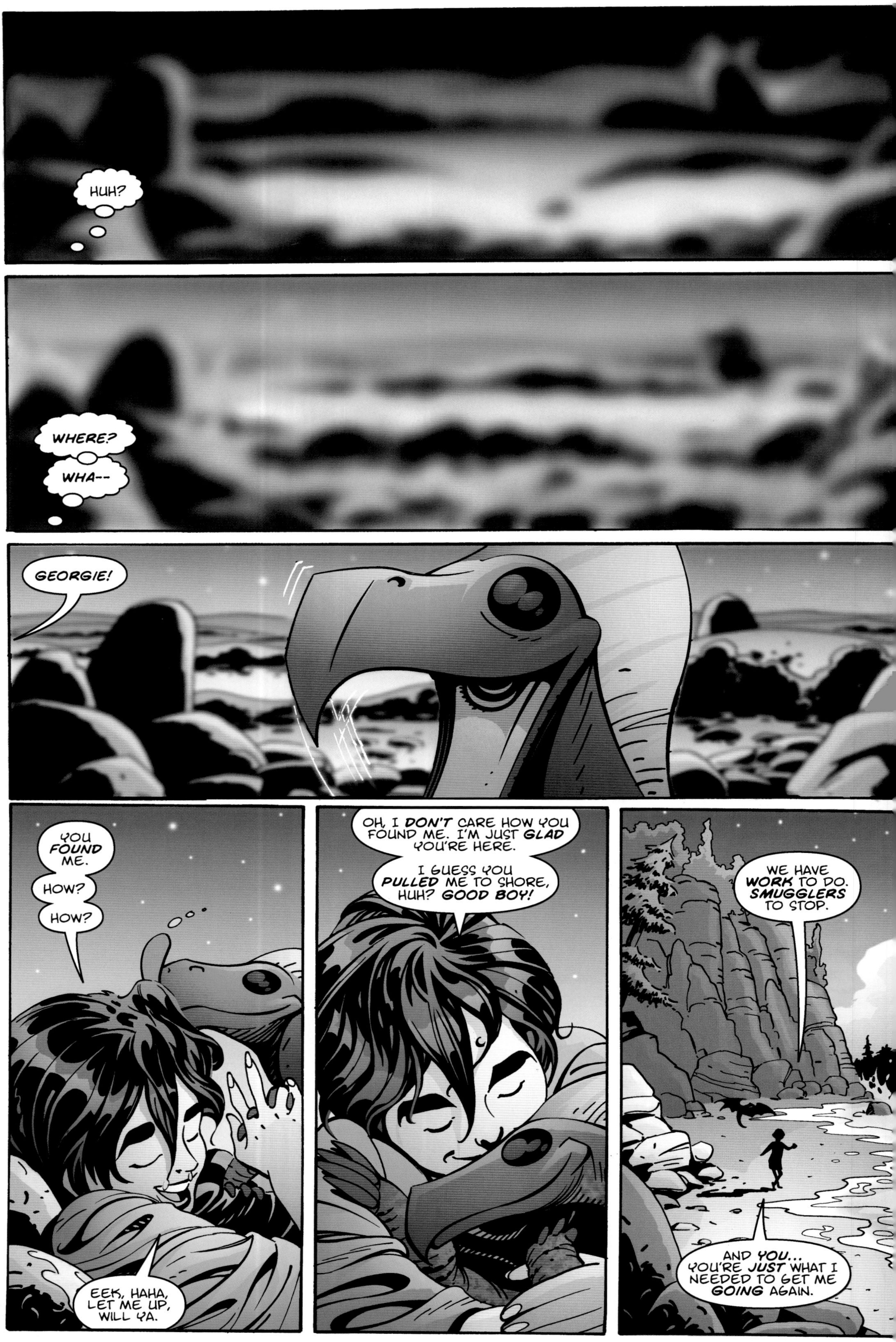
HUH?
WHERE?
WHA--
GEORGIE!
YOU FOUND ME.
HOW?
HOW?
EEK, HAHA, LET ME UP, WILL YA.
OH, I DON'T CARE HOW YOU FOUND ME. I'M JUST GLAD YOU'RE HERE.
I GUESS YOU PULLED ME TO SHORE, HUH? GOOD BOY!
WE HAVE WORK TO DO. SMUGGLERS TO STOP.
AND YOU... YOU'RE JUST WHAT I NEEDED TO GET ME GOING AGAIN.

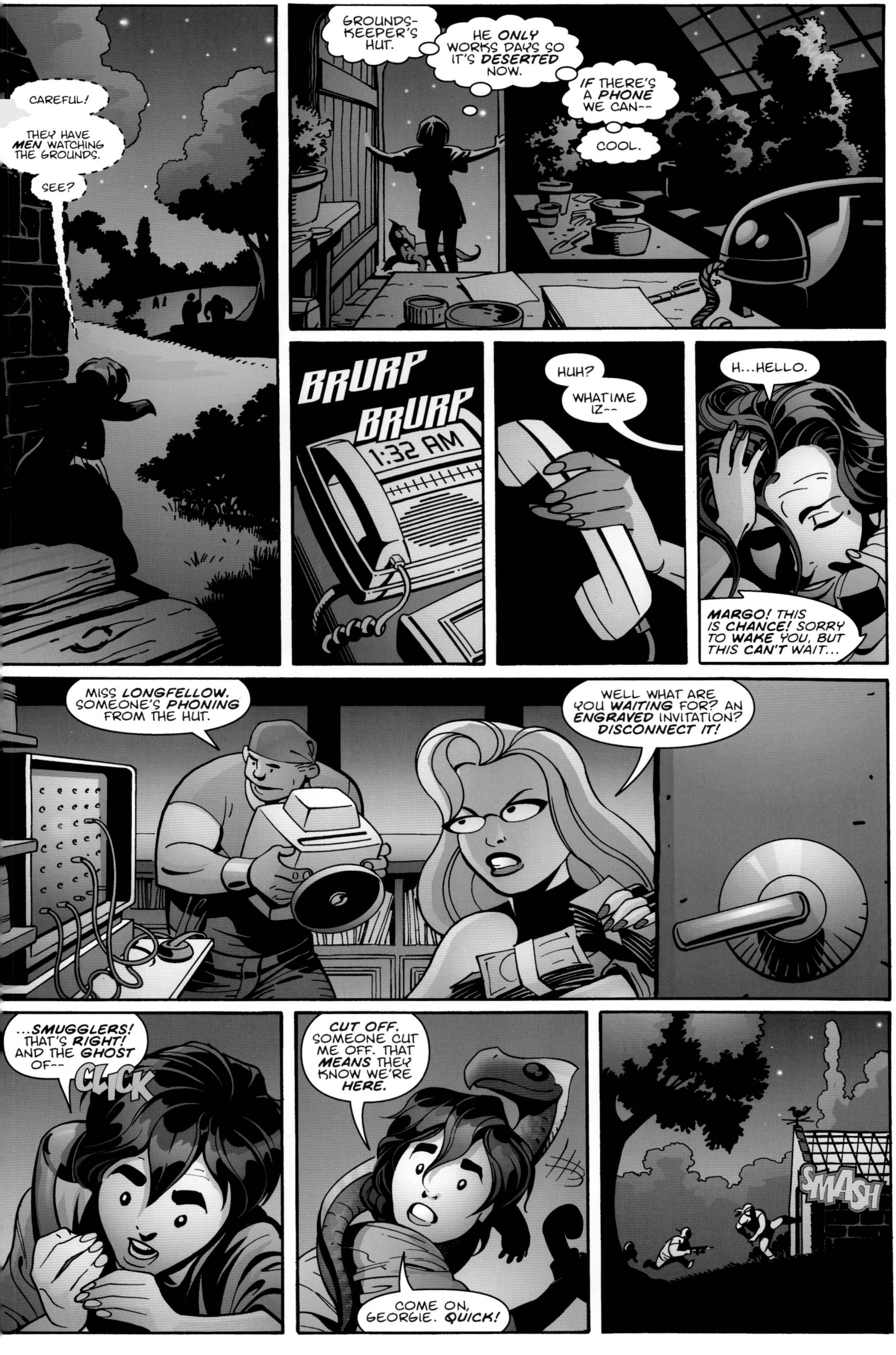

CAREFUL!
THEY HAVE MEN WATCHING THE GROUNDS.
SEE?
GROUNDS-KEEPER'S HUT.
HE ONLY WORKS DAYS SO IT'S DESERTED NOW.
IF THERE'S A PHONE WE CAN--
COOL.
BRURP
BRURP
1:32 AM
HUH?
WHATIME IZ--
H...HELLO.
MARGO! THIS IS CHANCE! SORRY TO WAKE YOU, BUT THIS CAN'T WAIT...
MISS LONGFELLOW. SOMEONE'S PHONING FROM THE HUT.
WELL WHAT ARE YOU WAITING FOR? AN ENGRAVED INVITATION? DISCONNECT IT!
...SMUGGLERS! THAT'S RIGHT! AND THE GHOST OF--
CLICK
CUT OFF. SOMEONE CUT ME OFF. THAT MEANS THEY KNOW WE'RE HERE.
COME ON, GEORGIE. QUICK!
SMASH

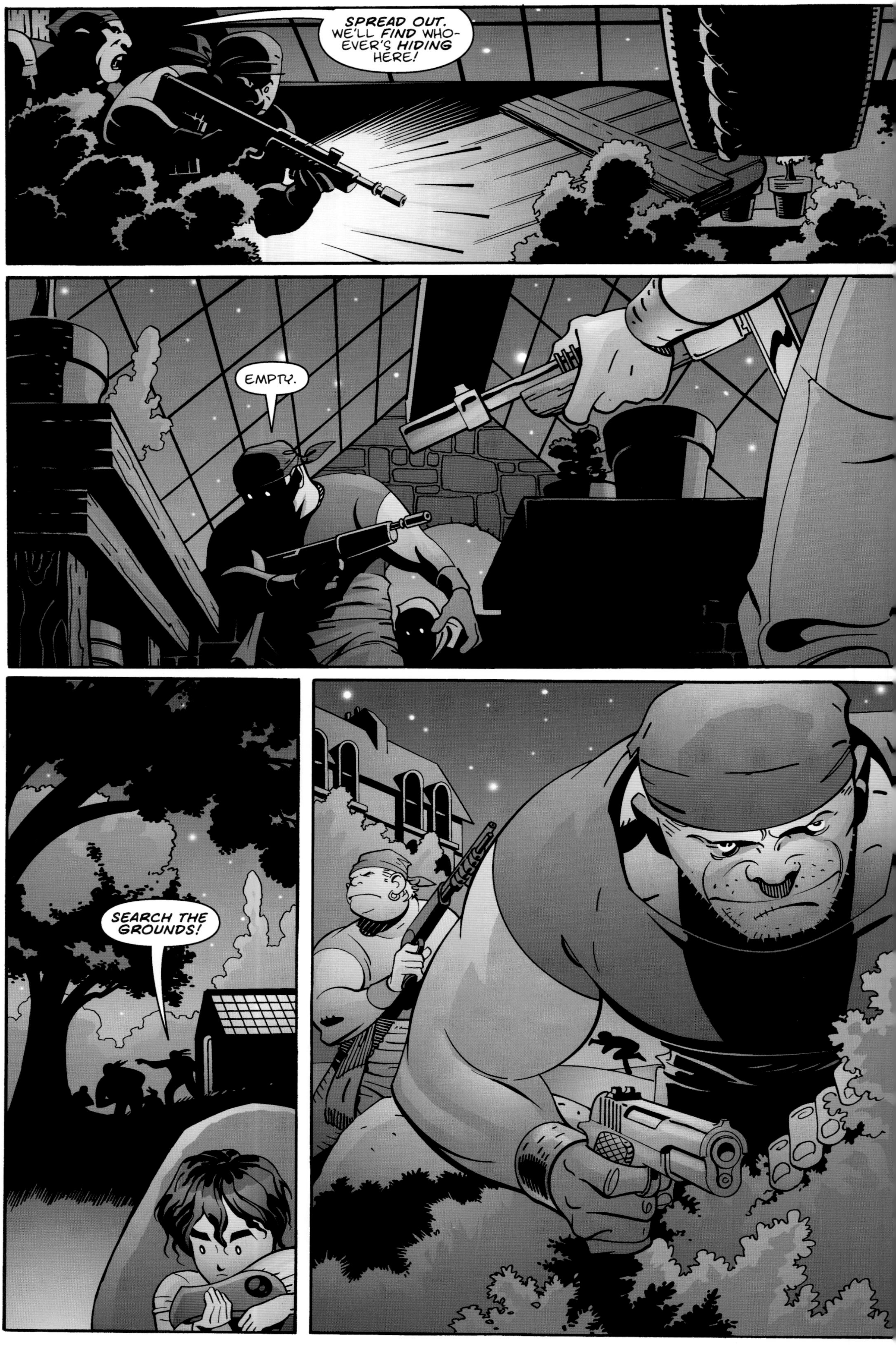
SPREAD OUT. WE'LL FIND WHO-EVER'S HIDING HERE!
EMPTY.
SEARCH THE GROUNDS!

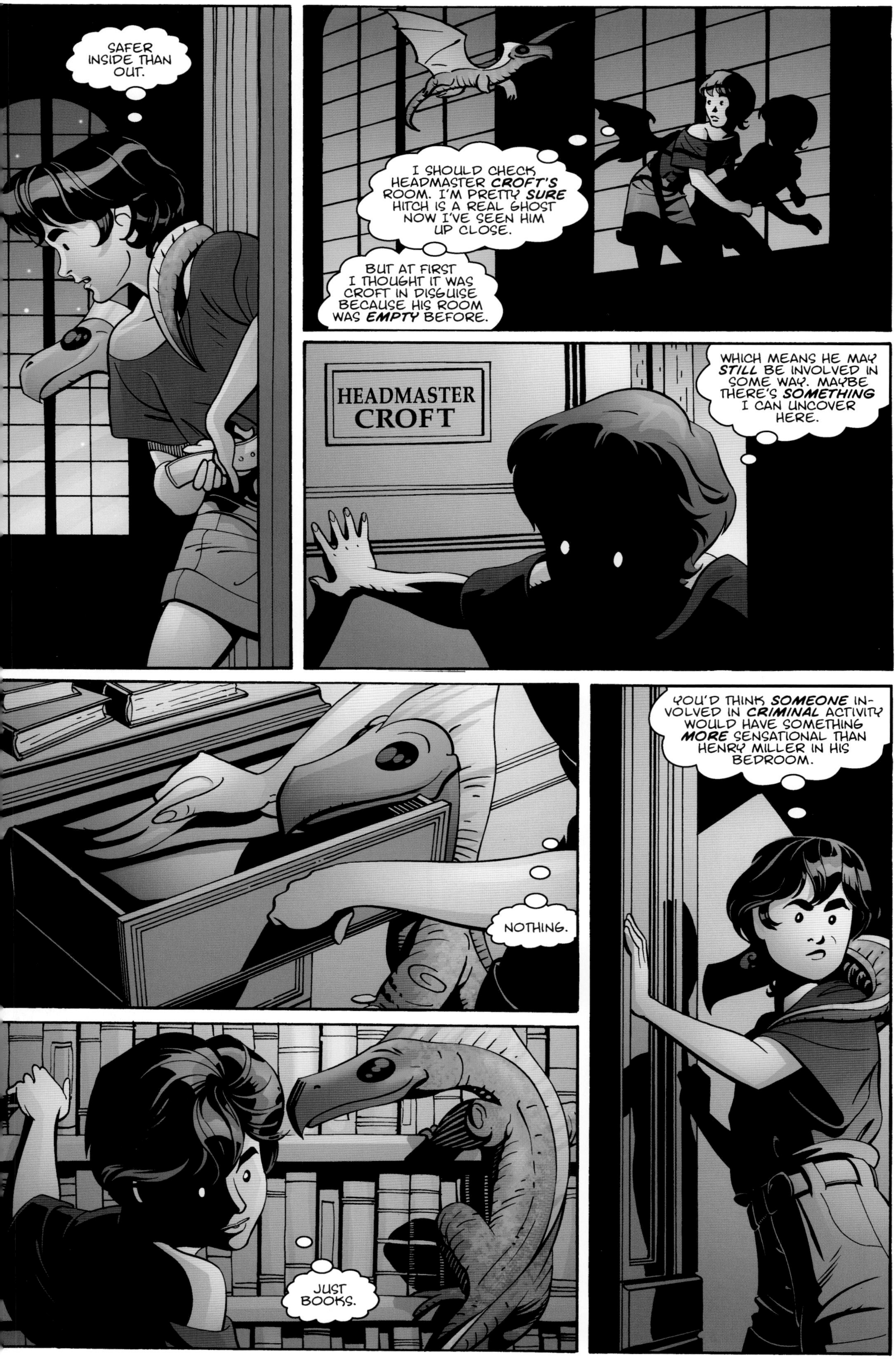
SAFER INSIDE THAN OUT.
I SHOULD CHECK HEADMASTER CROFT'S ROOM. I'M PRETTY SURE HITCH IS A REAL GHOST NOW I'VE SEEN HIM UP CLOSE.
BUT AT FIRST I THOUGHT IT WAS CROFT IN DISGUISE BECAUSE HIS ROOM WAS EMPTY BEFORE.
HEADMASTER CROFT
WHICH MEANS HE MAY STILL BE INVOLVED IN SOME WAY. MAYBE THERE'S SOMETHING I CAN UNCOVER HERE.
NOTHING.
JUST BOOKS.
YOU'D THINK SOMEONE IN-VOLVED IN CRIMINAL ACTIVITY WOULD HAVE SOMETHING MORE SENSATIONAL THAN HENRY MILLER IN HIS BEDROOM.

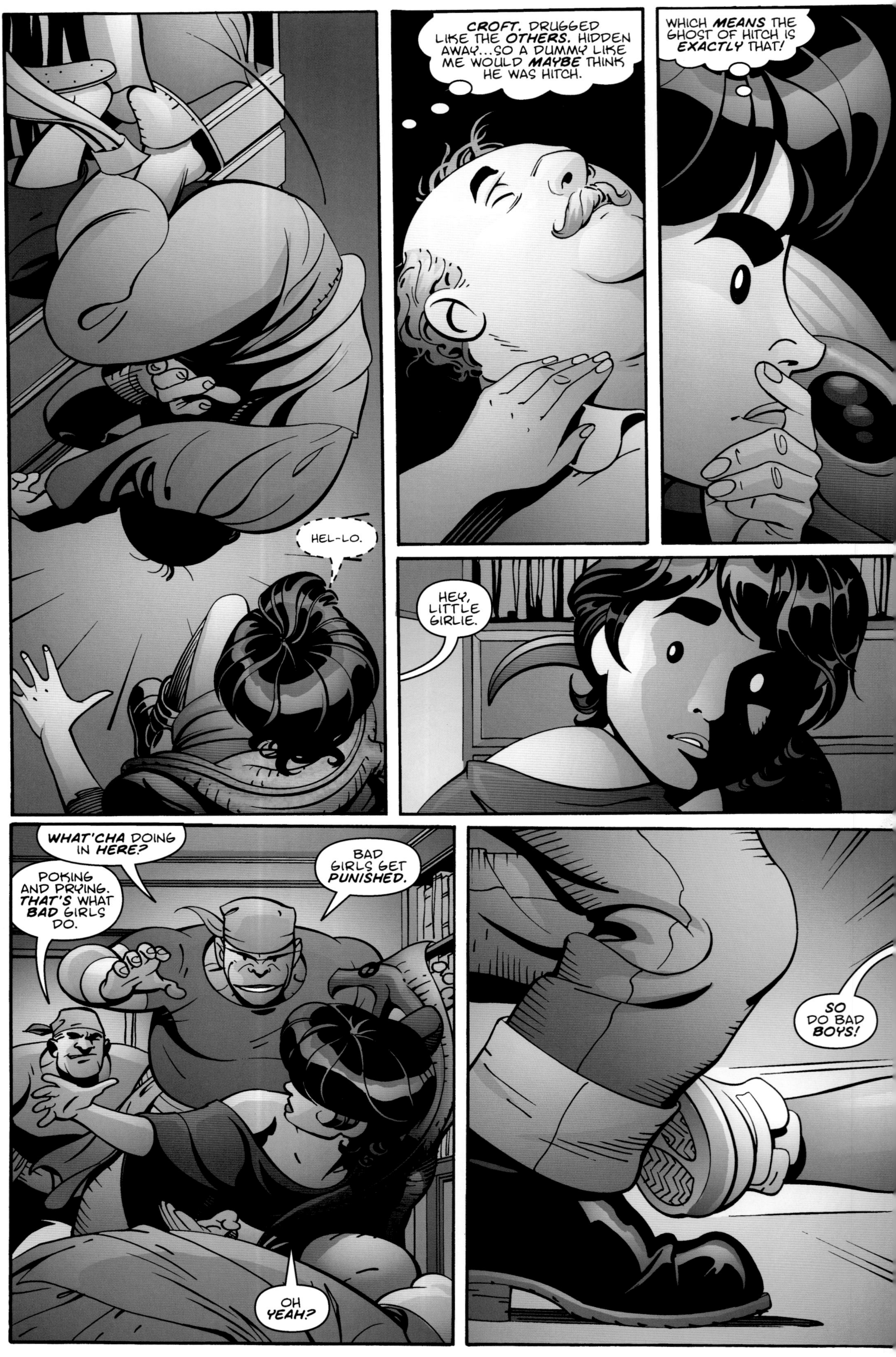
CROFT. DRUGGED LIKE THE OTHERS. HIDDEN AWAY...SO A DUMMY LIKE ME WOULD MAYBE THINK HE WAS HITCH.
WHICH MEANS THE GHOST OF HITCH IS EXACTLY THAT!
HEL-LO.
HEY, LITTLE GIRLIE.
WHAT'CHA DOING IN HERE?
POKING AND PRYING. THAT'S WHAT BAD GIRLS DO.
BAD GIRLS GET PUNISHED.
OH YEAH?
SO DO BAD BOYS!

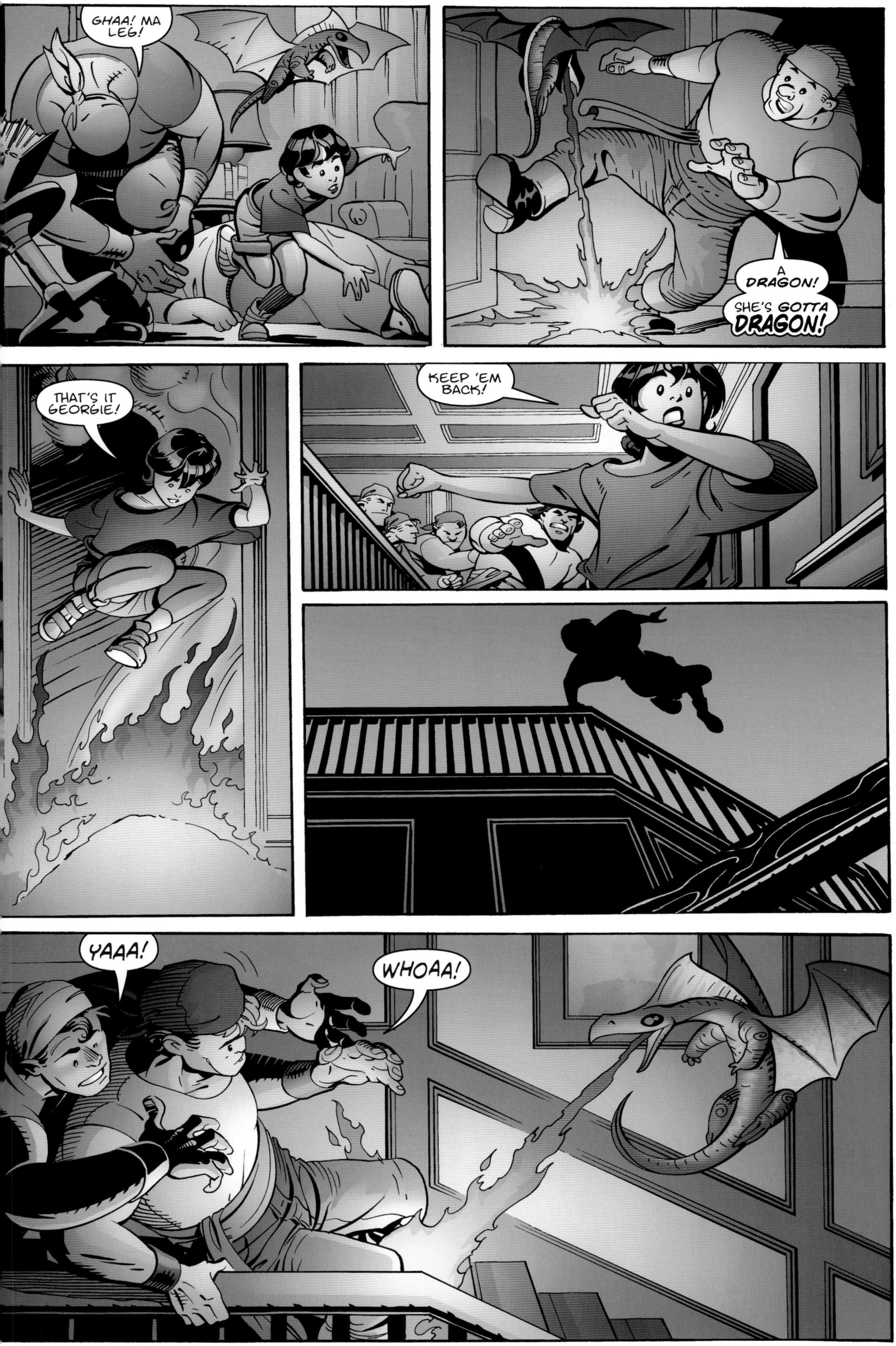
GHAA! MA LEG!
A DRAGON!
SHE'S GOTTA DRAGON!
THAT'S IT GEORGIE!
KEEP 'EM BACK!
YAAA!
WHOAA!

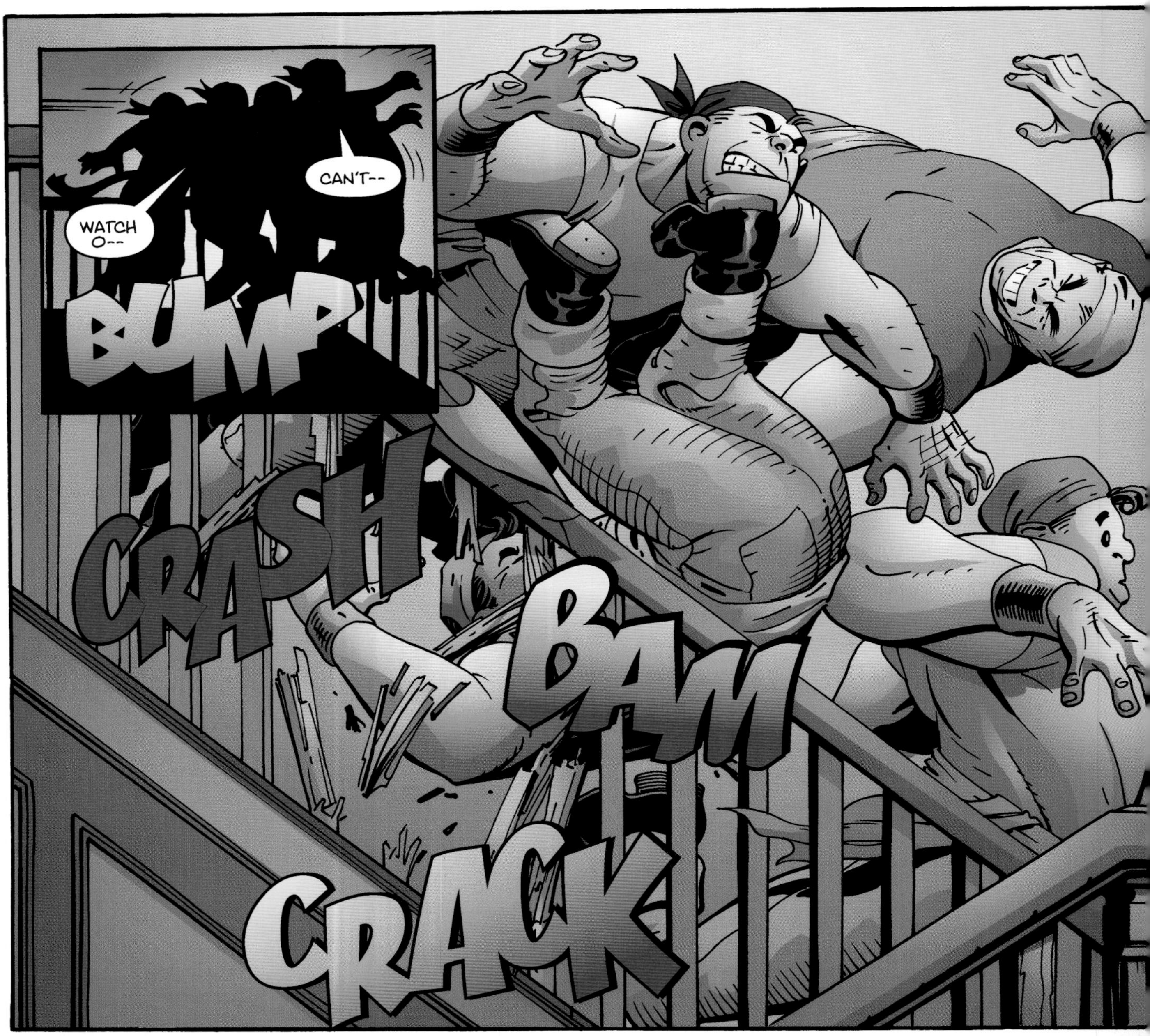
WATCH O--
CAN'T--
BUMP
CRASH
BAM
CRACK

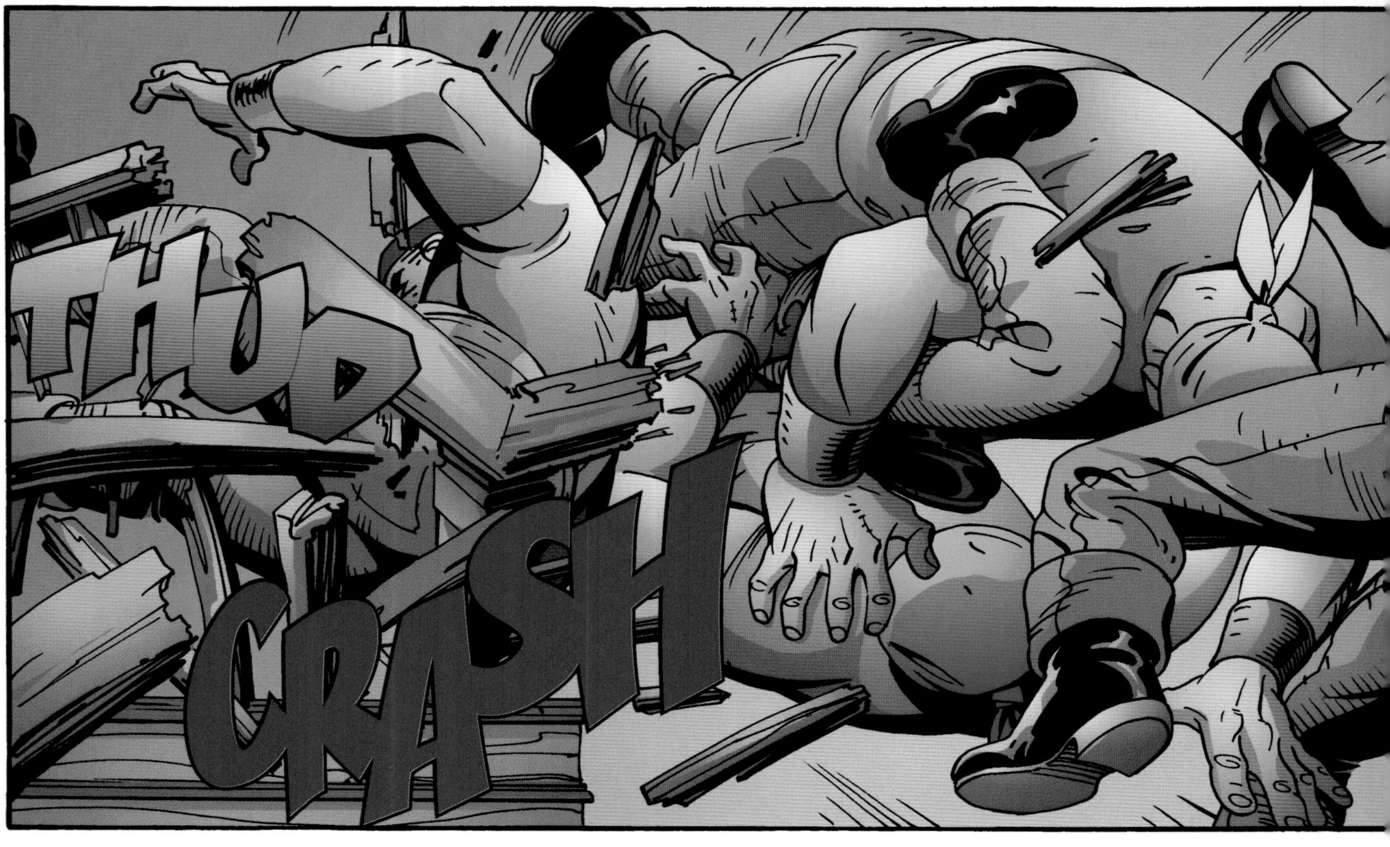
THUD
CRASH

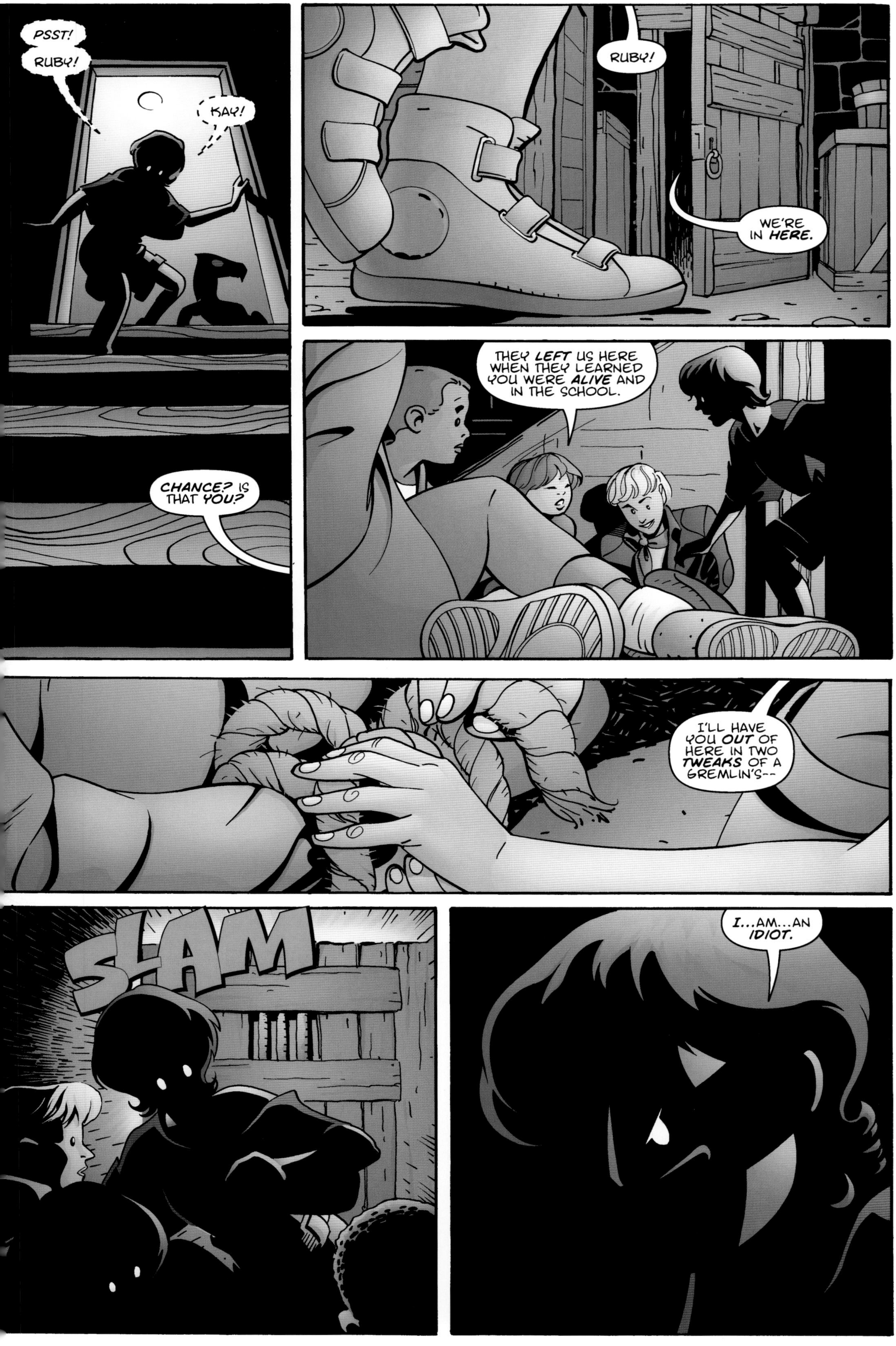
PSST!
RUBY!
KAY!
RUBY!
WE'RE IN HERE.
CHANCE? IS THAT YOU?
THEY LEFT US HERE WHEN THEY LEARNED YOU WERE ALIVE AND IN THE SCHOOL.
I'LL HAVE YOU OUT OF HERE IN TWO TWEAKS OF A GREMLIN'S--
SLAM
I...AM...AN IDIOT.

WE COULDN'T KILL YOU, BUT AT LEAST WE *CAPTURED* YOU.

*ALL OF YOU LOCKED AWAY, NICE AND TIGHT. EVEN THAT FLYING *LIZARD* YOU GOT.

HE'S A *DRAGON*. YOU'RE THE LIZARDS.

IT WAS ONLY *AFTER* WE SENT YOU OUT TO SEA, I REALIZED THAT *KILLING* THE DAUGHTER OF LUCAS FALCONER MIGHT *NOT* HAVE BEEN THE WISEST MOVE.

SO WE WERE *ALREADY* PREPARING TO PULL OUT WHEN YOU RE-APPEARED.

THIS SCHOOL HAS SERVED US *WELL*, BUT IF THE AUTHORITIES STARTED *SNIFFING* AROUND ABOUT YOUR DISAPPEARANCE... OR *WORST* STILL YOUR *FATHER* CAME...

...WELL, YOU CAN *IMAGINE* THAT WOULDN'T BE A GOOD THING.

NOW, I *DON'T* KNOW WHAT YOU SAID ON THE TELEPHONE OR TO *WHOM*, BUT I'M ASSUMING THE *AUTHORITIES* ARE ON THEIR WAY.

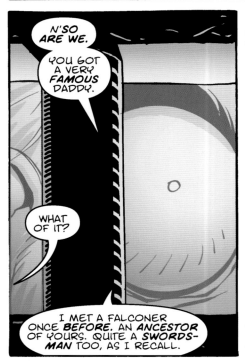

N'SO ARE WE.

YOU GOT A VERY *FAMOUS* DADDY.

WHAT OF IT?

I MET A FALCONER ONCE *BEFORE*. AN *ANCESTOR* OF YOURS. QUITE A *SWORDS-MAN* TOO, AS I RECALL.

NOT THAT IT MATTERS NOW.

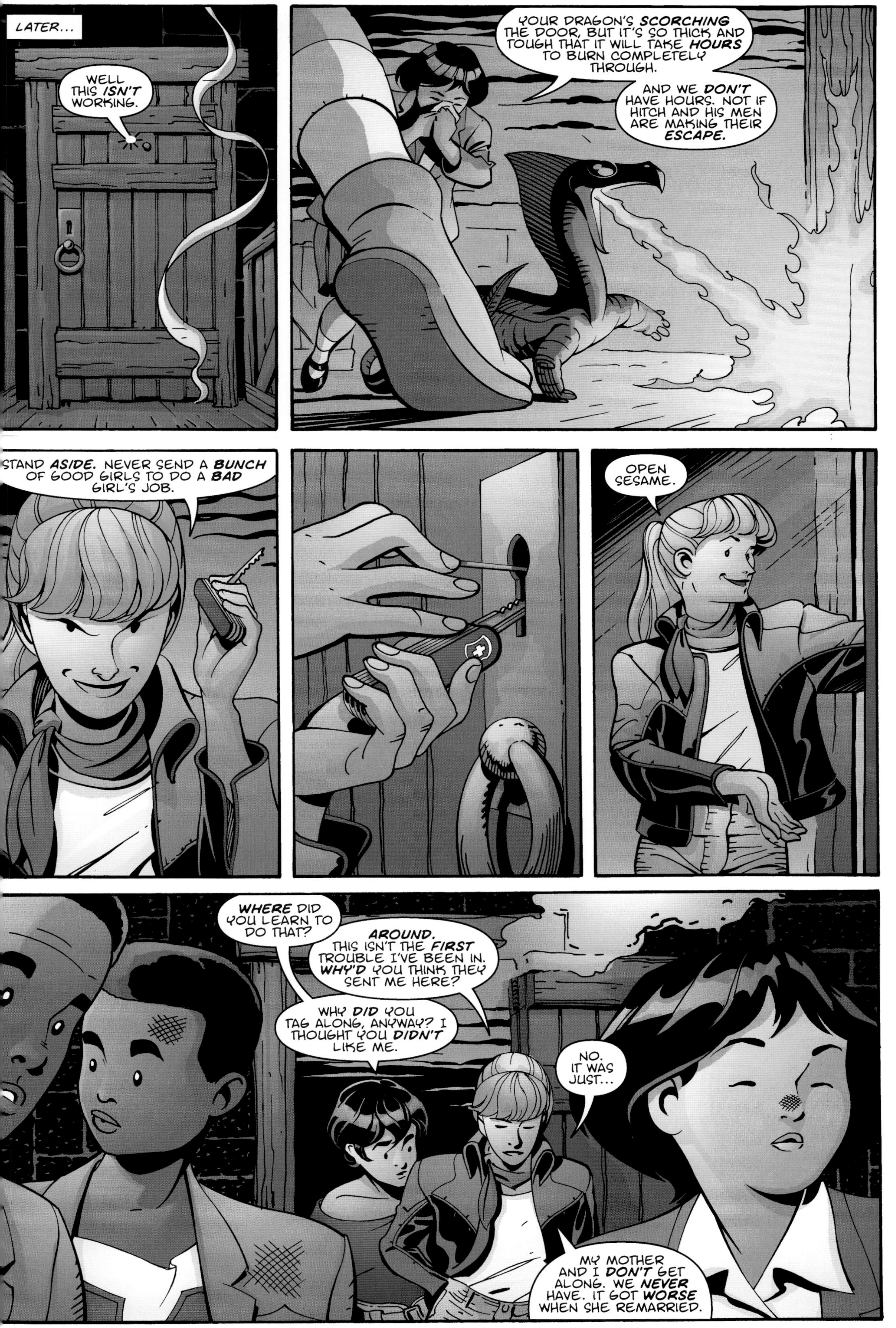
LATER...
WELL THIS *ISN'T* WORKING.
YOUR DRAGON'S *SCORCHING* THE DOOR, BUT IT'S SO THICK AND TOUGH THAT IT WILL TAKE *HOURS* TO BURN COMPLETELY THROUGH.
AND WE *DON'T* HAVE HOURS. NOT IF HITCH AND HIS MEN ARE MAKING THEIR *ESCAPE.*
STAND *ASIDE.* NEVER SEND A *BUNCH* OF GOOD GIRLS TO DO A *BAD* GIRL'S JOB.
OPEN SESAME.
WHERE DID YOU LEARN TO DO THAT?
AROUND. THIS ISN'T THE *FIRST* TROUBLE I'VE BEEN IN. *WHY'D* YOU THINK THEY SENT ME HERE?
WHY *DID* YOU TAG ALONG, ANYWAY? I THOUGHT YOU *DIDN'T* LIKE ME.
NO. IT WAS JUST...
MY MOTHER AND I *DON'T* GET ALONG. WE *NEVER* HAVE. IT GOT *WORSE* WHEN SHE REMARRIED.

MY *FATHER* DIED. MY *REAL* FATHER. I WAS *JEALOUS* OF YOU HAVING THE GREAT LUCAS FALCONER AS YOUR DAD.

SORRY I CALLED HIM A FREAK.

TRUTH IS, I THINK HE LOOKS KINDA *COOL.*

COME *ON.* HITCH WILL GET AWAY.

THE SMUGGLERS' CAVE...

THEY'RE GONE!

NO, *LOOK,* OUT THERE. I *SEE* THEM. THEY HAVEN'T GONE *TOO* FAR.

MY *FATHER* DIED. MY *REAL* FATHER.

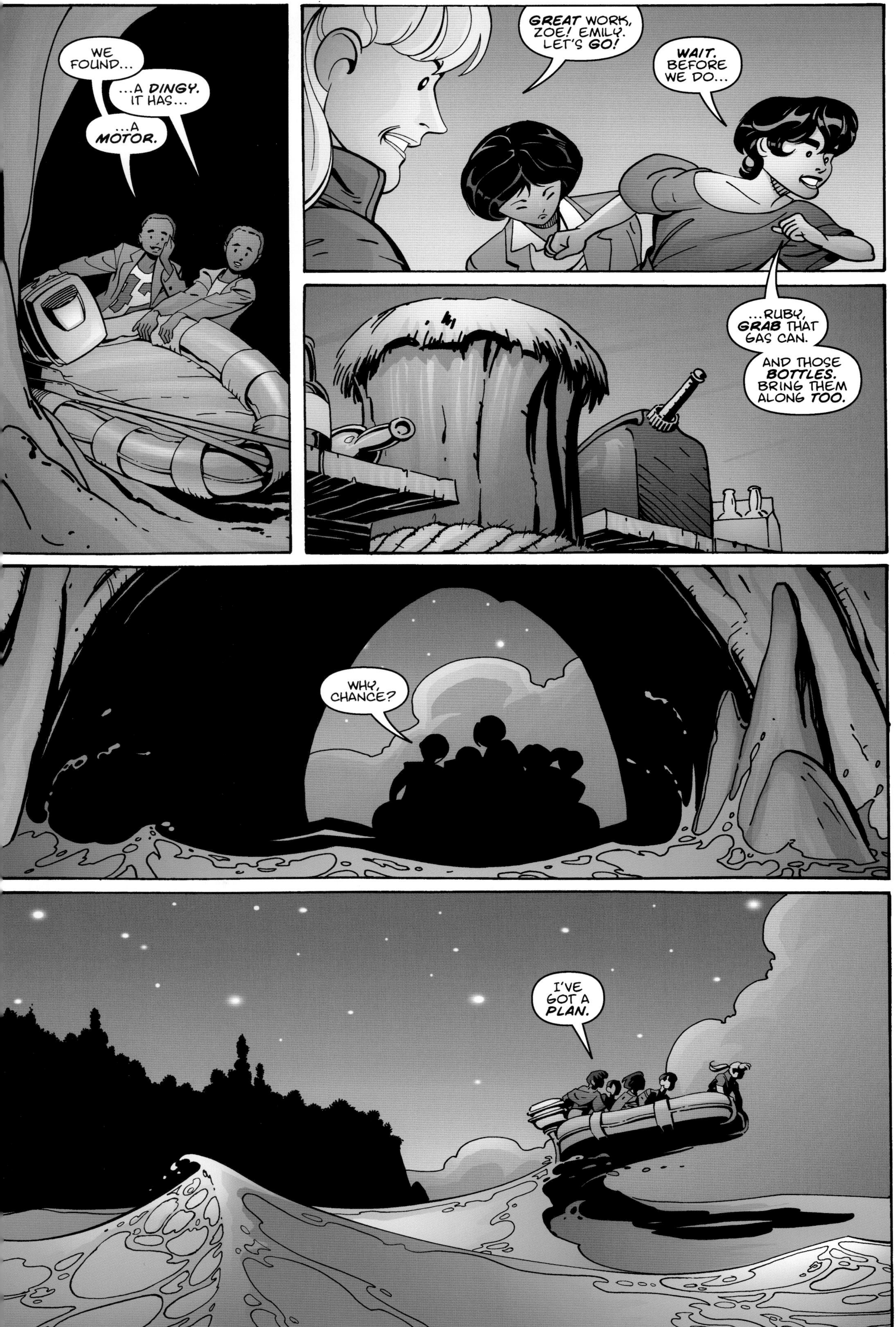
WE FOUND...
...A DINGY. IT HAS...
...A MOTOR.
GREAT WORK, ZOE! EMILY. LET'S GO!
WAIT. BEFORE WE DO...
...RUBY, GRAB THAT GAS CAN.
AND THOSE BOTTLES. BRING THEM ALONG TOO.
WHY, CHANCE?
I'VE GOT A PLAN.

I'M GOING *BELOW.* LOOKS LIKE WE GOT *AWAY* WITH IT BOYS.

WHERE ARE WE GOING, CAPTAIN?

DEVIL'S ECHO. THE FALCONER GIRL PUT ME IN *MIND* OF IT. *BOOTY* TO BE HAD THERE, FOR SURE.

WHAT ABOUT *LUCAS* FALCONER?

LET *ME* WORRY 'BOUT HIM, LONGFELLOW. *'SIDES,* BE A WHILE 'FORE HE'LL KNOW FOR *SURE* WE'RE EVEN *THERE.* N'WE'LL BE SET UP AND *RUNNING* BY THEN.

ANYWAY, WHAT HAVE I T'FEAR FROM *ANY* MAN? BAH. ONE OF LUCAS' *ANCESTORS* MAY INDEED'A BEEN THE *ONE* SENT ME T'DAVY JONES' *LOCKER,* AYE.

BUT HOW CAN *ANY* FALCONER HURT ME NOW THAT I'M *DEAD?*

THAT'S WHAT I INTEND TO *FIND* OUT.

HEY BOYS! WATCH YOUR *HEADS!* INCOMING!

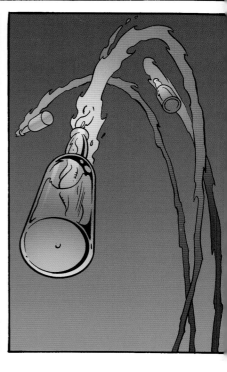

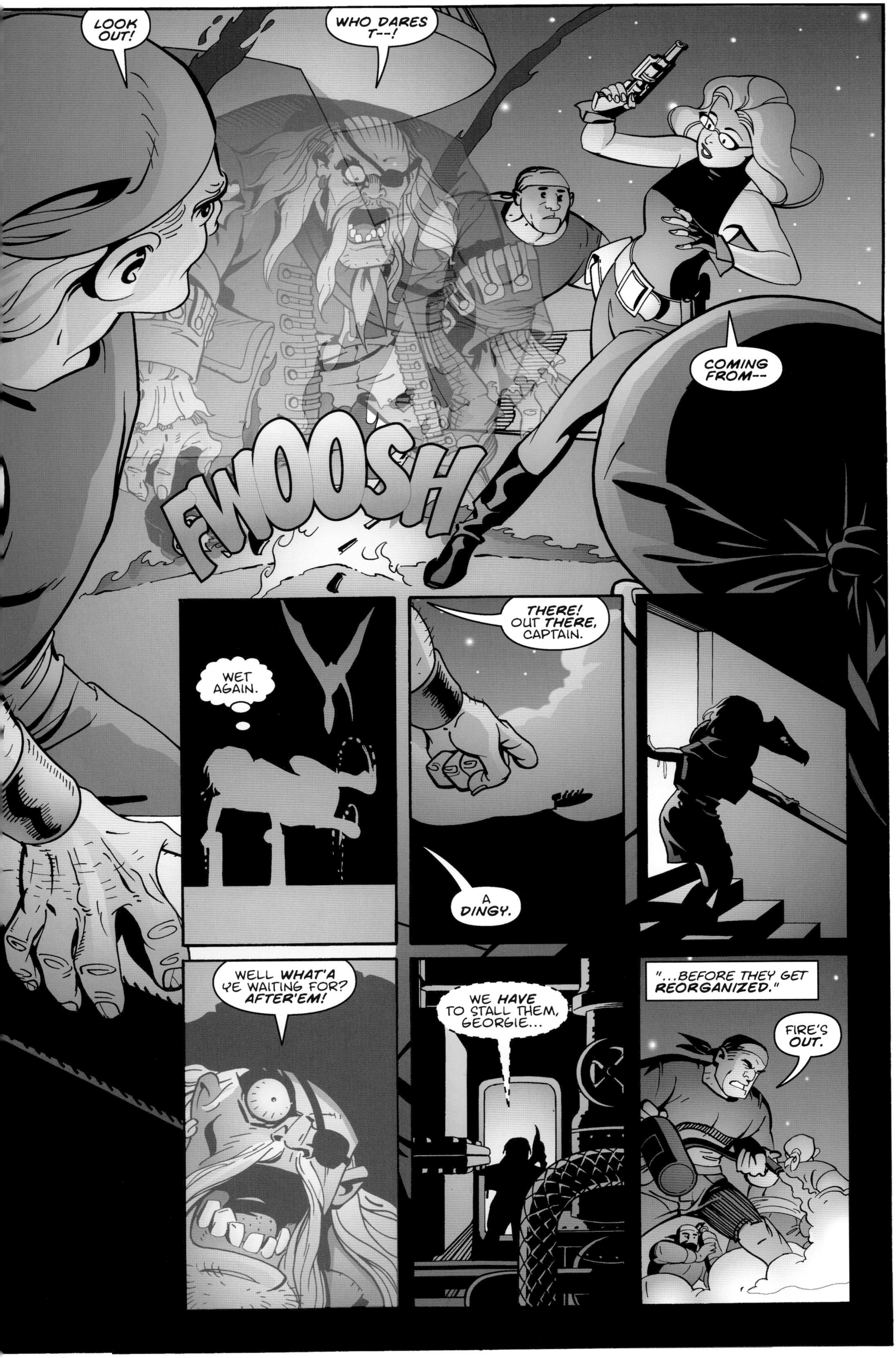
LOOK OUT!
WHO DARES T--!
COMING FROM--
FWOOSH
WET AGAIN.
THERE! OUT THERE, CAPTAIN.
A DINGY.
WELL WHAT'A YE WAITING FOR? AFTER'EM!
WE HAVE TO STALL THEM, GEORGIE...
"...BEFORE THEY GET REORGANIZED."
FIRE'S OUT.

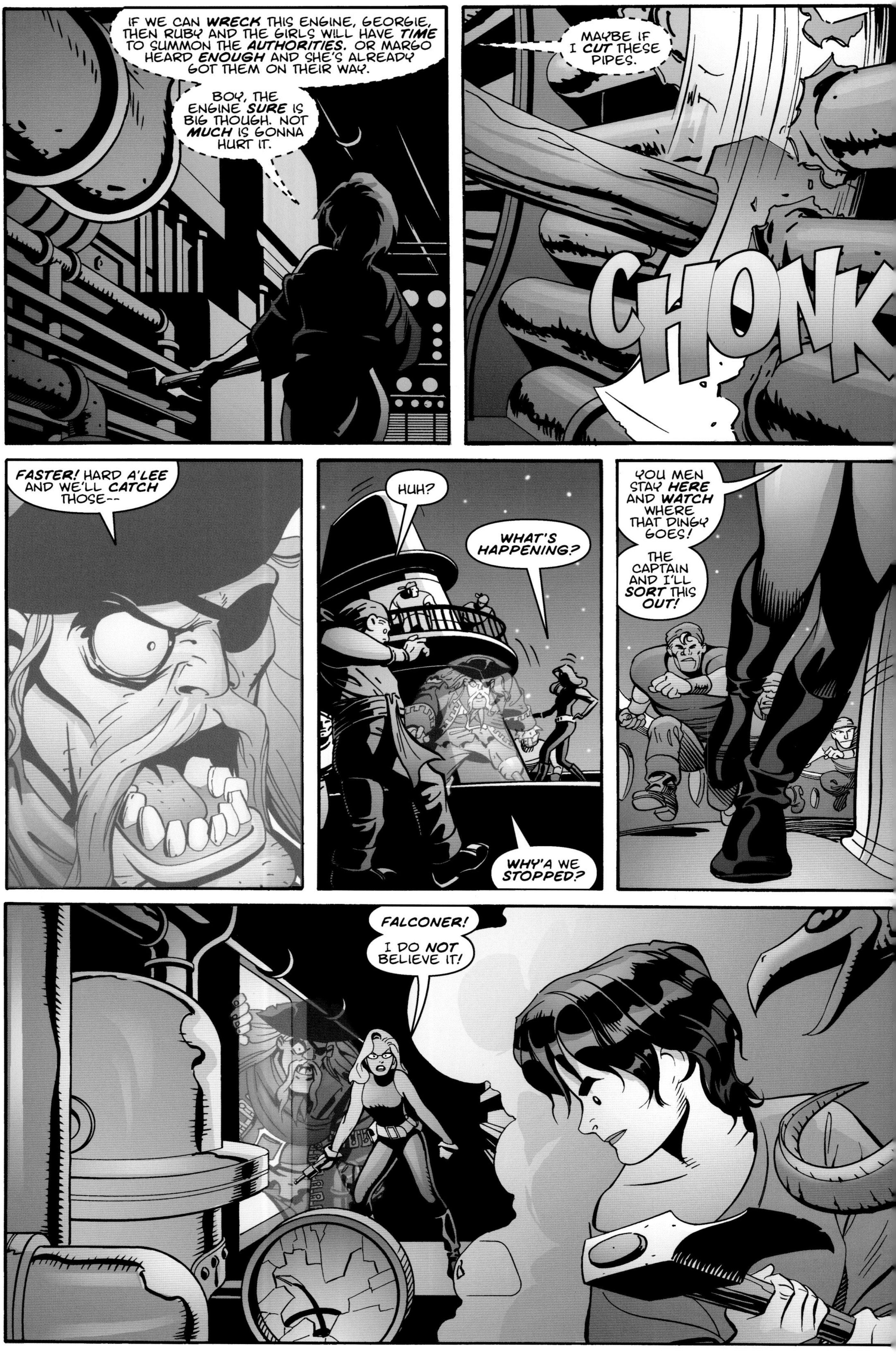
IF WE CAN WRECK THIS ENGINE, GEORGIE, THEN RUBY AND THE GIRLS WILL HAVE TIME TO SUMMON THE AUTHORITIES. OR MARGO HEARD ENOUGH AND SHE'S ALREADY GOT THEM ON THEIR WAY.
BOY, THE ENGINE SURE IS BIG THOUGH. NOT MUCH IS GONNA HURT IT.
MAYBE IF I CUT THESE PIPES.
CHONK
FASTER! HARD A'LEE AND WE'LL CATCH THOSE--
HUH?
WHAT'S HAPPENING?
WHY'A WE STOPPED?
YOU MEN STAY HERE AND WATCH WHERE THAT DINGY GOES!
THE CAPTAIN AND I'LL SORT THIS OUT!
FALCONER!
I DO NOT BELIEVE IT!

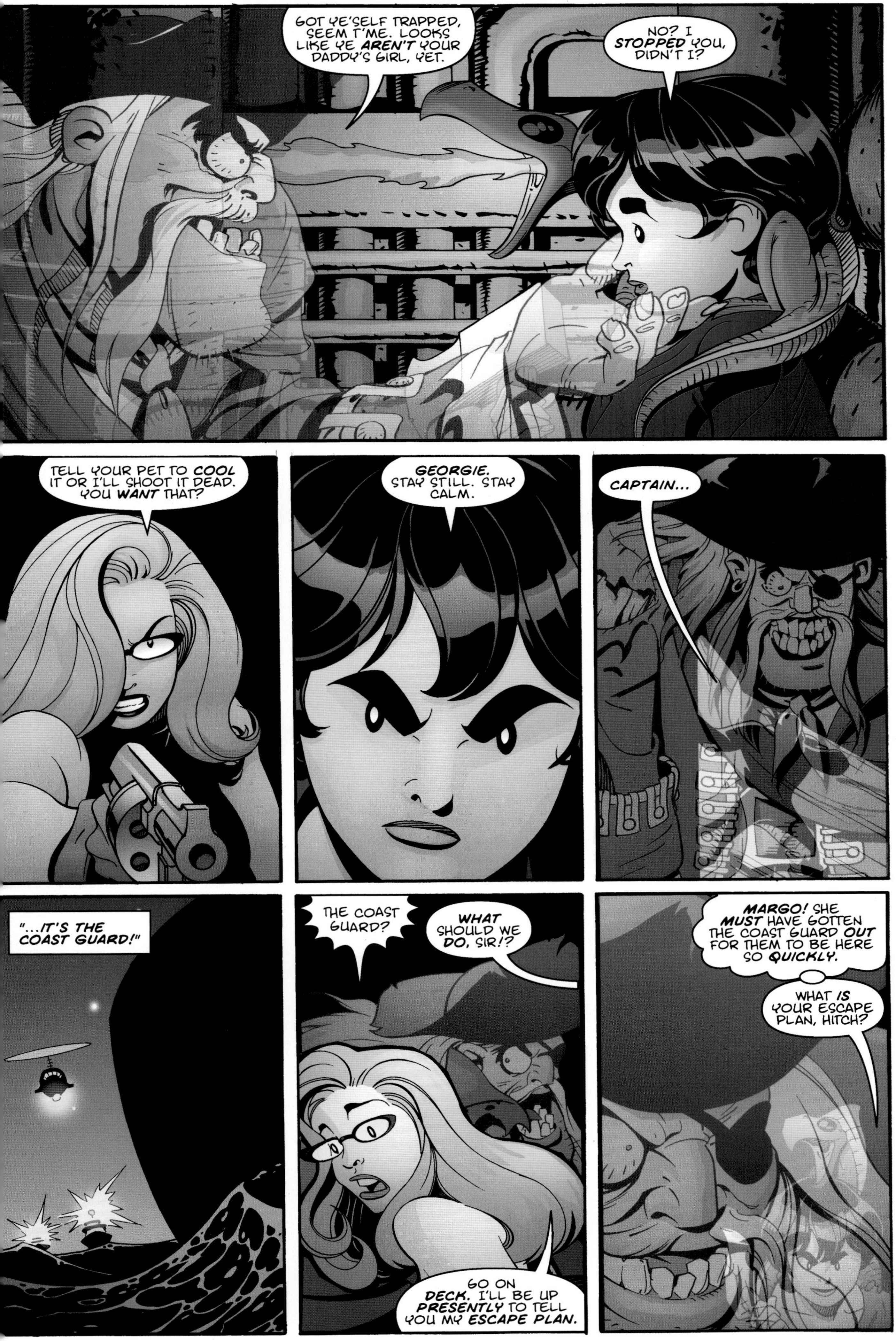
GOT YE'SELF TRAPPED, SEEM T'ME. LOOKS LIKE YE AREN'T YOUR DADDY'S GIRL, YET.
NO? I STOPPED YOU, DIDN'T I?
TELL YOUR PET TO COOL IT OR I'LL SHOOT IT DEAD. YOU WANT THAT?
GEORGIE. STAY STILL. STAY CALM.
CAPTAIN...
"...IT'S THE COAST GUARD!"
THE COAST GUARD?
WHAT SHOULD WE DO, SIR!?
GO ON DECK. I'LL BE UP PRESENTLY TO TELL YOU MY ESCAPE PLAN.
MARGO! SHE MUST HAVE GOTTEN THE COAST GUARD OUT FOR THEM TO BE HERE SO QUICKLY.
WHAT IS YOUR ESCAPE PLAN, HITCH?

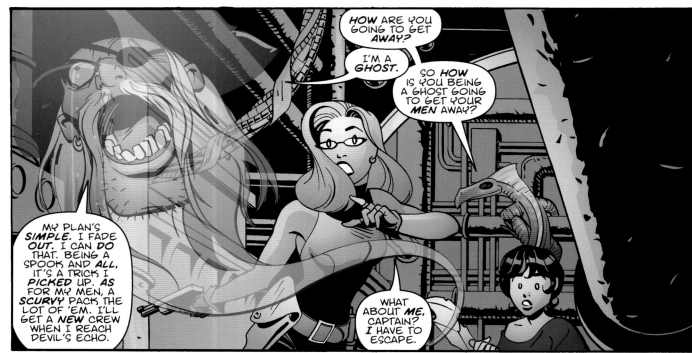

HOW ARE YOU GOING TO GET AWAY?

I'M A GHOST.

SO HOW IS YOU BEING A GHOST GOING TO GET YOUR MEN AWAY?

MY PLAN'S SIMPLE. I FADE OUT. I CAN DO THAT. BEING A SPOOK AND ALL, IT'S A TRICK I PICKED UP. AS FOR MY MEN, A SCURVY PACK THE LOT OF 'EM. I'LL GET A NEW CREW WHEN I REACH DEVIL'S ECHO.

WHAT ABOUT ME, CAPTAIN? I HAVE TO ESCAPE.

SORRY, LASS. YOU, I'LL MISS. YOU WERE A HELP. BUT THIS TIME THERE'S NO WAY. SMILE PRETTY AT THE JUDGE AND HE MIGHT GO EASY ON YOU.

HOW CAN YOU LEAVE ME?

I'M A PIRATE. I'M A VILLAIN...

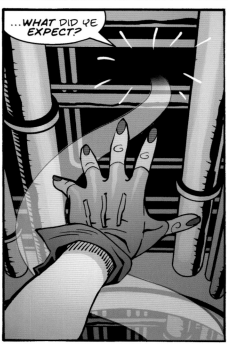

...WHAT DID YE EXPECT?

YOU MEDDLER! YOU LITTLE MEDDLER! LOOK WHAT YOU'VE DONE!

I'LL KILL YOU! YOU AND THAT STUPID LIZARD!

BLAM

BLAM

BLAM

LOOK OUT, GEORGIE! SHE'LL HIT THE--

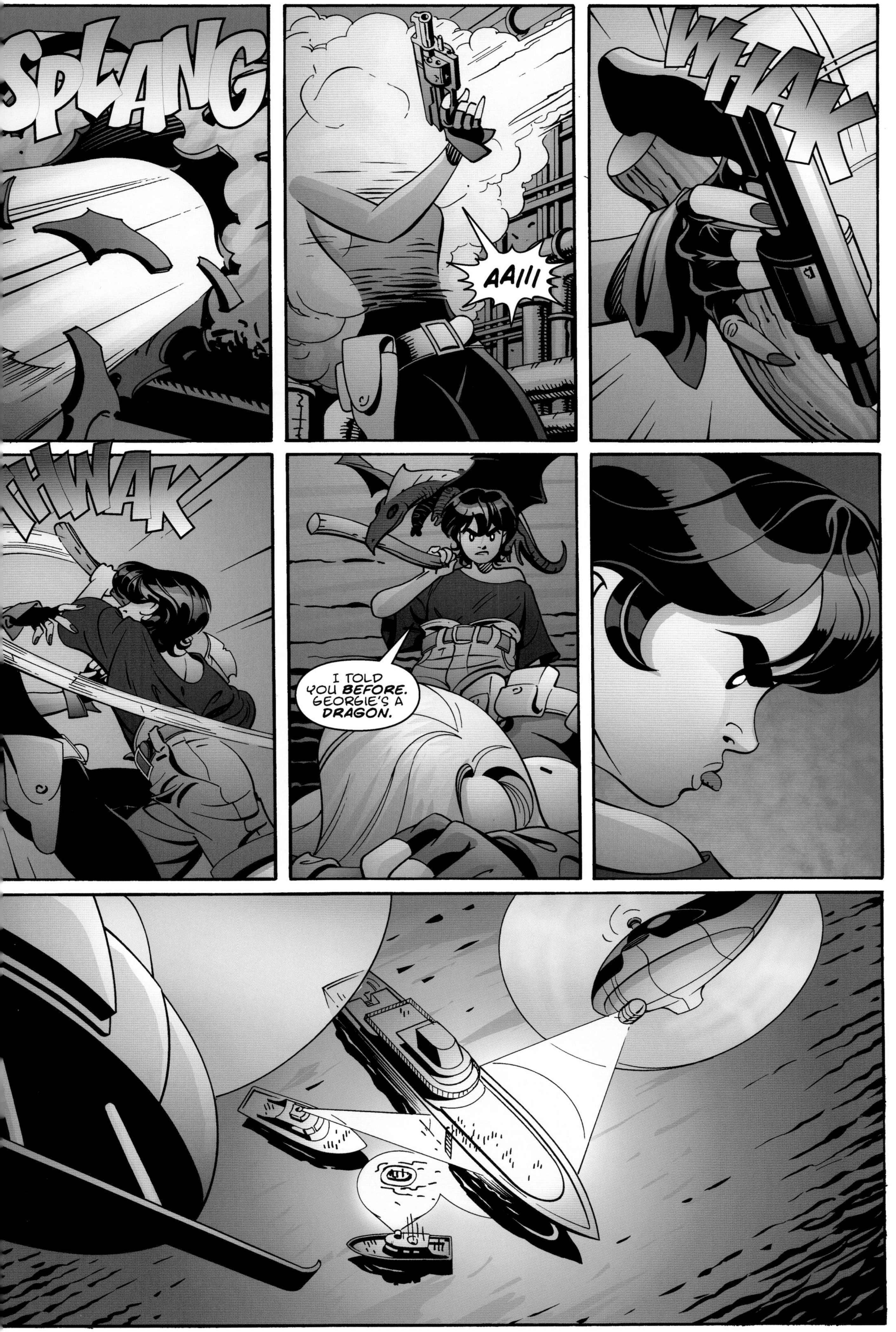
SPLANG
AAIII
WHAK
WHAK
I TOLD YOU BEFORE. GEORGIE'S A DRAGON.

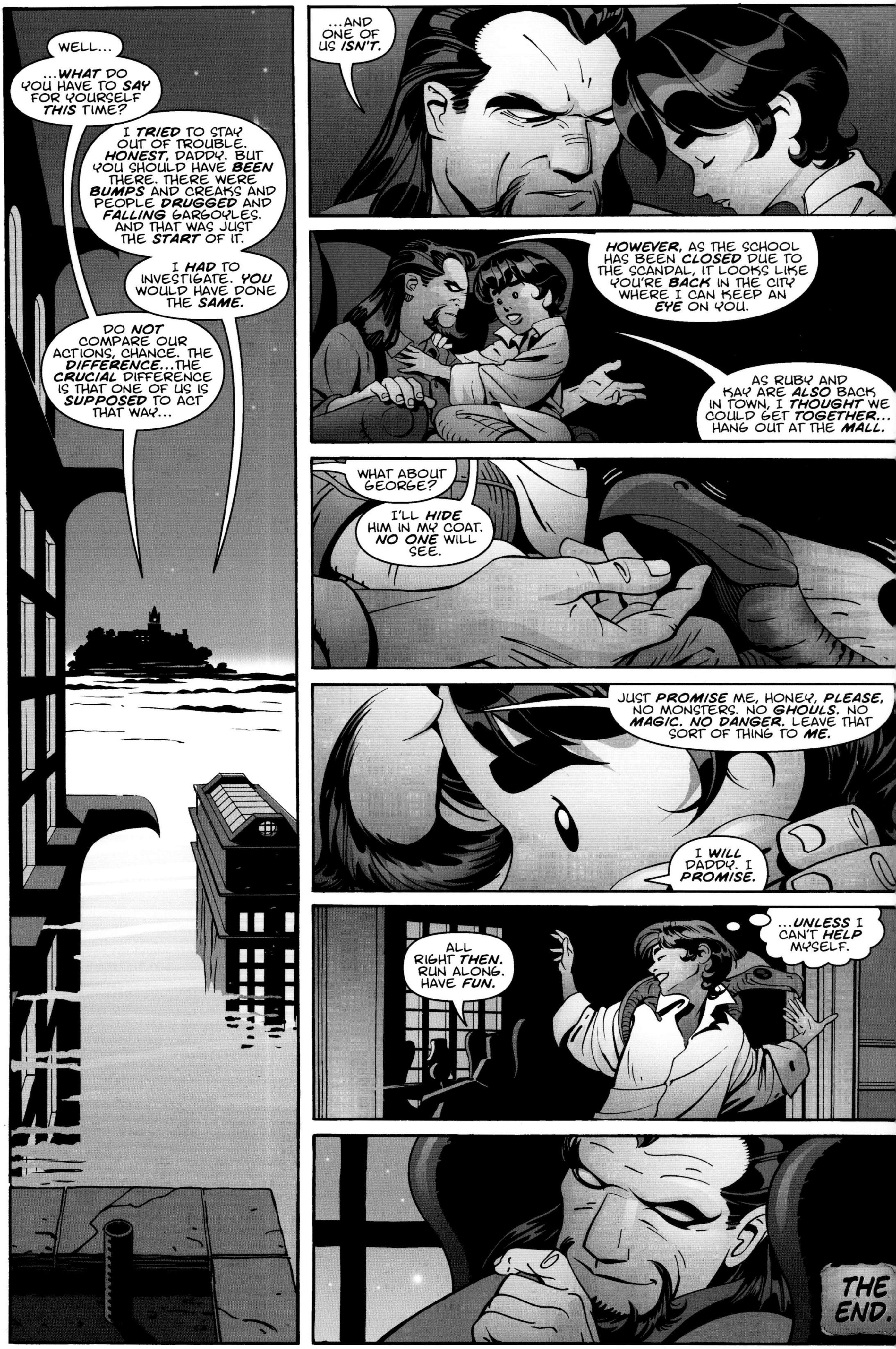
WELL...
...WHAT DO YOU HAVE TO SAY FOR YOURSELF THIS TIME?
I TRIED TO STAY OUT OF TROUBLE. HONEST, DADDY. BUT YOU SHOULD HAVE BEEN THERE. THERE WERE BUMPS AND CREAKS AND PEOPLE DRUGGED AND FALLING GARGOYLES. AND THAT WAS JUST THE START OF IT.
I HAD TO INVESTIGATE. YOU WOULD HAVE DONE THE SAME.
DO NOT COMPARE OUR ACTIONS, CHANCE. THE DIFFERENCE...THE CRUCIAL DIFFERENCE IS THAT ONE OF US IS SUPPOSED TO ACT THAT WAY...
...AND ONE OF US ISN'T.
HOWEVER, AS THE SCHOOL HAS BEEN CLOSED DUE TO THE SCANDAL, IT LOOKS LIKE YOU'RE BACK IN THE CITY WHERE I CAN KEEP AN EYE ON YOU.
AS RUBY AND KAY ARE ALSO BACK IN TOWN, I THOUGHT WE COULD GET TOGETHER... HANG OUT AT THE MALL.
WHAT ABOUT GEORGE?
I'LL HIDE HIM IN MY COAT. NO ONE WILL SEE.
JUST PROMISE ME, HONEY, PLEASE, NO MONSTERS. NO GHOULS. NO MAGIC. NO DANGER. LEAVE THAT SORT OF THING TO ME.
I WILL DADDY. I PROMISE.
ALL RIGHT THEN. RUN ALONG. HAVE FUN.
...UNLESS I CAN'T HELP MYSELF.
THE END.

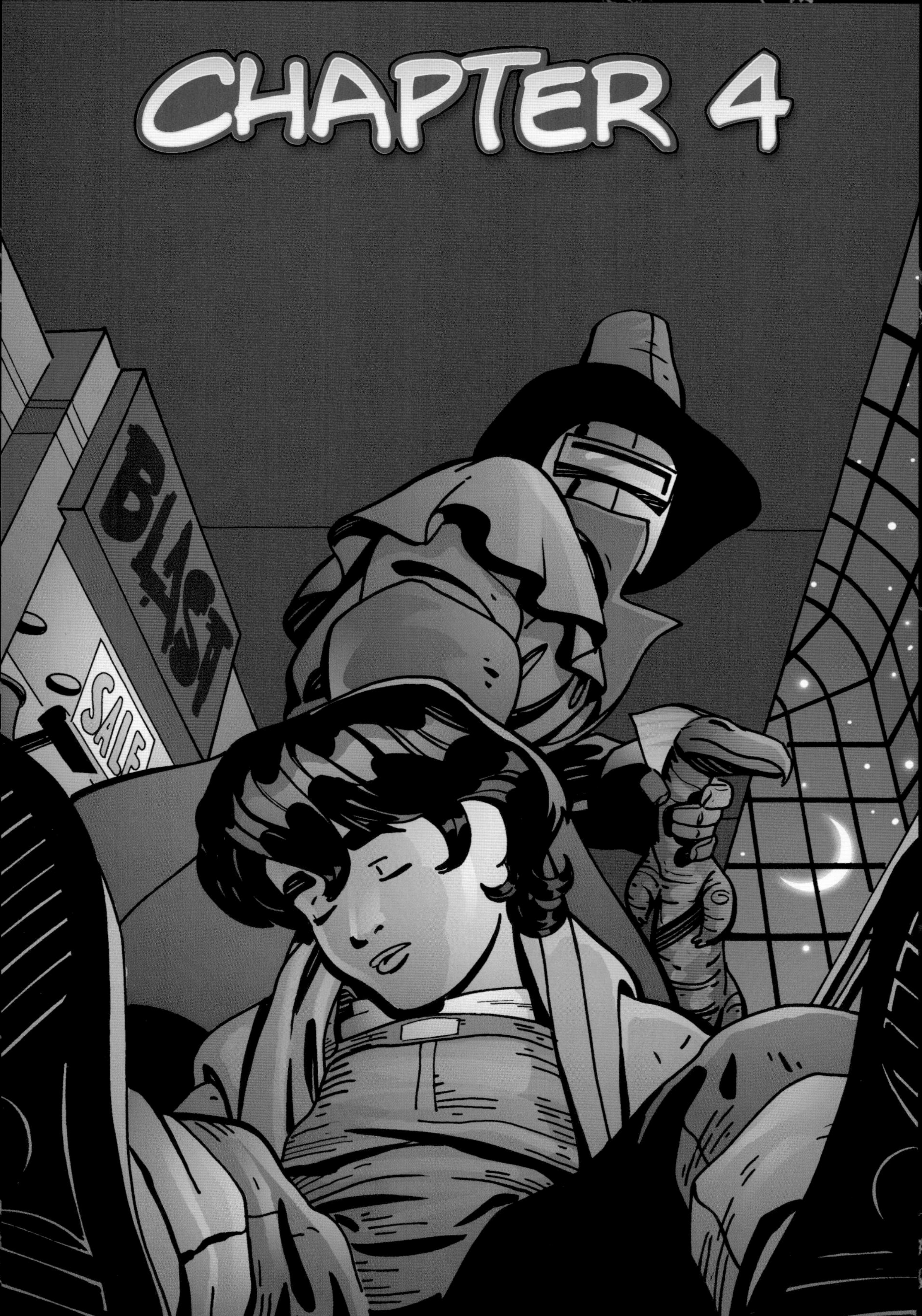
CHAPTER 4
BLAST
SALE

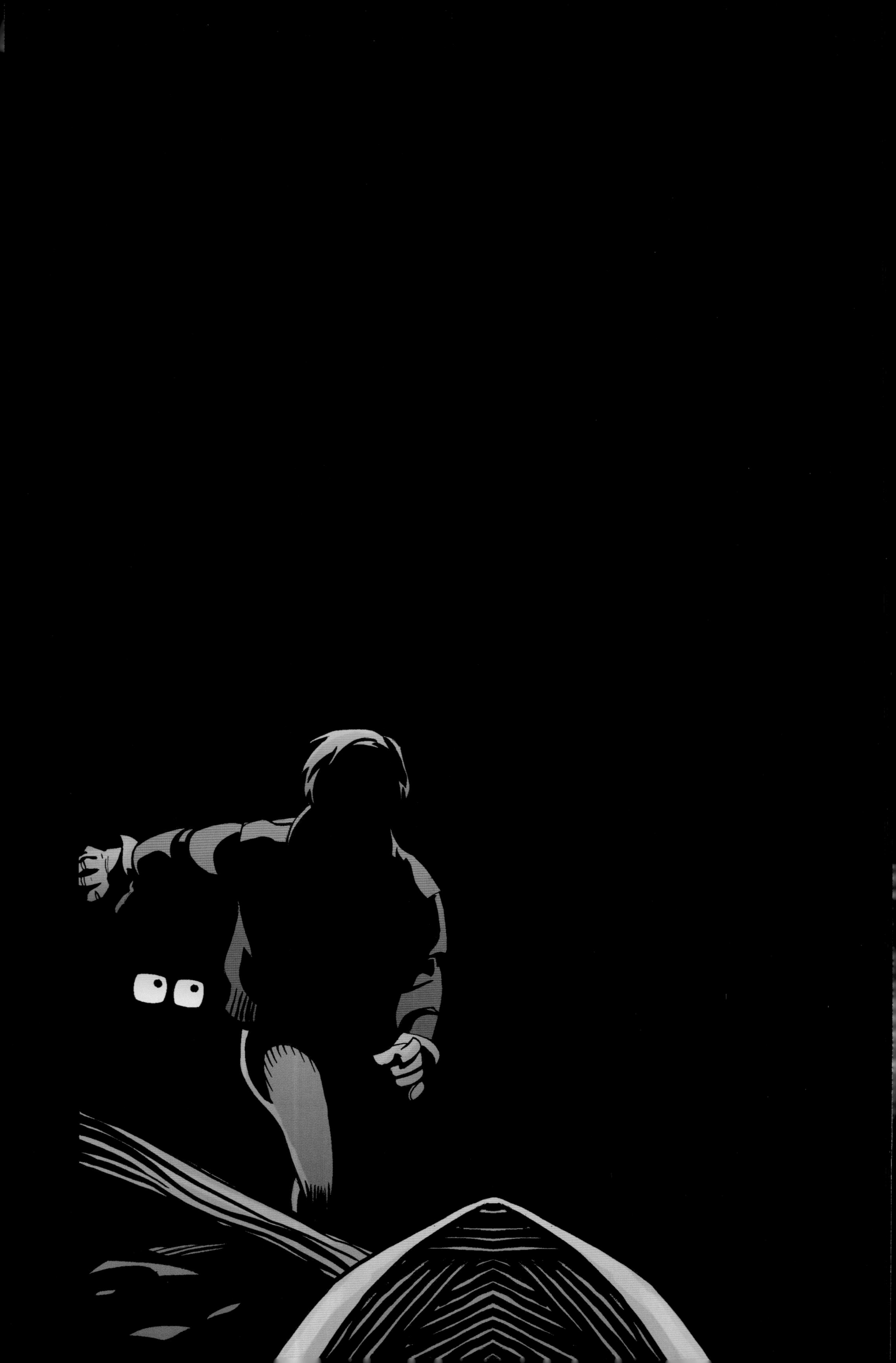

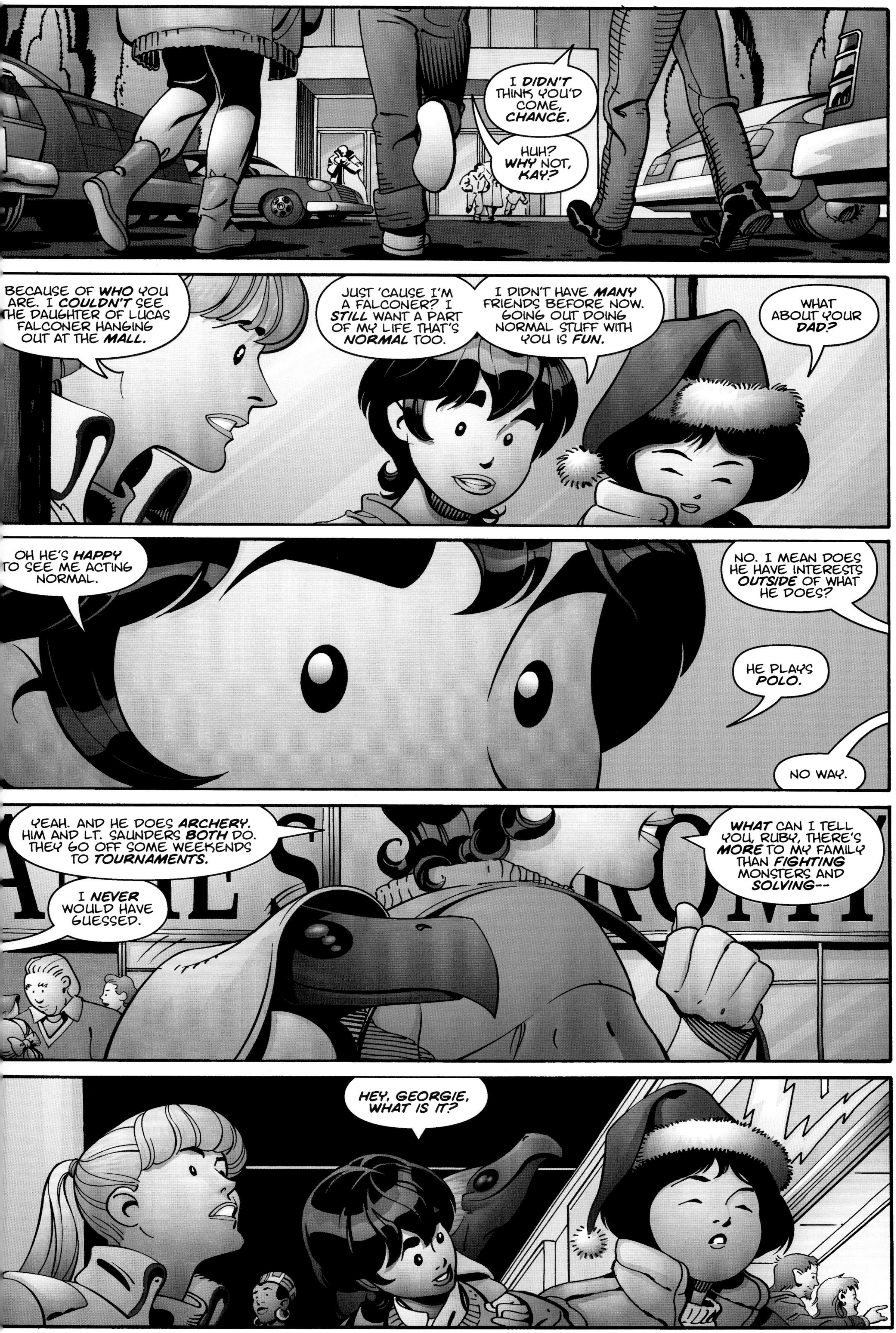
I DIDN'T THINK YOU'D COME, CHANCE.
HUH? WHY NOT, KAY?
BECAUSE OF WHO YOU ARE. I COULDN'T SEE THE DAUGHTER OF LUCAS FALCONER HANGING OUT AT THE MALL.
JUST 'CAUSE I'M A FALCONER? I STILL WANT A PART OF MY LIFE THAT'S NORMAL TOO.
I DIDN'T HAVE MANY FRIENDS BEFORE NOW. GOING OUT DOING NORMAL STUFF WITH YOU IS FUN.
WHAT ABOUT YOUR DAD?
OH HE'S HAPPY TO SEE ME ACTING NORMAL.
NO. I MEAN DOES HE HAVE INTERESTS OUTSIDE OF WHAT HE DOES?
HE PLAYS POLO.
NO WAY.
YEAH. AND HE DOES ARCHERY. HIM AND LT. SAUNDERS BOTH DO. THEY GO OFF SOME WEEKENDS TO TOURNAMENTS.
I NEVER WOULD HAVE GUESSED.
WHAT CAN I TELL YOU, RUBY, THERE'S MORE TO MY FAMILY THAN FIGHTING MONSTERS AND SOLVING--
HEY, GEORGIE, WHAT IS IT?

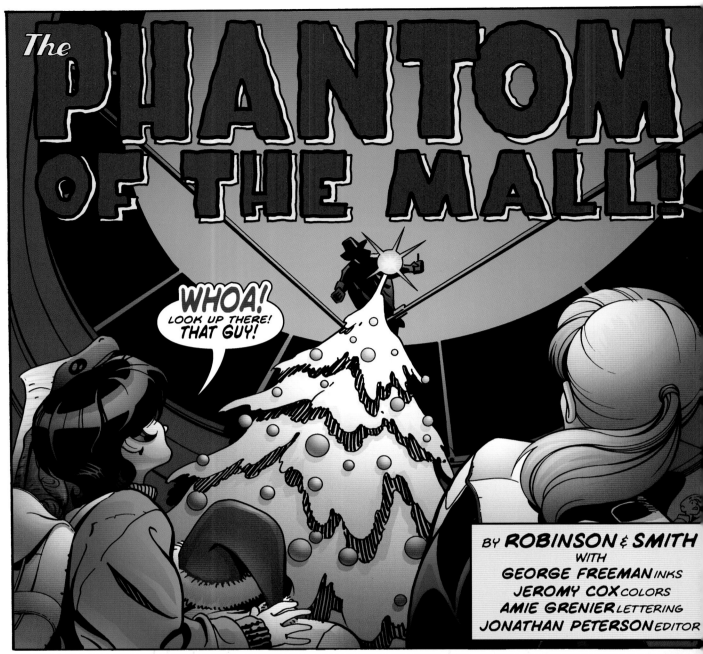

The PHANTOM OF THE MALL!

WHOA! LOOK UP THERE! THAT GUY!

BY **ROBINSON & SMITH**
WITH
GEORGE FREEMAN INKS
JEROMY COX COLORS
AMIE GRENIER LETTERING
JONATHAN PETERSON EDITOR

HE'S DOING SOMETHING TO THE TREE! HE'S--

GET OUT OF THE WAY! IT'S GONNA FALL!

BAMM

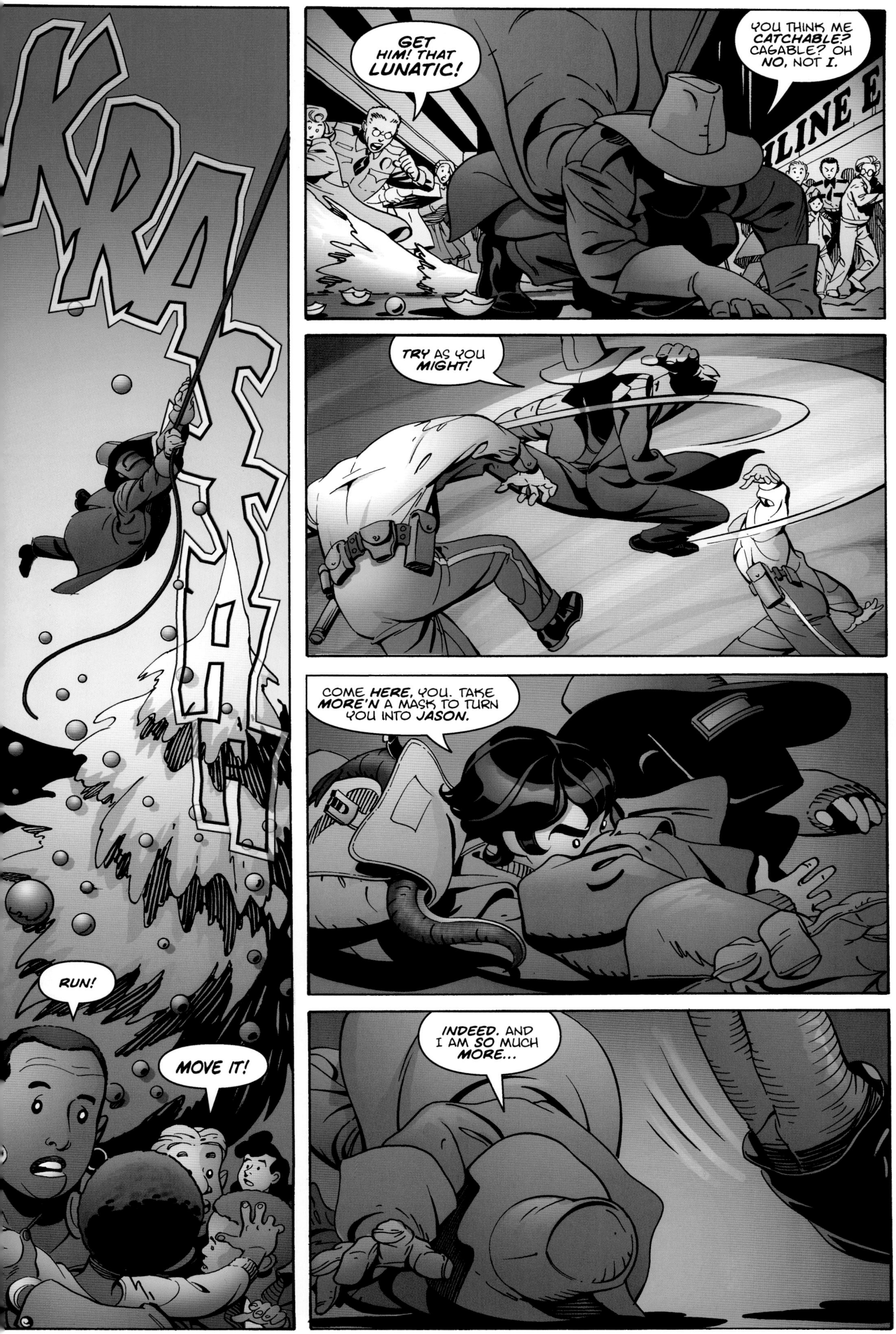
RUN!
MOVE IT!
GET HIM! THAT LUNATIC!
YOU THINK ME CATCHABLE? CAGABLE? OH NO, NOT I.
TRY AS YOU MIGHT!
COME HERE, YOU. TAKE MORE'N A MASK TO TURN YOU INTO JASON.
INDEED. AND I AM SO MUCH MORE...

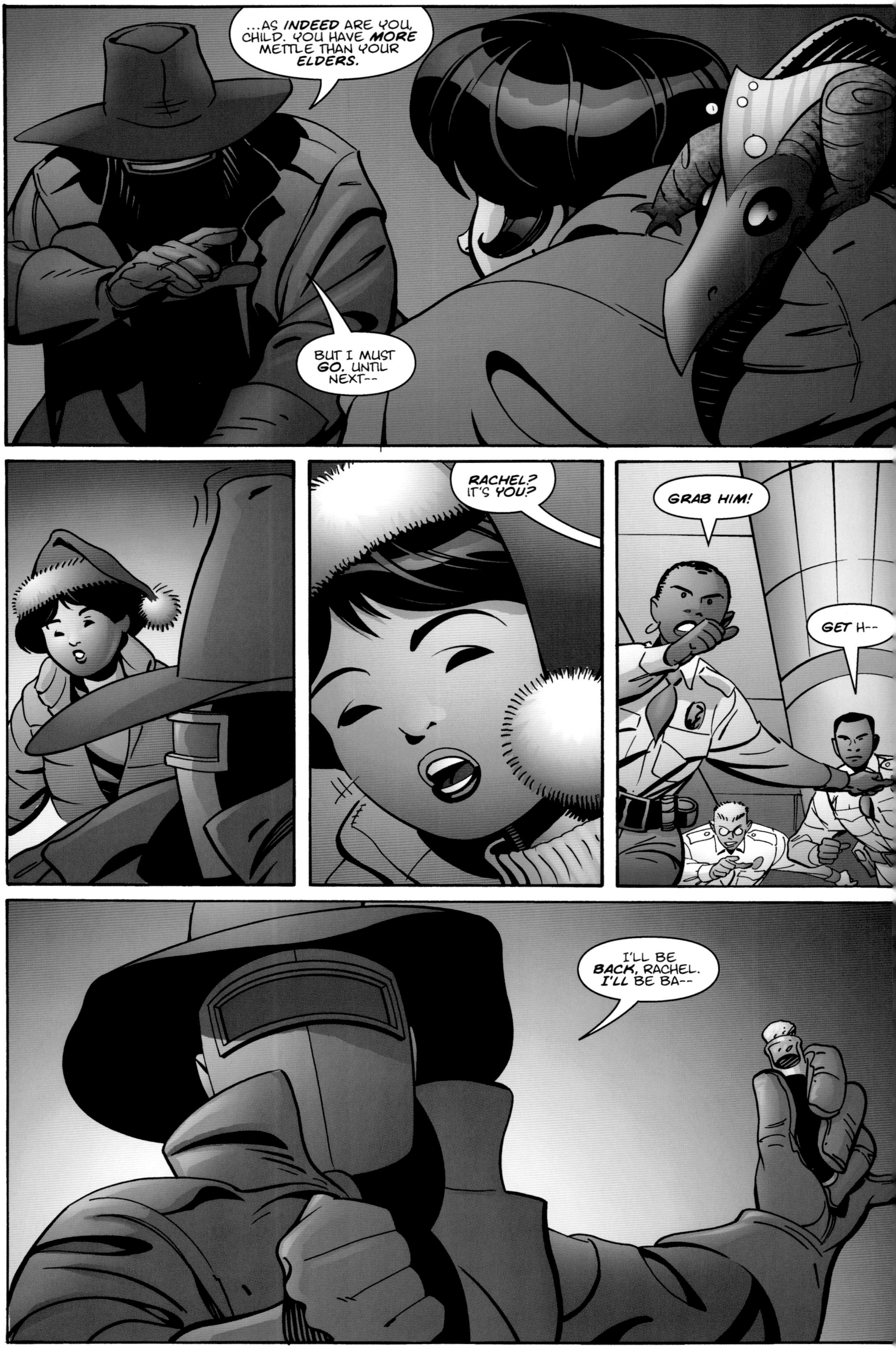
...AS *INDEED* ARE YOU, CHILD. YOU HAVE *MORE* METTLE THAN YOUR *ELDERS.*
BUT I MUST *GO.* UNTIL NEXT--
RACHEL? IT'S *YOU?*
GRAB HIM!
GET H--
I'LL BE *BACK,* RACHEL. *I'LL* BE BA--

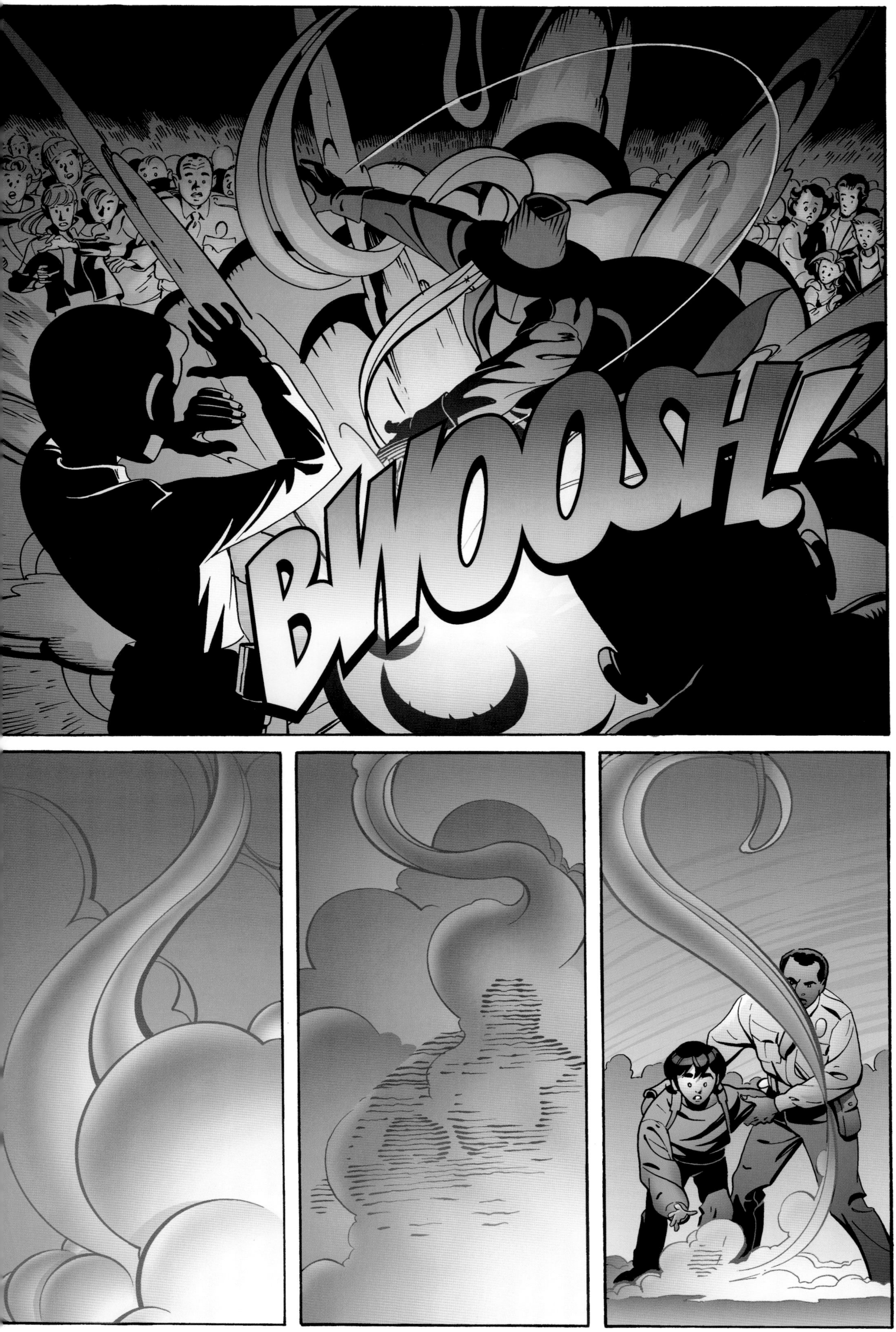
BWOOSH!

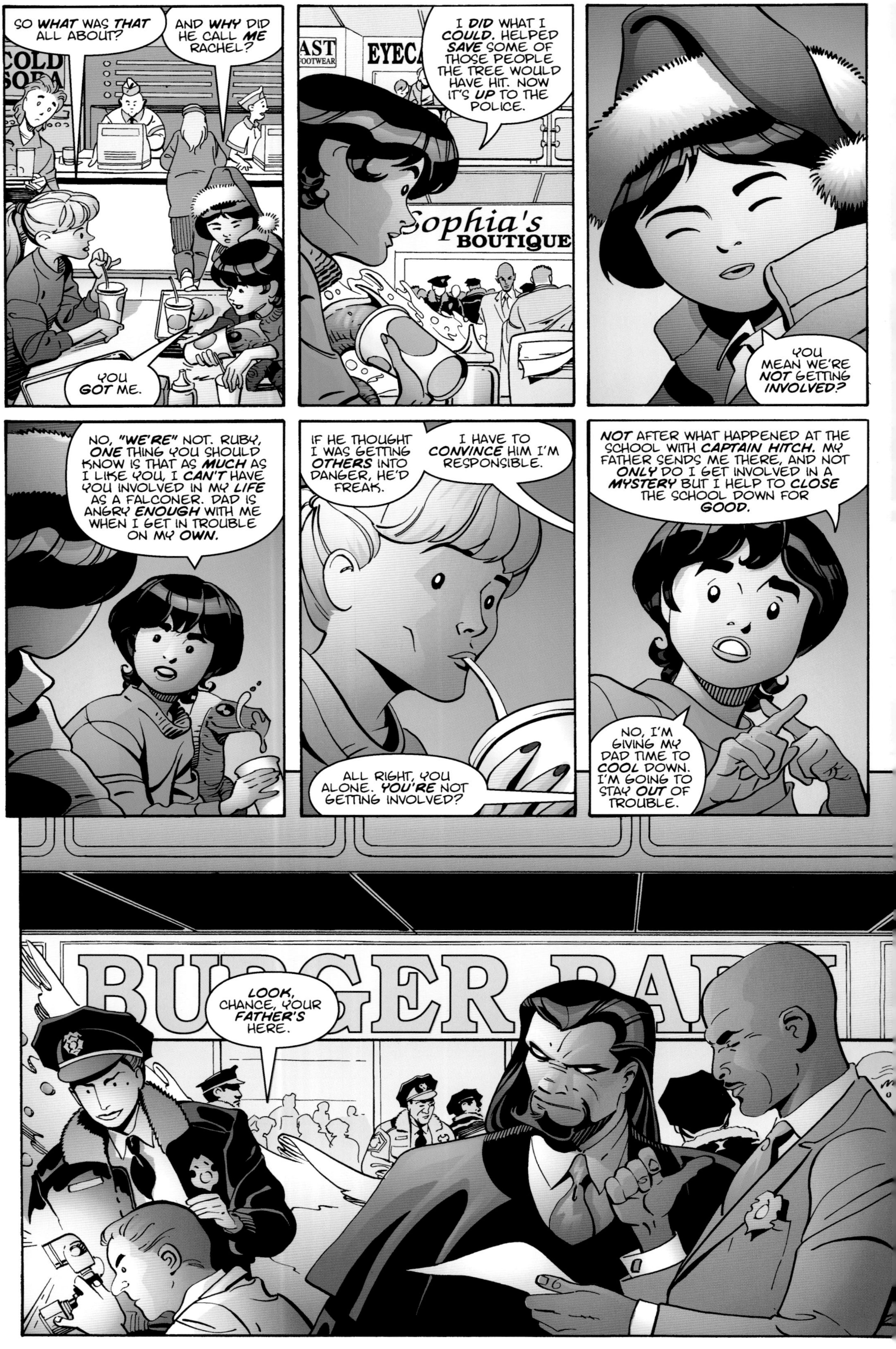
SO WHAT WAS THAT ALL ABOUT?
AND WHY DID HE CALL ME RACHEL?
COLD SODA
YOU GOT ME.
EAST FOOTWEAR
EYECA
I DID WHAT I COULD. HELPED SAVE SOME OF THOSE PEOPLE THE TREE WOULD HAVE HIT. NOW IT'S UP TO THE POLICE.
Sophia's BOUTIQUE
YOU MEAN WE'RE NOT GETTING INVOLVED?
NO, "WE'RE" NOT. RUBY, ONE THING YOU SHOULD KNOW IS THAT AS MUCH AS I LIKE YOU, I CAN'T HAVE YOU INVOLVED IN MY LIFE AS A FALCONER. DAD IS ANGRY ENOUGH WITH ME WHEN I GET IN TROUBLE ON MY OWN.
IF HE THOUGHT I WAS GETTING OTHERS INTO DANGER, HE'D FREAK.
I HAVE TO CONVINCE HIM I'M RESPONSIBLE.
ALL RIGHT, YOU ALONE. YOU'RE NOT GETTING INVOLVED?
NOT AFTER WHAT HAPPENED AT THE SCHOOL WITH CAPTAIN HITCH. MY FATHER SENDS ME THERE, AND NOT ONLY DO I GET INVOLVED IN A MYSTERY BUT I HELP TO CLOSE THE SCHOOL DOWN FOR GOOD.
NO, I'M GIVING MY DAD TIME TO COOL DOWN. I'M GOING TO STAY OUT OF TROUBLE.
LOOK, CHANCE, YOUR FATHER'S HERE.

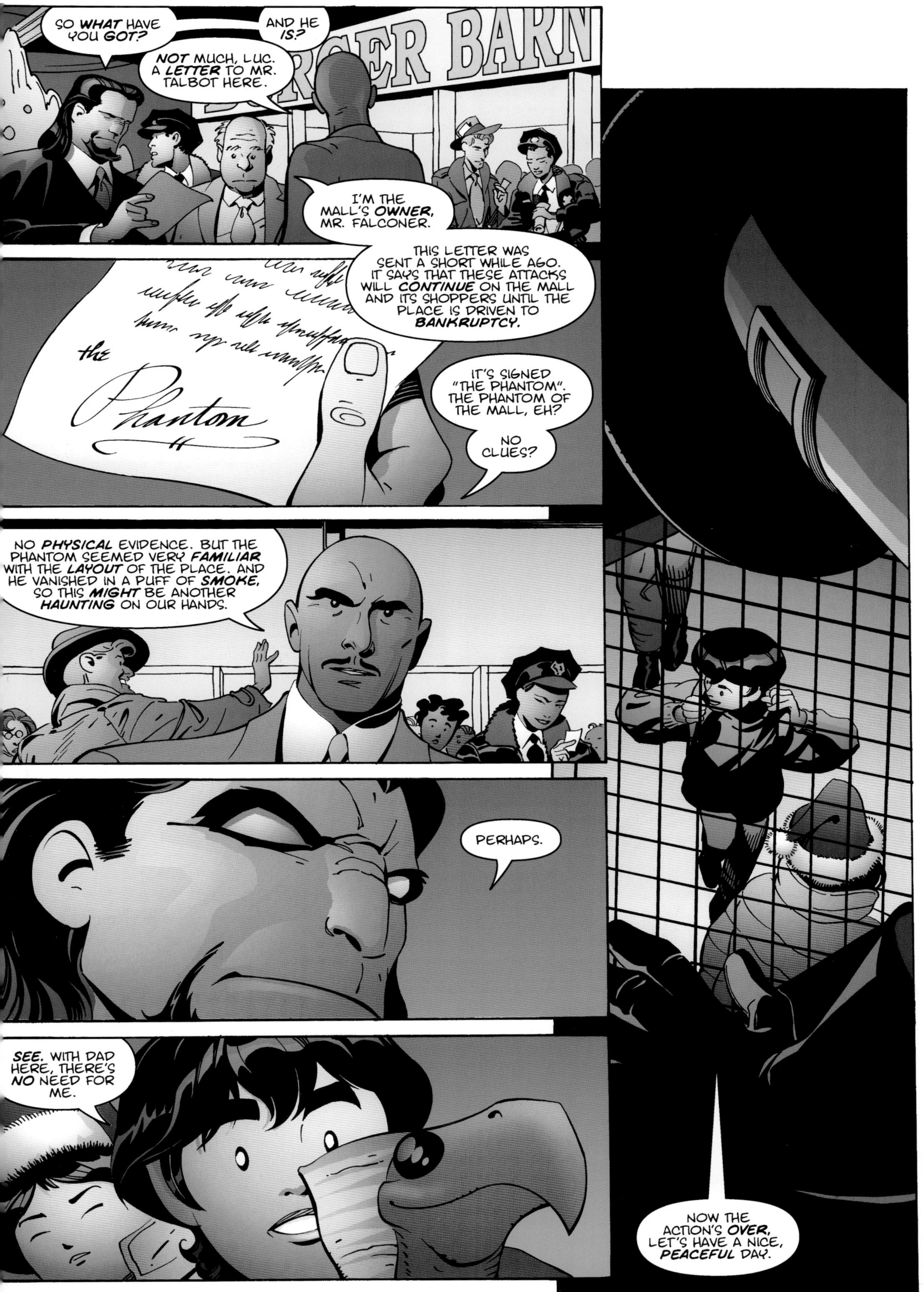
SO WHAT HAVE YOU GOT?
NOT MUCH, LUC. A LETTER TO MR. TALBOT HERE.
AND HE IS?
I'M THE MALL'S OWNER, MR. FALCONER.
THIS LETTER WAS SENT A SHORT WHILE AGO. IT SAYS THAT THESE ATTACKS WILL CONTINUE ON THE MALL AND ITS SHOPPERS UNTIL THE PLACE IS DRIVEN TO BANKRUPTCY.
the Phantom
IT'S SIGNED "THE PHANTOM". THE PHANTOM OF THE MALL, EH?
NO CLUES?
NO PHYSICAL EVIDENCE. BUT THE PHANTOM SEEMED VERY FAMILIAR WITH THE LAYOUT OF THE PLACE. AND HE VANISHED IN A PUFF OF SMOKE, SO THIS MIGHT BE ANOTHER HAUNTING ON OUR HANDS.
PERHAPS.
SEE. WITH DAD HERE, THERE'S NO NEED FOR ME.
NOW THE ACTION'S OVER, LET'S HAVE A NICE, PEACEFUL DAY.

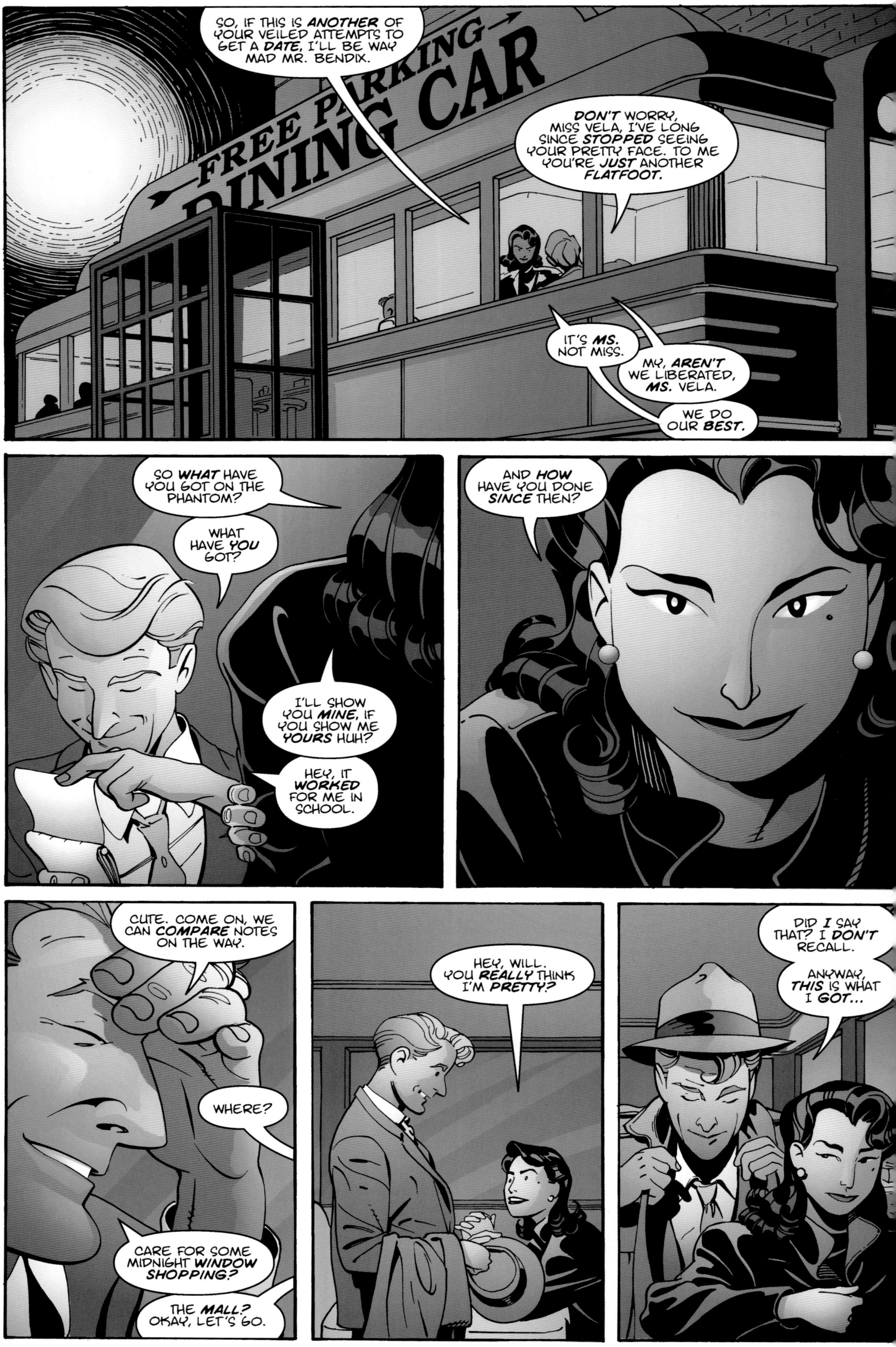
FREE PARKING
DINING CAR
SO, IF THIS IS ANOTHER OF YOUR VEILED ATTEMPTS TO GET A DATE, I'LL BE WAY MAD MR. BENDIX.
DON'T WORRY, MISS VELA, I'VE LONG SINCE STOPPED SEEING YOUR PRETTY FACE. TO ME YOU'RE JUST ANOTHER FLATFOOT.
IT'S MS. NOT MISS.
MY, AREN'T WE LIBERATED, MS. VELA.
WE DO OUR BEST.
SO WHAT HAVE YOU GOT ON THE PHANTOM?
WHAT HAVE YOU GOT?
I'LL SHOW YOU MINE, IF YOU SHOW ME YOURS HUH?
HEY, IT WORKED FOR ME IN SCHOOL.
AND HOW HAVE YOU DONE SINCE THEN?
CUTE. COME ON, WE CAN COMPARE NOTES ON THE WAY.
WHERE?
CARE FOR SOME MIDNIGHT WINDOW SHOPPING?
THE MALL? OKAY, LET'S GO.
HEY, WILL. YOU REALLY THINK I'M PRETTY?
DID I SAY THAT? I DON'T RECALL.
ANYWAY, THIS IS WHAT I GOT...

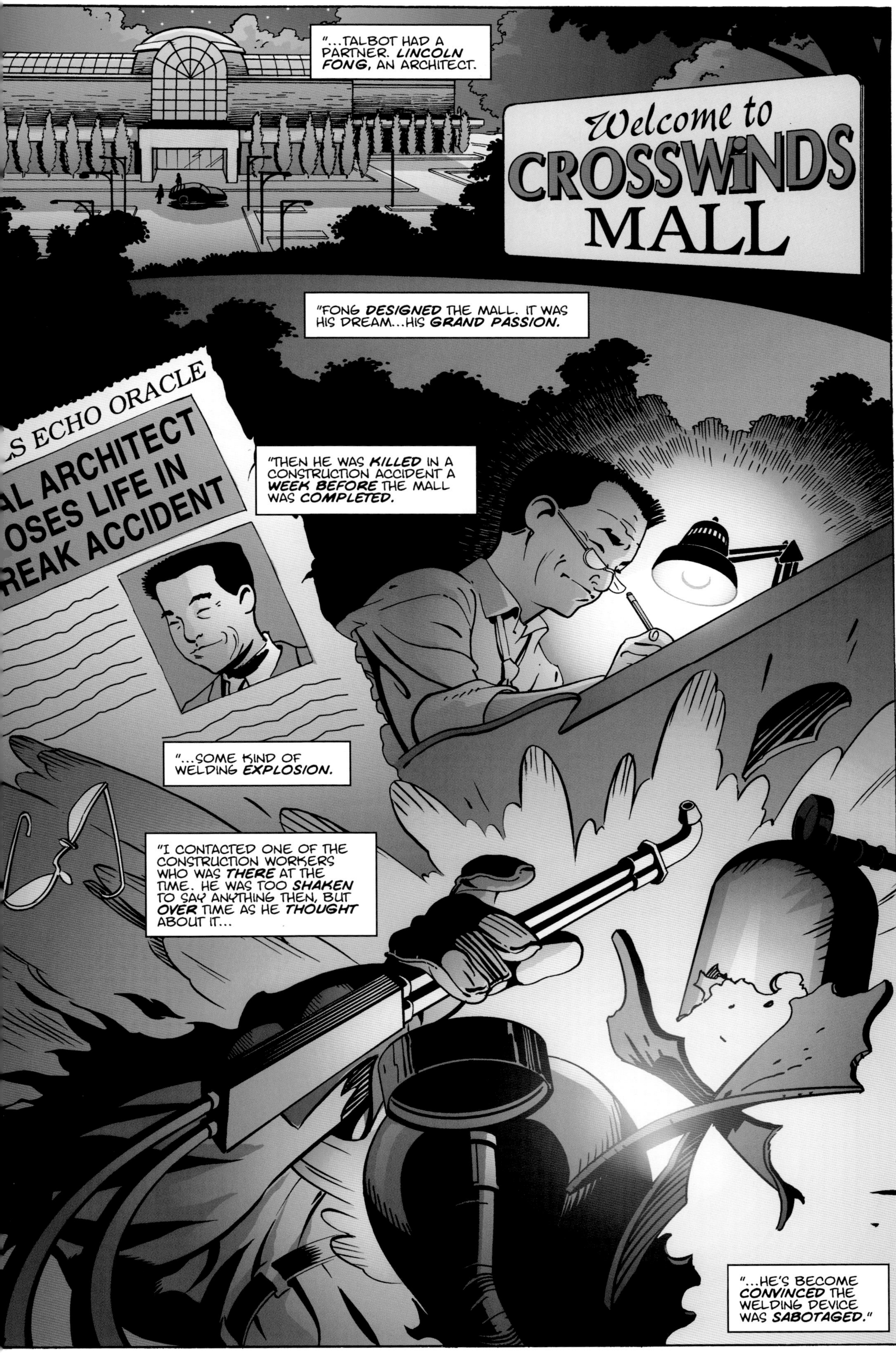
"...TALBOT HAD A PARTNER. LINCOLN FONG, AN ARCHITECT.
Welcome to CROSSWINDS MALL
"FONG DESIGNED THE MALL. IT WAS HIS DREAM...HIS GRAND PASSION.
ECHO ORACLE
AL ARCHITECT OSES LIFE IN REAK ACCIDENT
"THEN HE WAS KILLED IN A CONSTRUCTION ACCIDENT A WEEK BEFORE THE MALL WAS COMPLETED.
"...SOME KIND OF WELDING EXPLOSION.
"I CONTACTED ONE OF THE CONSTRUCTION WORKERS WHO WAS THERE AT THE TIME. HE WAS TOO SHAKEN TO SAY ANYTHING THEN, BUT OVER TIME AS HE THOUGHT ABOUT IT...
"...HE'S BECOME CONVINCED THE WELDING DEVICE WAS SABOTAGED."

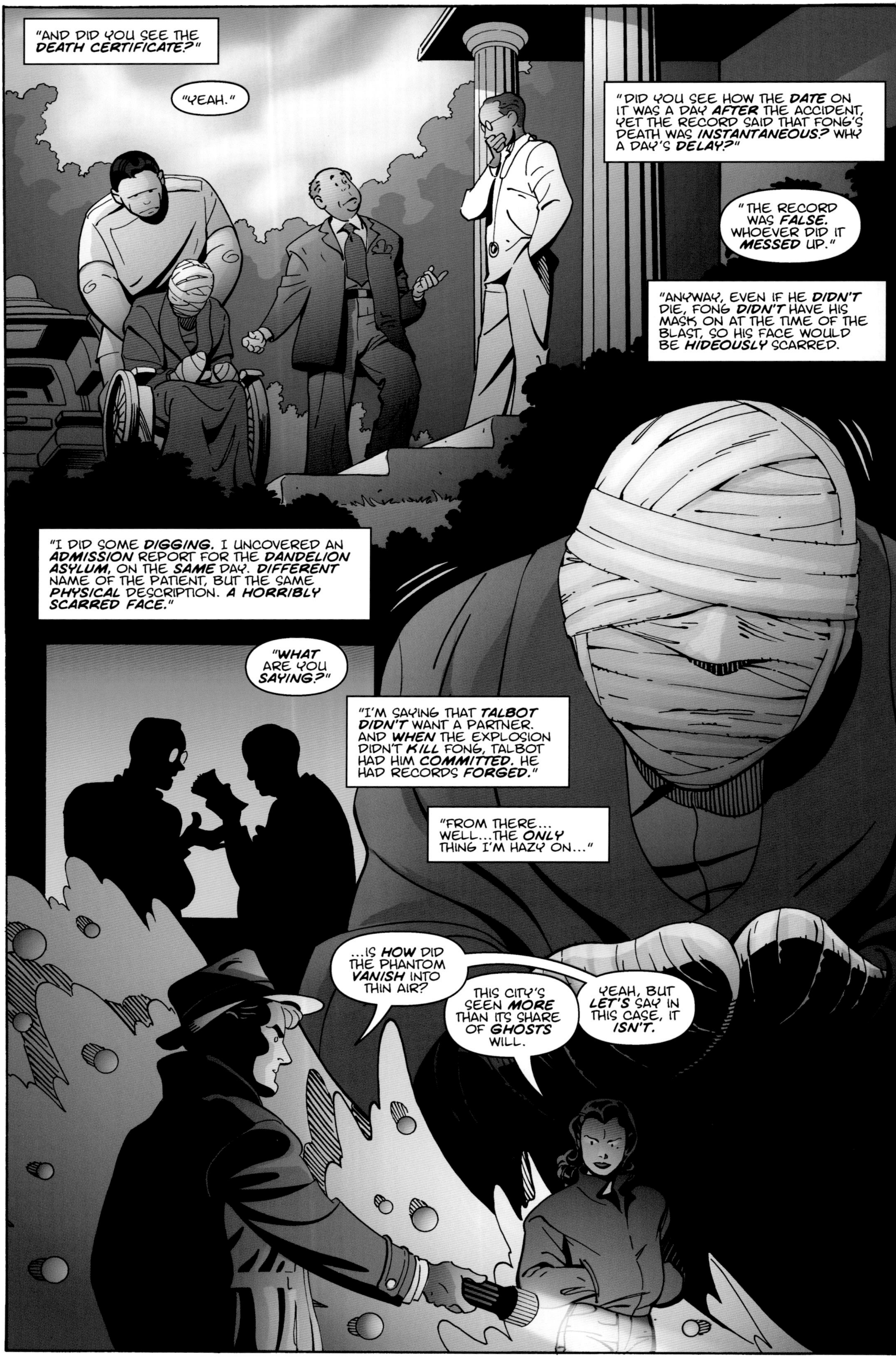
"AND DID YOU SEE THE DEATH CERTIFICATE?"
"YEAH."
"DID YOU SEE HOW THE DATE ON IT WAS A DAY AFTER THE ACCIDENT, YET THE RECORD SAID THAT FONG'S DEATH WAS INSTANTANEOUS? WHY A DAY'S DELAY?"
"THE RECORD WAS FALSE. WHOEVER DID IT MESSED UP."
"ANYWAY, EVEN IF HE DIDN'T DIE, FONG DIDN'T HAVE HIS MASK ON AT THE TIME OF THE BLAST, SO HIS FACE WOULD BE HIDEOUSLY SCARRED.
"I DID SOME DIGGING. I UNCOVERED AN ADMISSION REPORT FOR THE DANDELION ASYLUM, ON THE SAME DAY. DIFFERENT NAME OF THE PATIENT, BUT THE SAME PHYSICAL DESCRIPTION. A HORRIBLY SCARRED FACE."
"WHAT ARE YOU SAYING?"
"I'M SAYING THAT TALBOT DIDN'T WANT A PARTNER. AND WHEN THE EXPLOSION DIDN'T KILL FONG, TALBOT HAD HIM COMMITTED. HE HAD RECORDS FORGED."
"FROM THERE... WELL...THE ONLY THING I'M HAZY ON..."
...IS HOW DID THE PHANTOM VANISH INTO THIN AIR?
THIS CITY'S SEEN MORE THAN ITS SHARE OF GHOSTS WILL.
YEAH, BUT LET'S SAY IN THIS CASE, IT ISN'T.

THERE! WHERE THE PHANTOM DISAPPEARED. A HIDDEN *TRAPDOOR.* YOU CAN *BARELY* SEE IT WHEN IT'S *CLOSED.* EASY FOR EVERY-ONE TO *MISS.*

COME ON! LET'S *CHECK* IT OUT.

IF THIS IS AN *EXAMPLE* OF FONG'S DESIGNS, THEN HE COULD HAVE *LACED* THIS WHOLE STRUCTURE WITH TRAPDOORS AND PASSAGES.

YOU THINK HE'S HERE *NOW?*

I HOPE SO.

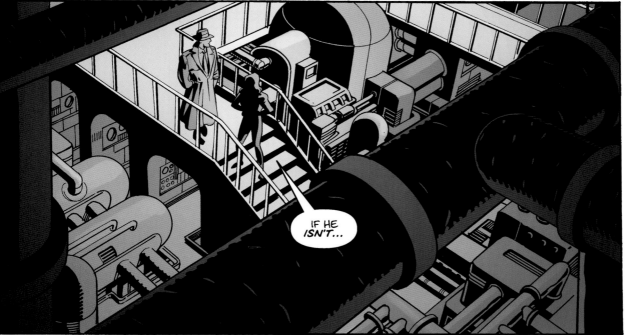

IF HE *ISN'T...*

"...THEN *GOD* KNOWS *WHAT* HE'S UP TO."

THANKS FOR SLEEPING OVER, GUYS.

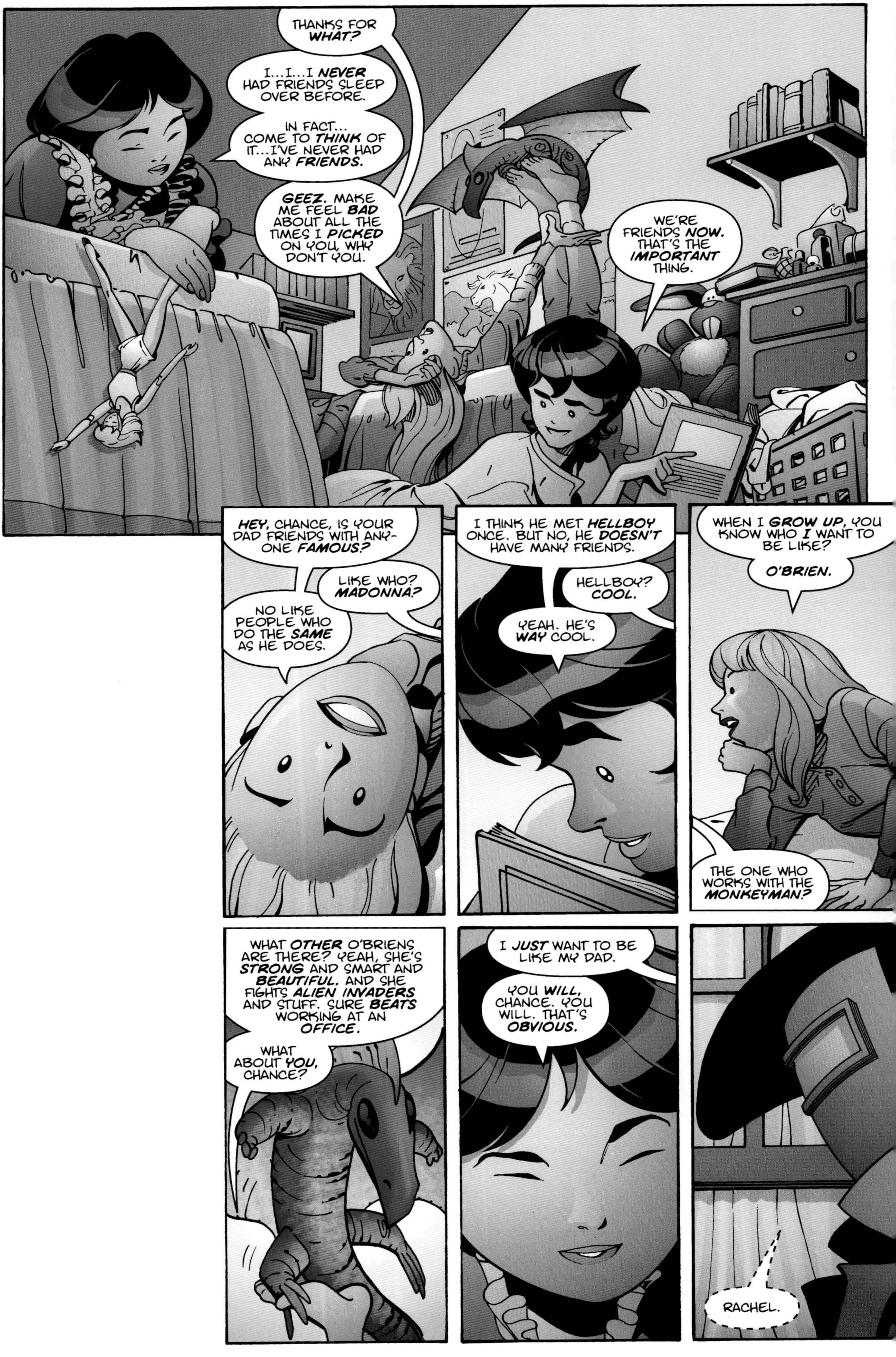
THANKS FOR WHAT?
I...I...I NEVER HAD FRIENDS SLEEP OVER BEFORE.
IN FACT... COME TO THINK OF IT...I'VE NEVER HAD ANY FRIENDS.
GEEZ. MAKE ME FEEL BAD ABOUT ALL THE TIMES I PICKED ON YOU, WHY DON'T YOU.
WE'RE FRIENDS NOW. THAT'S THE IMPORTANT THING.
HEY, CHANCE, IS YOUR DAD FRIENDS WITH ANY-ONE FAMOUS?
LIKE WHO? MADONNA?
NO LIKE PEOPLE WHO DO THE SAME AS HE DOES.
I THINK HE MET HELLBOY ONCE. BUT NO, HE DOESN'T HAVE MANY FRIENDS.
HELLBOY? COOL.
YEAH. HE'S WAY COOL.
WHEN I GROW UP, YOU KNOW WHO I WANT TO BE LIKE?
O'BRIEN.
THE ONE WHO WORKS WITH THE MONKEYMAN?
WHAT OTHER O'BRIENS ARE THERE? YEAH, SHE'S STRONG AND SMART AND BEAUTIFUL. AND SHE FIGHTS ALIEN INVADERS AND STUFF. SURE BEATS WORKING AT AN OFFICE.
WHAT ABOUT YOU, CHANCE?
I JUST WANT TO BE LIKE MY DAD.
YOU WILL, CHANCE. YOU WILL. THAT'S OBVIOUS.
RACHEL.

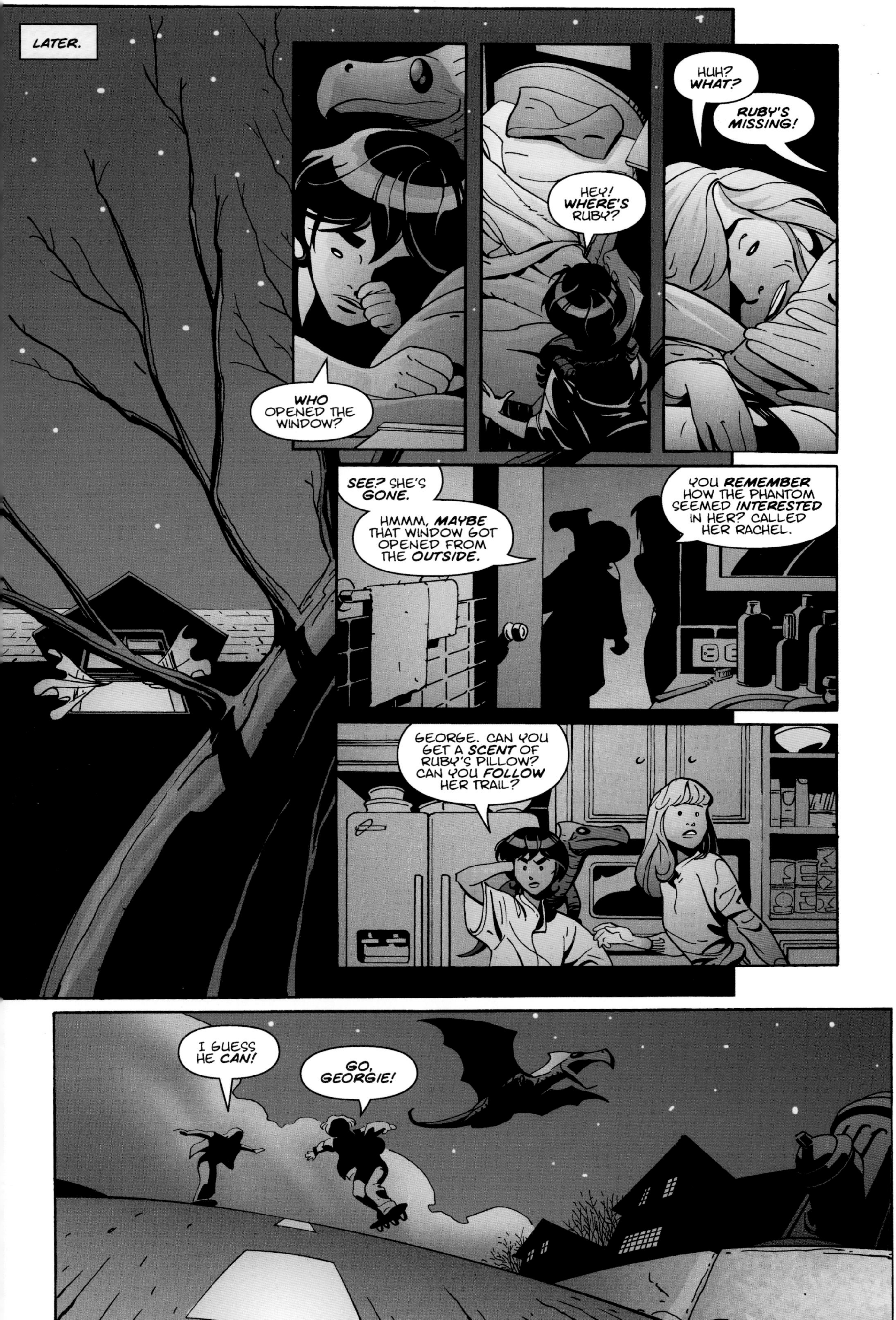
LATER.
WHO OPENED THE WINDOW?
HEY! WHERE'S RUBY?
HUH? WHAT?
RUBY'S MISSING!
SEE? SHE'S GONE.
HMMM, MAYBE THAT WINDOW GOT OPENED FROM THE OUTSIDE.
YOU REMEMBER HOW THE PHANTOM SEEMED INTERESTED IN HER? CALLED HER RACHEL.
GEORGE. CAN YOU GET A SCENT OF RUBY'S PILLOW? CAN YOU FOLLOW HER TRAIL?
I GUESS HE CAN!
GO, GEORGIE!

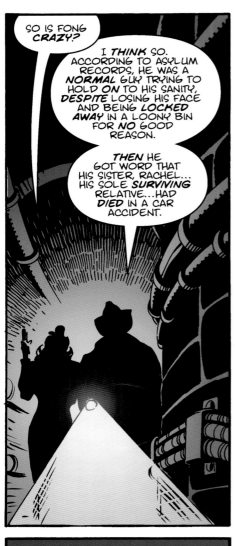

SO IS FONG *CRAZY*?

I *THINK* SO. ACCORDING TO ASYLUM RECORDS, HE WAS A *NORMAL GUY* TRYING TO HOLD *ON* TO HIS SANITY, DESPITE LOSING HIS FACE AND BEING *LOCKED AWAY* IN A LOONY BIN FOR *NO GOOD* REASON.

THEN HE GOT WORD THAT HIS SISTER, RACHEL... HIS SOLE *SURVIVING* RELATIVE...HAD *DIED* IN A CAR ACCIDENT.

OH *RACHEL*, YOU'VE COME *BACK* TO ME. I THOUGHT I'D LOST YOU *FOREVER*.

I'M *NOT* RACHEL. MY NAME'S *RUBY*. KEEP *AWAY* FROM ME!

WE'RE *BACK* AT THE MALL.

WHICH WAY NOW?

FOLLOW GEORGIE.

DON'T THINK I'D *HARM* YOU. HUSH. AS *SOON* AS MY WORK IS DONE *HERE*, WE'LL GO AWAY AND BE BROTHER AND SISTER *AGAIN*.

BUT I'M NOT--

SECRET OPENING. GOOD WORK, GEORGIE.

WOW!

COME ON!

AND THAT NEWS OF HIS SISTER'S DEATH *UNHINGED* HIM?

IT WAS HIS *LAST* LINK TO THE OUTSIDE. HE HAD NOTHING *ELSE* TO STAY SANE FOR.

THEN A MONTH AGO, FONG *ESCAPED*.

A MONTH TO *PLAN* HIS *REVENGE* ON TALBOT.

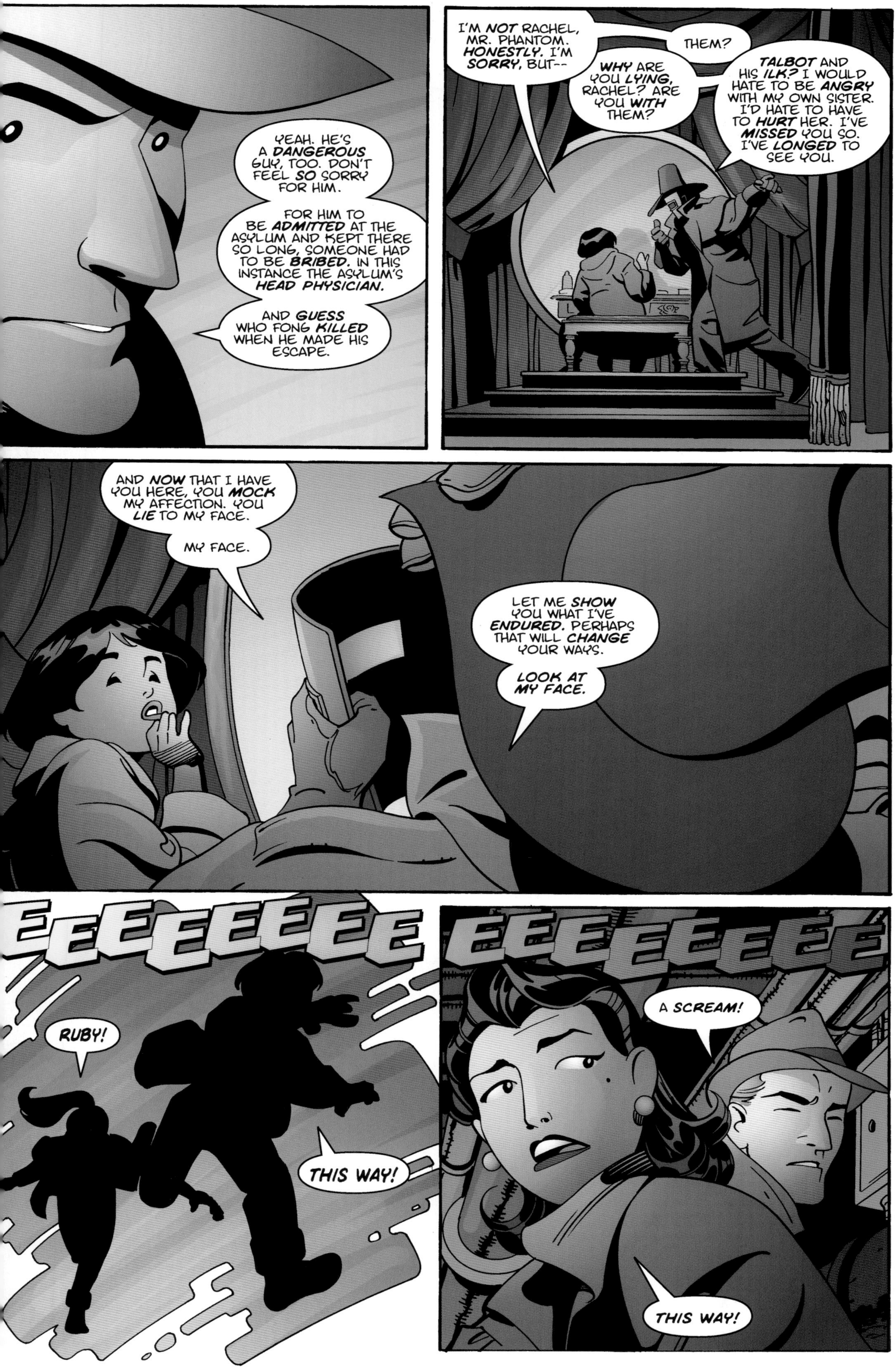
YEAH. HE'S A DANGEROUS GUY, TOO. DON'T FEEL SO SORRY FOR HIM.
FOR HIM TO BE ADMITTED AT THE ASYLUM AND KEPT THERE SO LONG, SOMEONE HAD TO BE BRIBED. IN THIS INSTANCE THE ASYLUM'S HEAD PHYSICIAN.
AND GUESS WHO FONG KILLED WHEN HE MADE HIS ESCAPE.
I'M NOT RACHEL, MR. PHANTOM. HONESTLY. I'M SORRY, BUT--
WHY ARE YOU LYING, RACHEL? ARE YOU WITH THEM?
THEM?
TALBOT AND HIS ILK? I WOULD HATE TO BE ANGRY WITH MY OWN SISTER. I'D HATE TO HAVE TO HURT HER. I'VE MISSED YOU SO. I'VE LONGED TO SEE YOU.
AND NOW THAT I HAVE YOU HERE, YOU MOCK MY AFFECTION. YOU LIE TO MY FACE.
MY FACE.
LET ME SHOW YOU WHAT I'VE ENDURED. PERHAPS THAT WILL CHANGE YOUR WAYS.
LOOK AT MY FACE.
EEEEEEEEE
RUBY!
THIS WAY!
EEEEEEEEEE
A SCREAM!
THIS WAY!

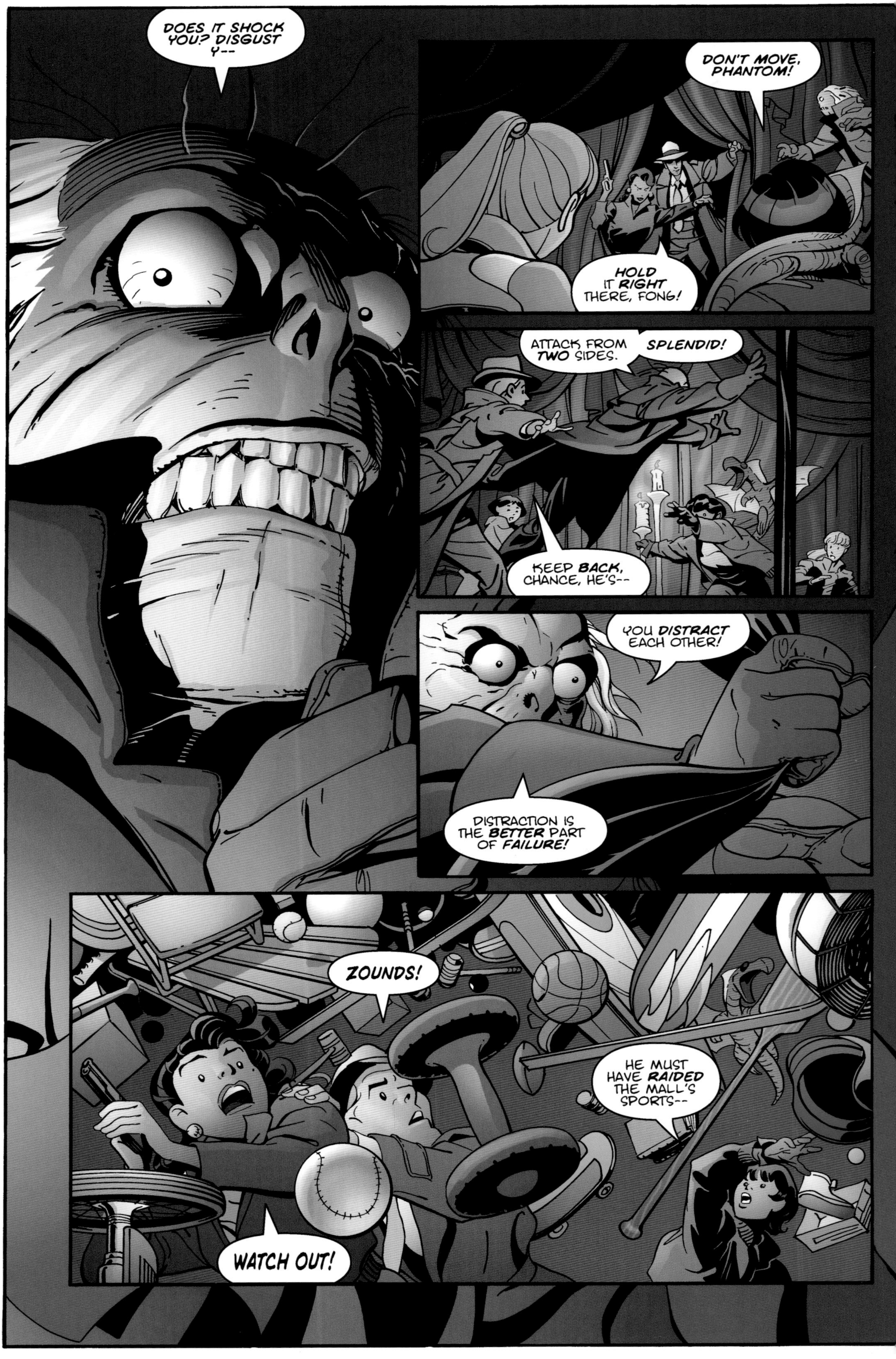
DOES IT SHOCK YOU? DISGUST Y--
DON'T MOVE, PHANTOM!
HOLD IT RIGHT THERE, FONG!
ATTACK FROM TWO SIDES.
SPLENDID!
KEEP BACK, CHANCE, HE'S--
YOU DISTRACT EACH OTHER!
DISTRACTION IS THE BETTER PART OF FAILURE!
ZOUNDS!
HE MUST HAVE RAIDED THE MALL'S SPORTS--
WATCH OUT!

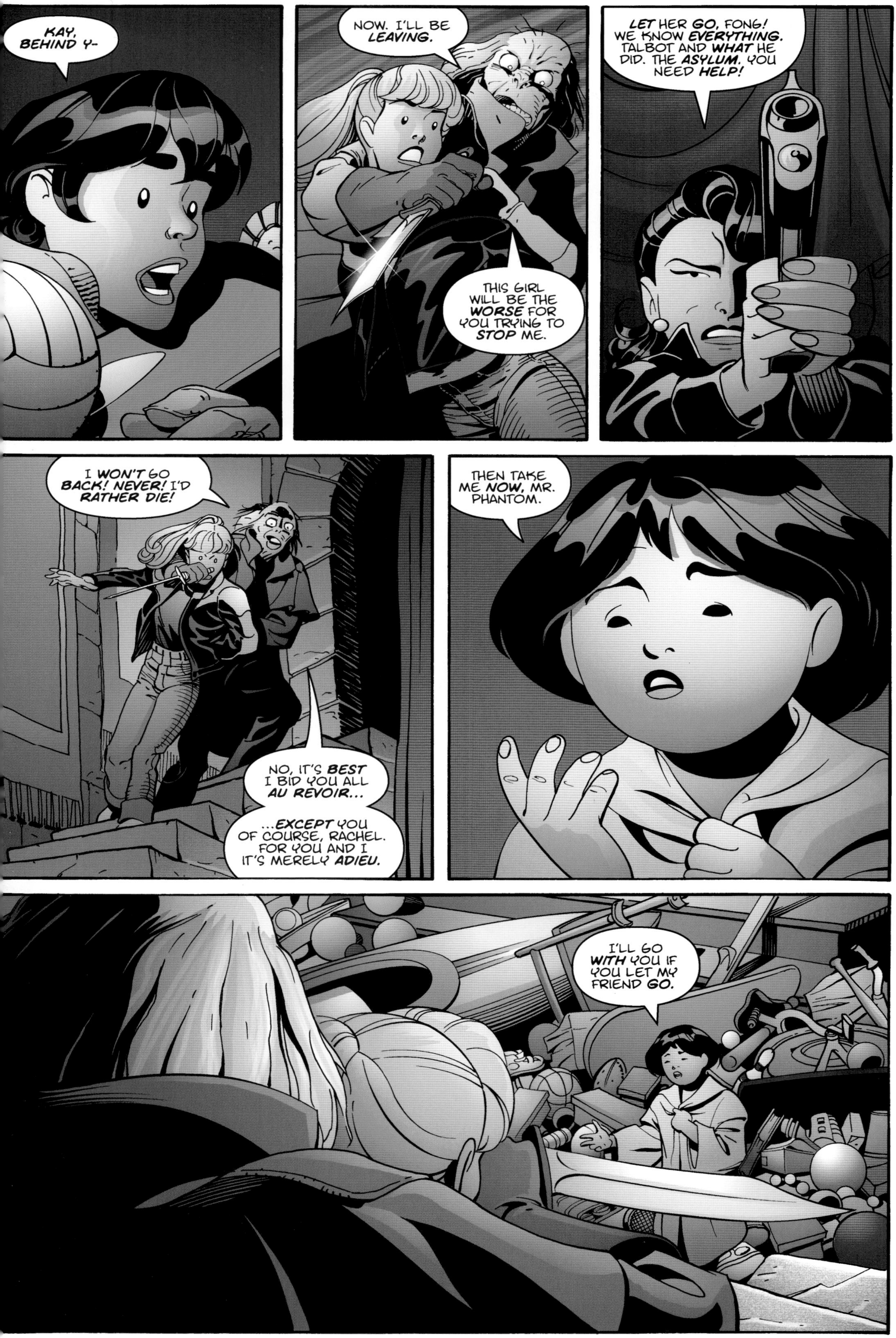
KAY, BEHIND Y-
NOW. I'LL BE LEAVING.
THIS GIRL WILL BE THE WORSE FOR YOU TRYING TO STOP ME.
LET HER GO, FONG! WE KNOW EVERYTHING. TALBOT AND WHAT HE DID. THE ASYLUM. YOU NEED HELP!
I WON'T GO BACK! NEVER! I'D RATHER DIE!
NO, IT'S BEST I BID YOU ALL AU REVOIR...
...EXCEPT YOU OF COURSE, RACHEL. FOR YOU AND I IT'S MERELY ADIEU.
THEN TAKE ME NOW, MR. PHANTOM.
I'LL GO WITH YOU IF YOU LET MY FRIEND GO.

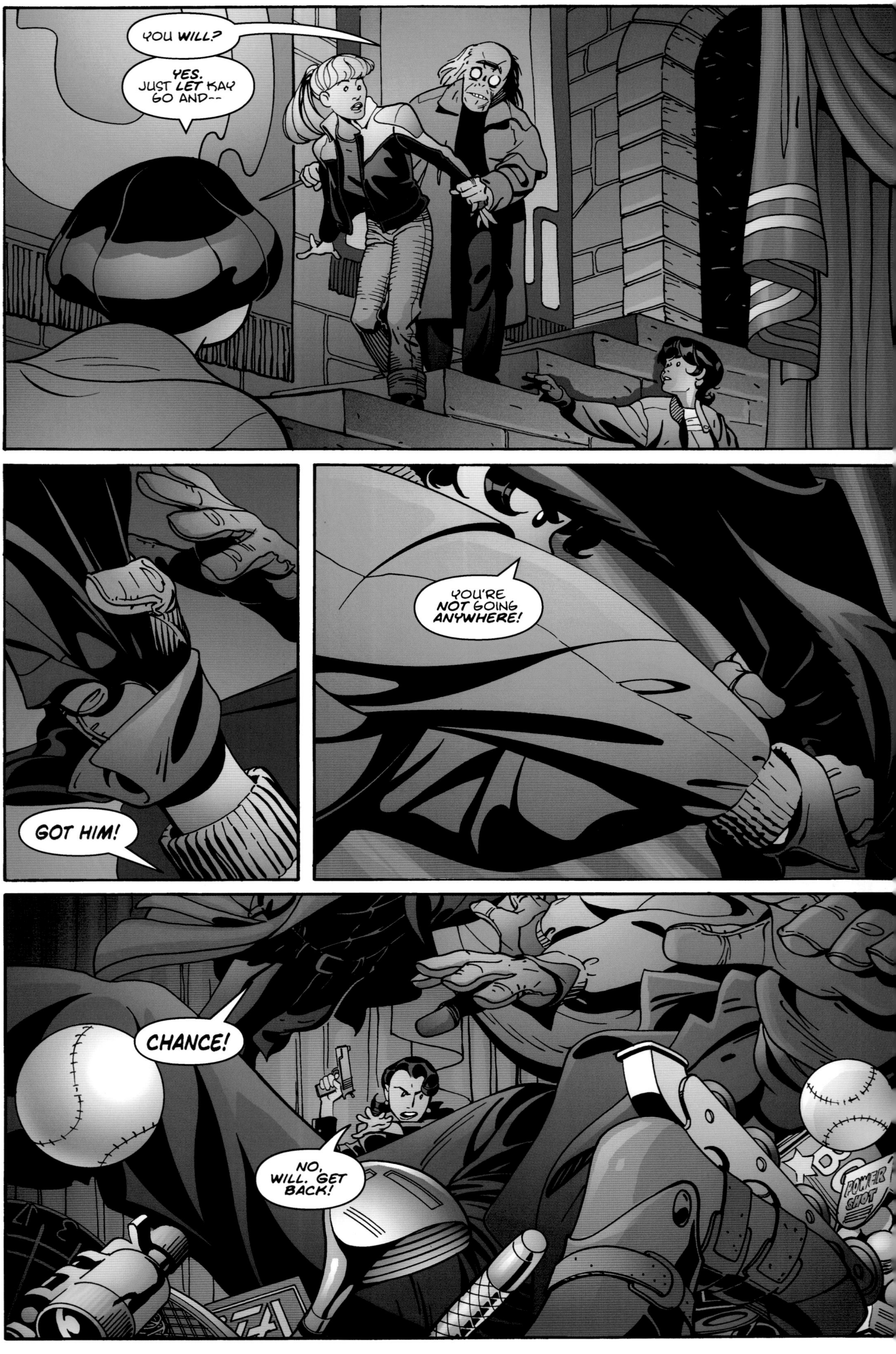

YOU WILL?
YES. JUST LET KAY GO AND--
GOT HIM!
YOU'RE NOT GOING ANYWHERE!
CHANCE!
NO, WILL. GET BACK!
POWER SHOT

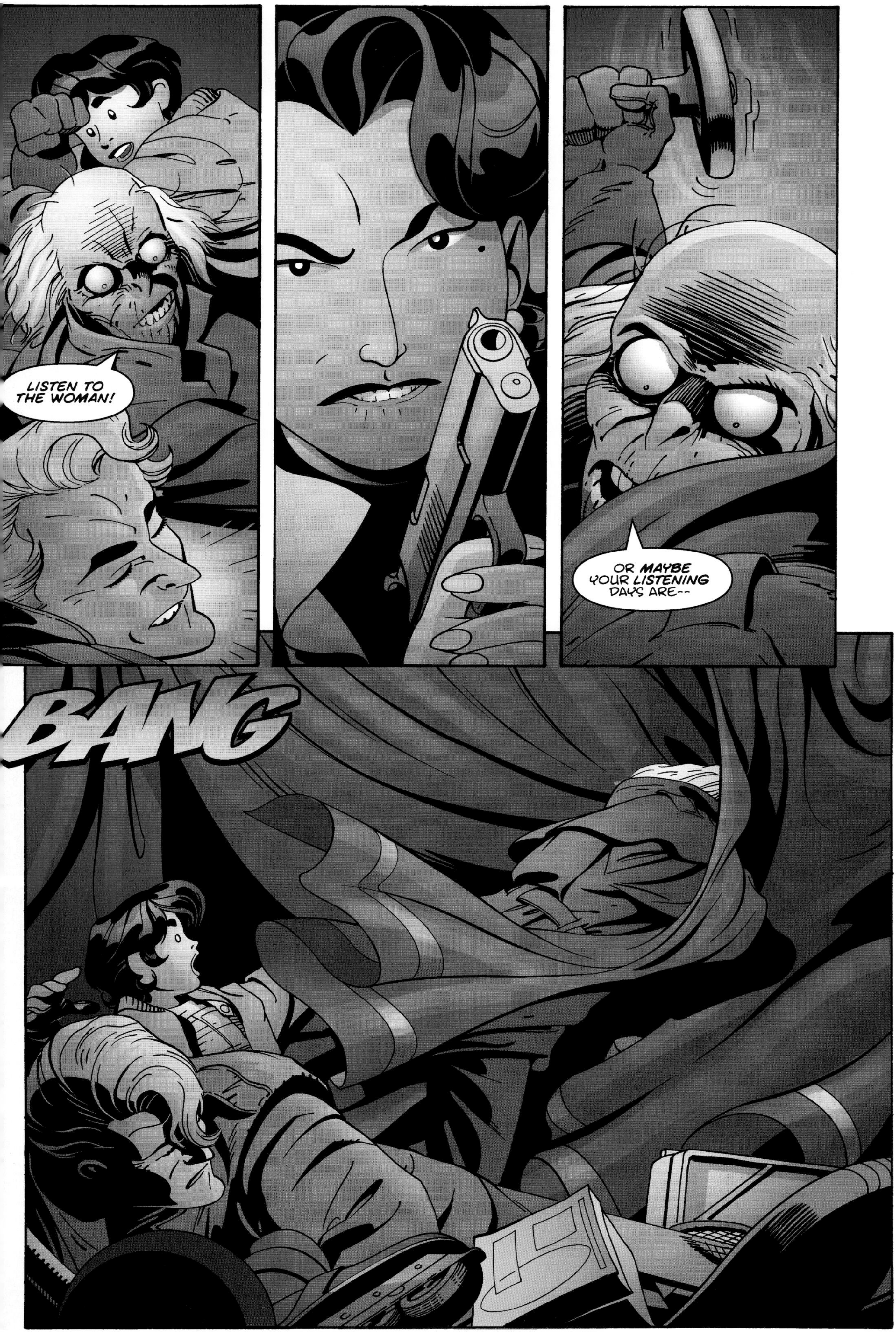
LISTEN TO THE WOMAN!
OR MAYBE YOUR LISTENING DAYS ARE--
BANG

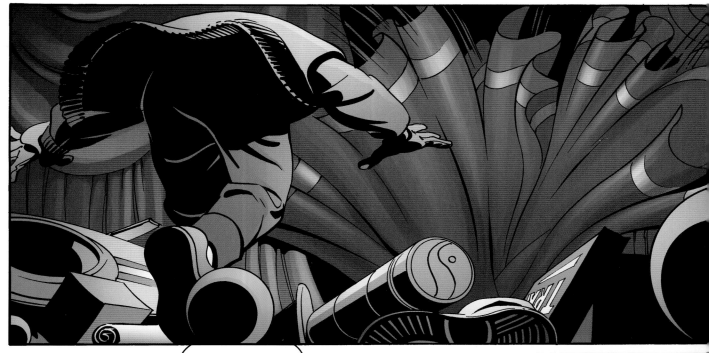

YOU GOT HIM, MARGO!

DID I *KILL* HIM? I *HOPE* I DIDN'T--

NO, MARGO.

...YOU *DIDN'T* KILL HIM.

THIS IS JUST HIS *CLOAK.* THERE'S A *LITTLE* BLOOD.

...BUT *NOTHING* MORE.

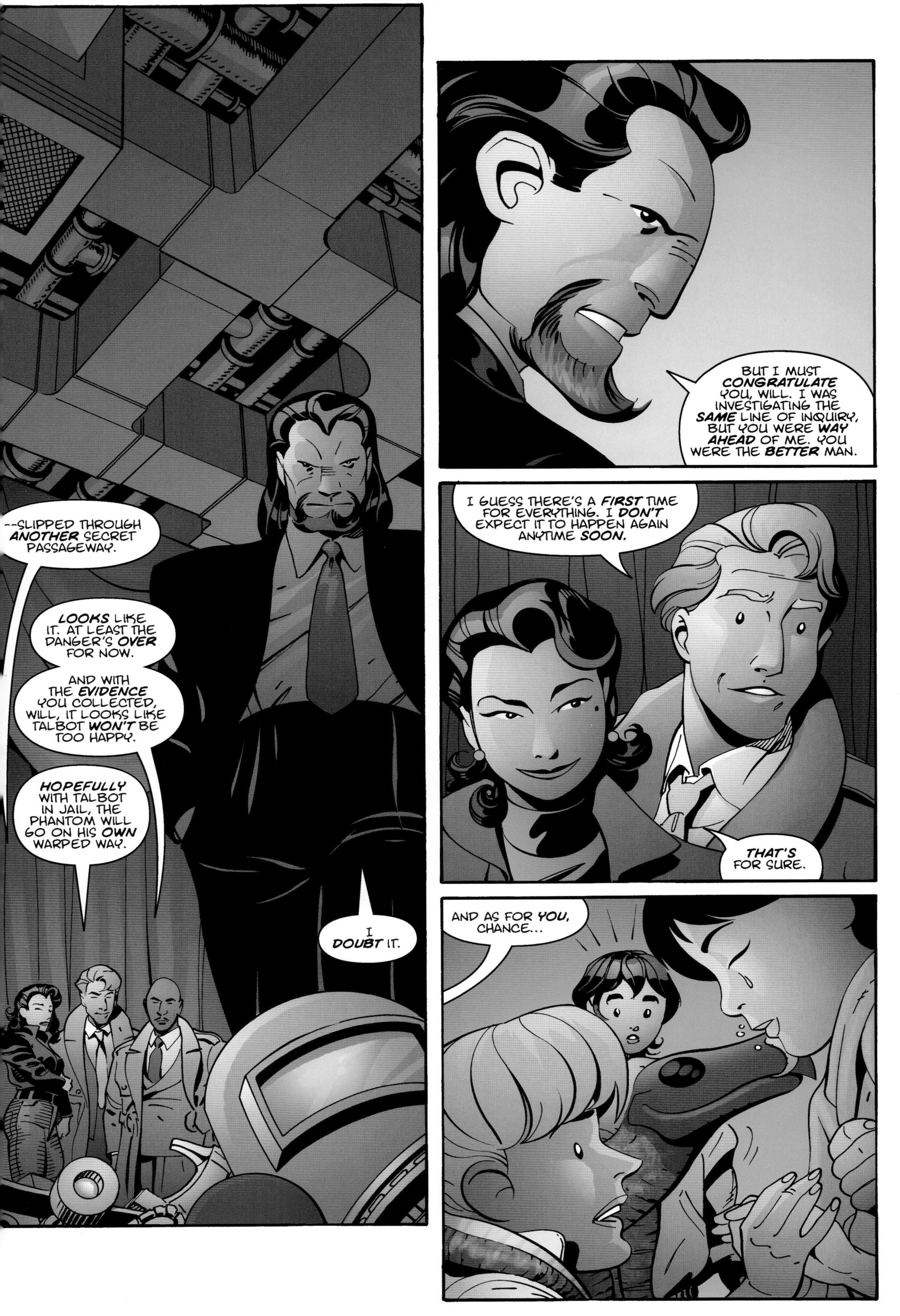
--SLIPPED THROUGH ANOTHER SECRET PASSAGEWAY.
LOOKS LIKE IT. AT LEAST THE DANGER'S OVER FOR NOW.
AND WITH THE EVIDENCE YOU COLLECTED, WILL, IT LOOKS LIKE TALBOT WON'T BE TOO HAPPY.
HOPEFULLY WITH TALBOT IN JAIL, THE PHANTOM WILL GO ON HIS OWN WARPED WAY.
I DOUBT IT.
BUT I MUST CONGRATULATE YOU, WILL. I WAS INVESTIGATING THE SAME LINE OF INQUIRY, BUT YOU WERE WAY AHEAD OF ME. YOU WERE THE BETTER MAN.
I GUESS THERE'S A FIRST TIME FOR EVERYTHING. I DON'T EXPECT IT TO HAPPEN AGAIN ANYTIME SOON.
THAT'S FOR SURE.
AND AS FOR YOU, CHANCE...

I TRIED TO STAY OUT OF IT, DADDY! HONEST, BUT WHEN RUBY GOT KIDNAPPED, I HAD TO--

HAD TO? HAD TO? GOD FORBID THAT YOU CALLED ME.

I DIDN'T THINK. I'M SORRY.

YOU WERE CONCERNED FOR YOUR FRIEND. I UNDERSTAND.

YOU DO?

THIS ONE TIME. THAT DOES NOT MEAN I EXPECT YOU TO MAKE A HABIT OF IT.

YOU OKAY, RUBY?

I'M A BIT SCARED. WHAT IF THE PHANTOM COMES BACK FOR ME?

IF HE DOES THEN HE'LL HAVE ME TO DEAL WITH TOO. YOU WOULD HAVE RISKED YOURSELF FOR ME. I'LL NEVER FORGET THAT.

I FEEL SORRY FOR HIM. HE MAY HAVE BEEN NUTS BUT HE WAS SAD TOO. THIS WILL SOUND CRAZY, AFTER HE KIDNAPPED ME AND SCARED ME WITH HIS FACE AND ALL.

YEAH?

BUT WHEREVER HE IS...

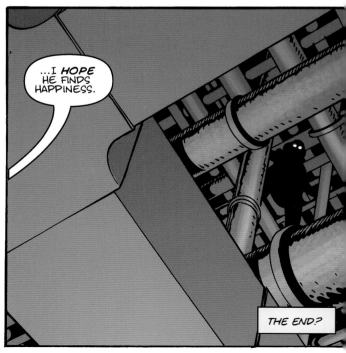

...I HOPE HE FINDS HAPPINESS.

THE END?

SKETCHBOOK

PAUL OPENED HIS SKETCHBOOK TO GIVE US A RARE BEHIND-THE-SCENES LOOK AT THE CHARACTERS -THE FRIENDS AND THE FOES- AND AN IDEA OF THEIR DEVELOPMENT.

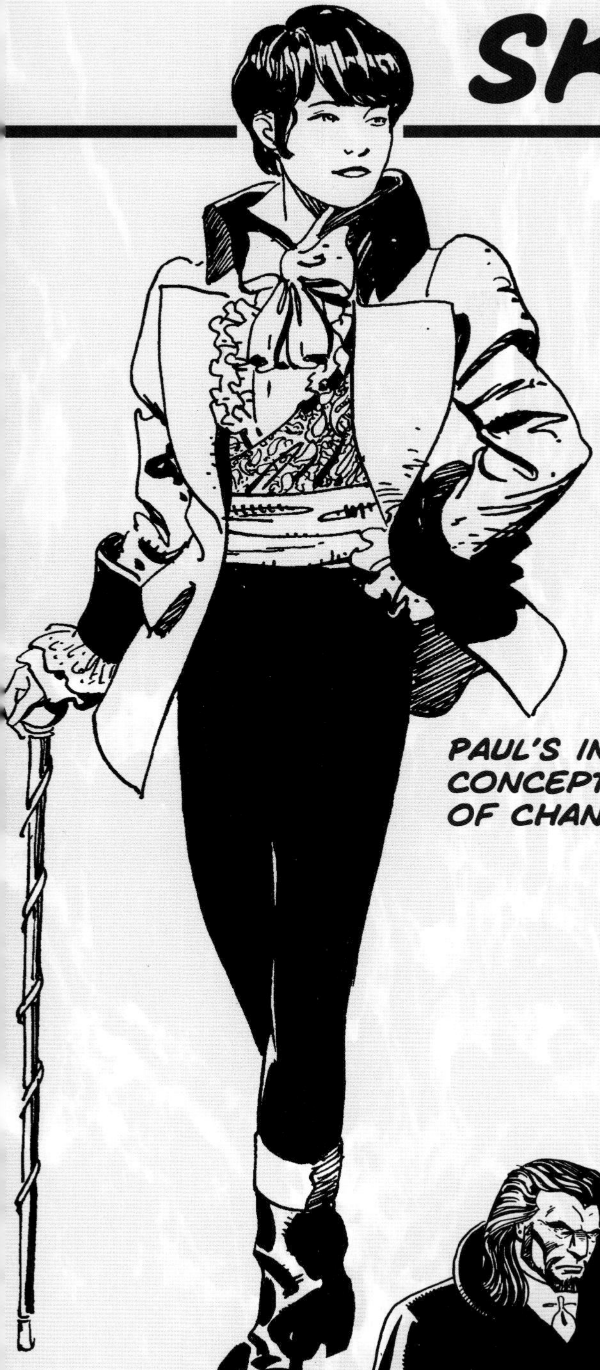

PAUL'S INITIAL CONCEPTION OF CHANCE...

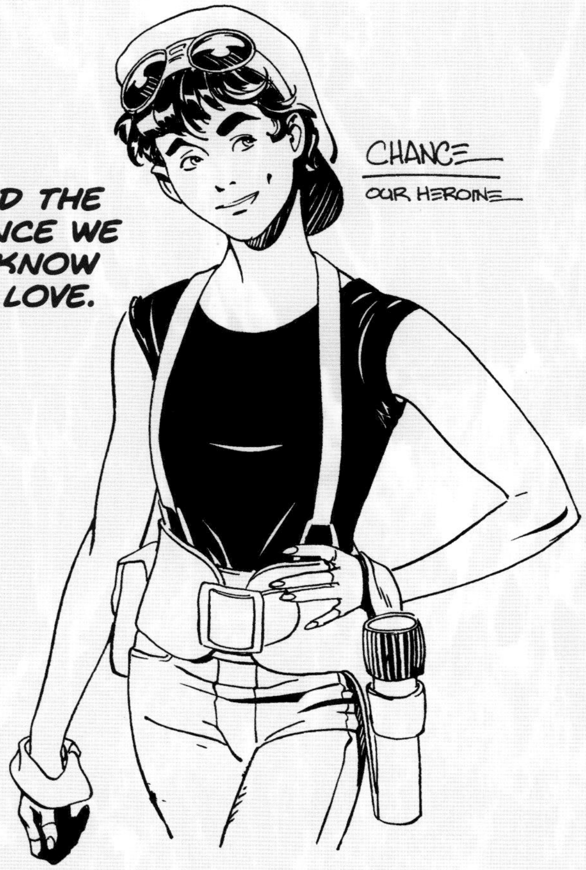
CHANCE
OUR HEROINE

...AND THE CHANCE WE ALL KNOW AND LOVE.

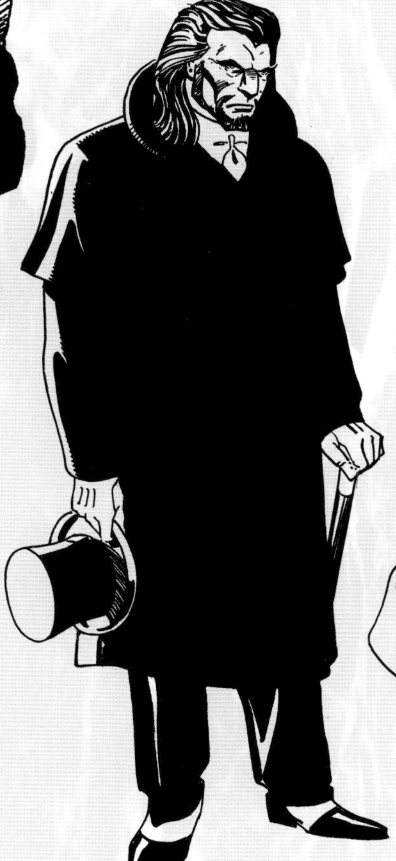

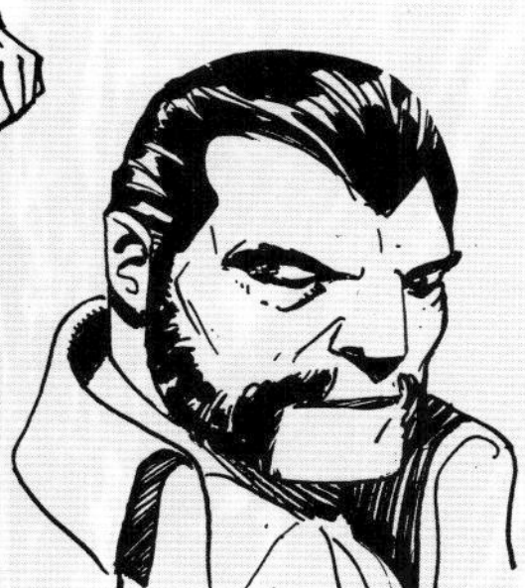
LUCAS FALCONER
CHANCE'S FATHER

THEN...

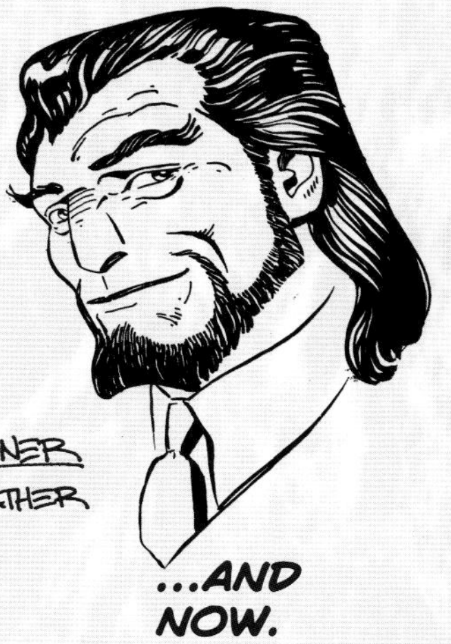

...AND NOW.

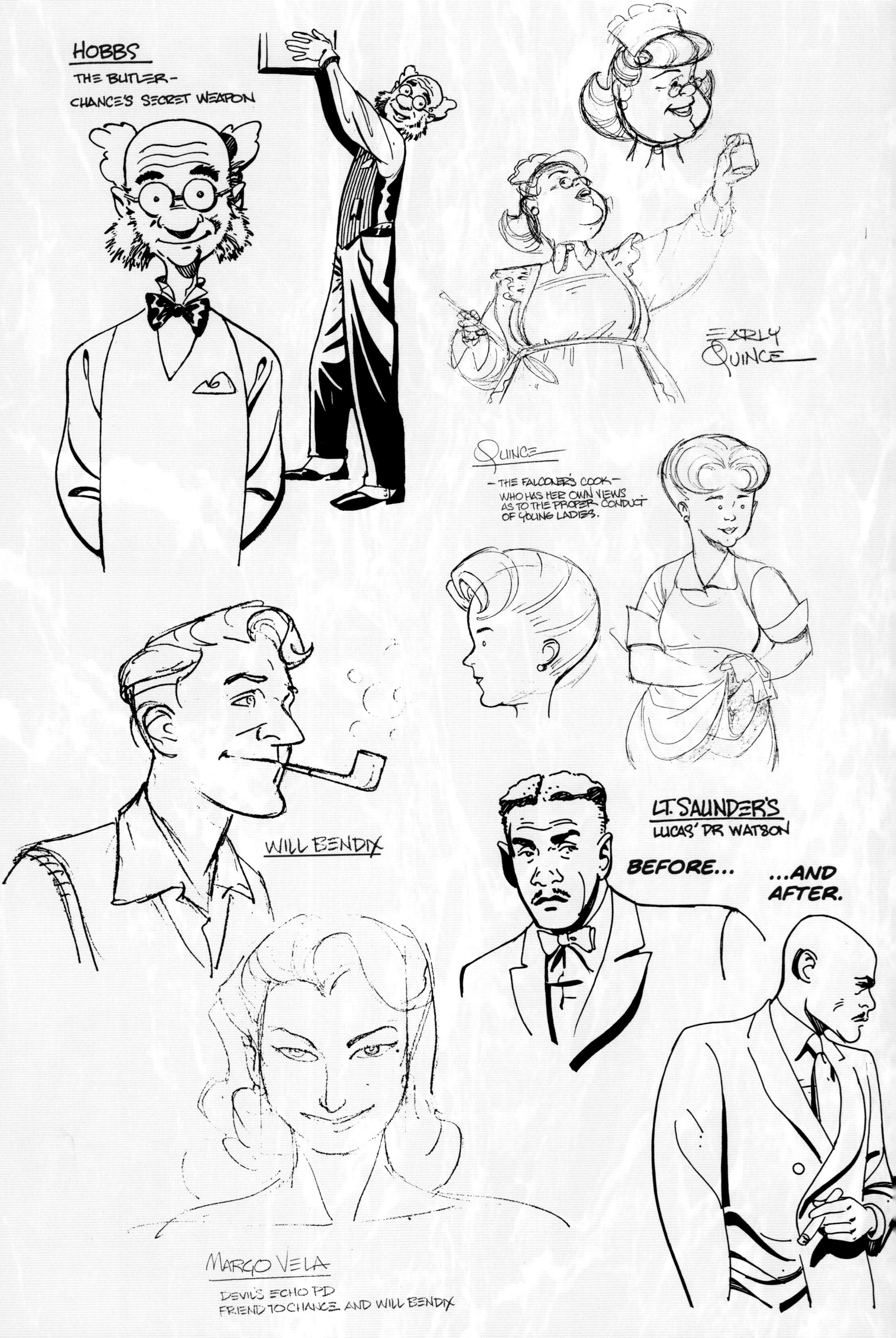
HOBBS
THE BUTLER -
CHANCE'S SECRET WEAPON
EARLY QUINCE
QUINCE
- THE FALCONER'S COOK -
WHO HAS HER OWN VIEWS
AS TO THE PROPER CONDUCT
OF YOUNG LADIES.
WILL BENDIX
LT. SAUNDER'S
LUCAS' DR WATSON
BEFORE...
...AND
AFTER.
MARGO VELA
DEVIL'S ECHO PD
FRIEND TO CHANCE AND WILL BENDIX

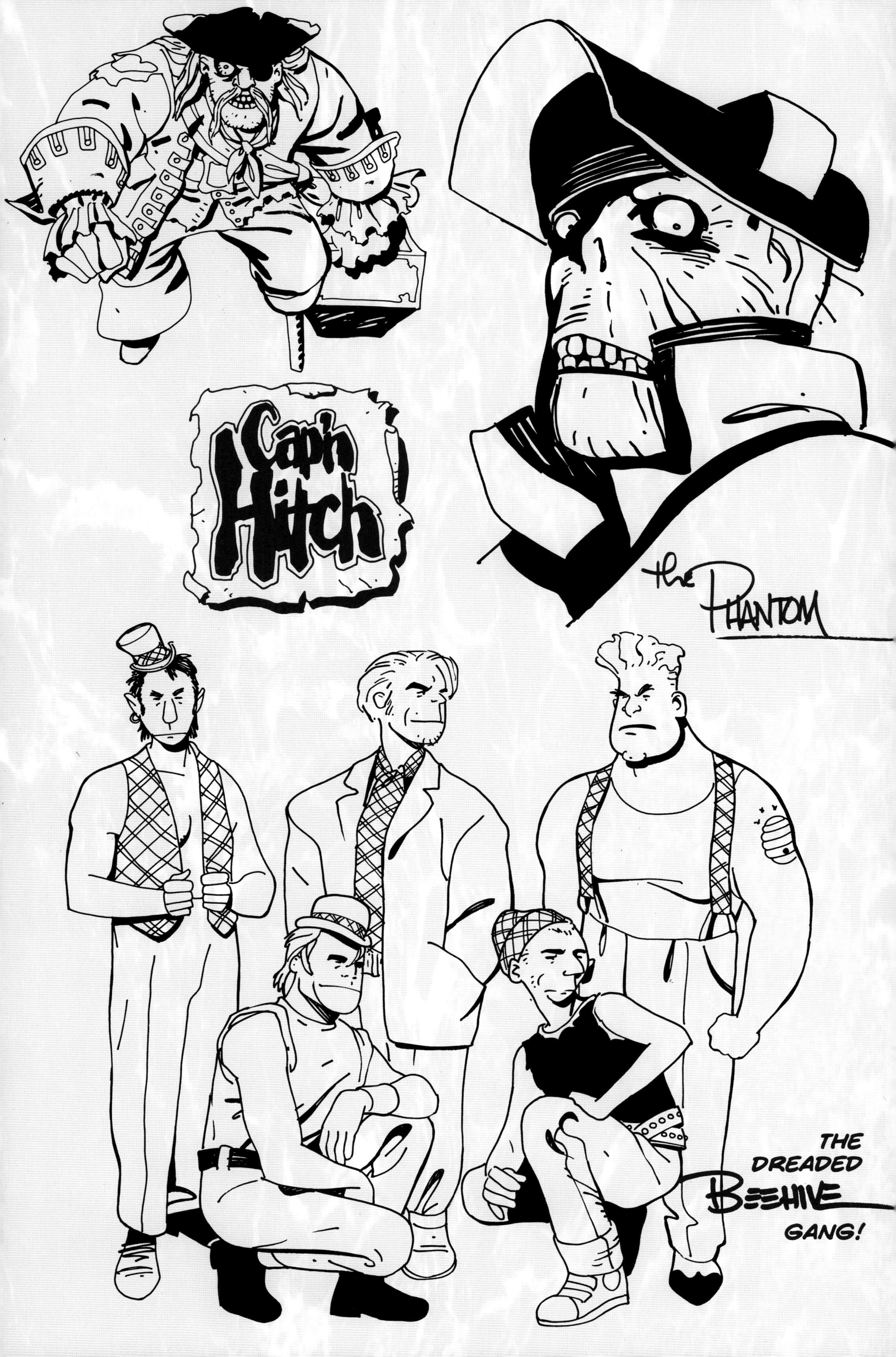
Cap'n Hitch
the PHANTOM
THE DREADED BEEHIVE GANG!

LEAVE IT TO
CHANCE™
BOOK ONE:
SHAMAN'S
RAIN
BY
JAMES
ROBINSON
&
PAUL
SMITH
WITH
JEROMY
COX

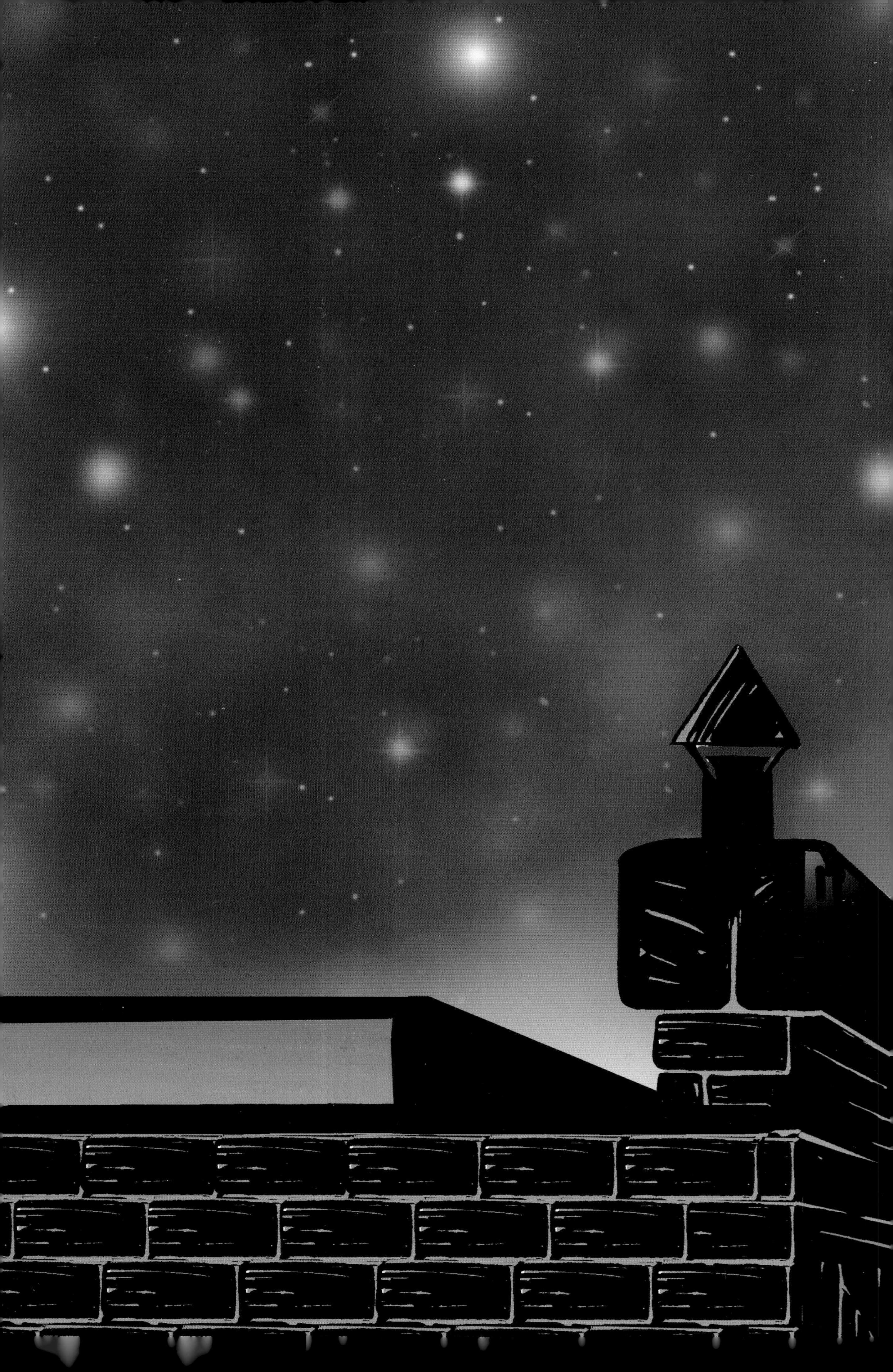